Lectures on Job

17TH CENTURY PRESBYTERIANS. *Lectures on Job* by James Durham is the second title in a uniform collection of books by 17th Century Presbyterians to be published by Naphtali Press.

Volumes previously published.

A Dispute Against the English Popish Ceremonies, by George Gillespie (1993).

Jus Divinum Regiminis Ecclesiastici or The Divine Right of Church-Government by sundry ministers of London (1654). (1995).

Lectures on Job

by James Durham

A New Edition

Edited by Christopher Coldwell

Naphtali Press
P. O. Box 141084
Dallas, TX 75214

Lectures on Job by James Durham

This New Edition Copyright © 1995 by Christopher Coldwell.

All Rights reserved

The text of this edition was taken from *AN EXPOSITION OF THE WHOLE BOOK OF JOB, With Practical Observations. By the late Rev. and Learned Mr. James Durham, Sometime Minister of the Gospel in Glasgow . . . . All carefully revised and corrected from a Manuscript Copy, never before published* (Glasgow: Printed by J. Bryce and D. Paterson, 1759).

17th Century Presbyterians Series Hardcover Edition

ISBN 0-941075-20-6

About This Edition

The text of this edition of Durham's *Lectures on Job* is based on the only printing of 1759.[1] It has been revised in so far as possible without marring the author's work, to reflect contemporary spelling, punctuation, and usage. Words or insertions supplied by the editor are in brackets []. Bracketed words or phrases that are italicized replace the original archaic or Scottish word or phrase (see list below), or define the preceding word or phrase if underlined. Scripture citations are italicized. The author's paraphrasing of the text is noted by single quotation marks. Archaic spellings and what appeared to be obvious misspellings have been corrected without any notice. If there was any doubt about a word the mistake is footnoted, and the most reasonable guess provided in the text. The numbering of points has been added to or converted, in order to clarify the outline of these lectures, and are not noted as insertions unless significantly adding to the text. Extraneous words or phrases have been deleted without mention where they confused or added nothing to the text. One or two parenthetic phrases of the author have been moved to footnotes, and these begin with "Durham:" to distinguish them from all the other footnotes of an editorial nature.

Many of the following Scottish words are replaced throughout the text.

addercop	[*spider*]
anent	[*about*]
aught	[*anything*]

---

1   *AN EXPOSITION OF THE WHOLE BOOK OF JOB, With Practical Observations. By the late Rev. and Learned Mr. James Durham, Sometime Minister of the Gospel in Glasgow . . . . All carefully revised and corrected from a Manuscript Copy, never before published* (Glasgow: Printed by J. Bryce and D. Paterson, 1759). The reader is referred to the various introductory articles in Durham's *A Treatise Concerning Scandal* (Dallas: Naphtali Press, 1990) for biographical information on the author. Also, many of the old editions of Durham's works contain biographical information. A short modern treatment by way of biography is George Christie's "James Durham as Courtier and Preacher," *Records of the Scottish Church History Society*, vol. IV, Part I.

ay	[*always; ever*]
besom	[*broom*]
big	[*build*]
contemn	[*despise*]
din	[*noise*]
dow	[*can*]
evanish	[*vanish*, or *disappear*]
exponed	[*interpreted, expounded*]
fain	[*most*]
feekless	[*frail; feeble*]
gar	[*make*]
gate	[*way*]
jangling	[*wrangling*]
kyth	[*appear, show*],
learn	[*teach*]
lippen	[*trust*]
meet	[*suitable*]
midses	[*means*]
misken	[*misunderstand*]
nor	[*than*]
outgate	[*outcome*]
propones	[*proposes*]
rub; rubbing	[*reflect;* to make a charge upon someone].
sey	[*assay; trial*]
smoor	[*smother*]
take up	[*understand*]
take with	[*admit; own; acknowledge*]
thir	[*these*]
trow	[*trust*]
uses to	[*normally*]
wale	[*choose*]
want	[*lack*]
without	[*outside*]

To The Reader

The Publishers of Mr. Durham's valuable writings candidly observe that he was always wholly taken up with the importance of his subject, and dived unto the heart of the best matter, but was less curious about some ornamental circumstances, as a labored elegance, smooth periods, and other things, which may be overlooked.[1] As there were few expositions or commentaries upon the holy Scriptures in this nation, about an hundred and twenty years ago, so the most learned and eminent ministers agreed, about the year 1650, to print some plain and short expositions of the principal books in the Old and New Testament. Mr. George Hutcheson accordingly published his expositions upon Job, the lesser prophets, and the Gospel of John. Mr. Alexander Nisbet printed his exposition of Ecclesiastes, and the Epistles of Peter; Mr. David Dickson, his expositions upon the Psalms, the Gospel of Matthew, and the Epistle to the Hebrews, and his Latin Commentaries on all the Epistles were also printed; Mr. James Ferguson, his exposition upon the Galatians, and the five following epistles were also published; and Mr. Durham's exposition of the Song of Solomon was printed sometime after his death. Mr. Robert Blair wrote an exposition upon the Proverbs for the press, but it is not printed; with many other expositions of the inspired writings, which were also prepared about that time for publication, and are yet in private hands.

Mr. Durham's exposition of the elegant book of Job would have been probably printed by Mr. Carstairs if he had lived some longer.

---

1 This is a portion of the original preface of the 1759 edition. James Durham (1622-1658) was a Scottish Presbyterian minister who served in the ministry a brief ten years, yet left behind quite a legacy. His books were very popular in Scotland and new editions of his works were published as late as 1840. According to George Christie, "in each decade between his death and the beginning of the nineteenth century at least one of his books was printed" ("Scripture Exposition in Scotland in the Seventeenth Century: Bibliography of James Durham, 1622-1658," *S.C.H.S. Records*, I, 97-111). No new edition of any of his works appeared until 1990, when Naphtali Press published his *Treatise Concerning Scandal*. For a list of Durham's works, see the insertion at the end of the next page.

The original copy, many years ago, was sent by Mr. Thomas Hog, a worthy minister in the North country, to the deceased Mr. Robert Wodrow, to be transcribed, and accordingly, it was faithfully copied by David Evandale, schoolmaster in Glasgow, one of the best and most accurate writers in that town. He might perhaps have altered the spelling of some words, and substituted some English words in place of the old Scots ones, as Mr. Carstairs did, but the candid reader will easily forgive such a trivial omission, and make the most favorable allowances for some unavoidable mistakes, peculiar to the posthumous writings of the most eminent divines.

[The following are the published works of James Durham. Many sermons also were left behind in manuscript — the notes of faithful hearers. For a complete identification of the editions of Durham's books, see Christie's article referenced in the footnote on the pervious page. Only the first two works were overseen by the author, who died during the preparation for the press of *A Treatise Concerning Scandal,* hence also known as *The Dying Man's Testament,* etc.

1. *A Commentarie upon the Book of Revelation.* 1658.
2. *The Dying man's Testament: or, A Treatise concerning Scandal.* 1659.
3. *Clavis Cantici: An Exposition of the Song of Solomon.* 1668.
4. *A Practical Exposition of the Ten Commandments.* 1675.
5. *The Blessednesse of the Death of these that die in the Lord.* 1681.
6. *Christ Crucified: or the Marrow of the Gospel.* 1683.
7. *The Unsearchable Riches of Christ.* 1685.
8. *Heaven upon Earth: the Joy of a good Conscience.* 1685.
9. *The Great Gain of Contenting Godliness.* 1685.
10. *The Great Corruption of Subtile Self.* 1686.
11. *An Exposition of the Book of Job.* 1759.

Naphtali Press is currently preparing new editions of the *Commentary on Revelation,* and *Christ Crucified* (72 Sermons on Isaiah 53). If the Lord pleases they will be published as part of this series. Naphtali Press also has published the sermons on death (#5) in *An Anthology of Presbyterian & Reformed Literature,* v. 1 #1-2.]

Lectures on Job

1

We will not enter on the debates and questions that are about this book; these things are clear to warrant us to ground our faith on it:

1. That it is a true story, and no parable; a story of the affliction of a gracious man, and the <u>outgate</u> [*outcome*]. 2. Be the writer who will, it is the Spirit who is the inditer, who has left it to us for a spiritual jewel, as is clear from Ezek. 14:14 and James 5:11. 3. It is clear who this man was by his friends, [who were][1] of the posterity of Abraham by Keturah, to whom he gave gifts, and sent them to the East (Gen. 25:6), and while religion stayed among them, Job, furnished with spiritual and temporal riches, stays among them. 4. For the time, it is evident to be when Israel was in Egypt, before the law, which is clear by Job's sacrificing in the land of Uz, which under the law was unlawful for him to have done, as also never <u>meddling</u> [*dealing*] with written scripture, nor evidences of God's power in overthrowing Pharaoh, when so many other things, and the old worlds drowning, is <u>meddled</u> [*dealt*] with, which prove it to be before.

The scope is: 1. To set out God's sovereignty and special hand in disposing of the afflictions and trials of his children, in the manner, measure and <u>outgate</u> [*issue*]. 2. How commendable a thing patience is, under the sharpest trials. 3. The happy outgate that patience under trials will have, as James 5:11, intimating the use that believers would make of affliction (Submit to God without fretting); and the end why afflictions are sent (to [set] folks [up]right, and draw them to this spiritual temper). 4. More particularly, to vindicate God's grace in Job as a real thing, which Satan calumniates: <u>To give the devil a lie</u> [*to*

---

1   Originally, "It is clear who this man was by his friends. Lot was of the posterity of Abraham by Keturah," etc. This is probably a transcriber's or editor's mistake. Durham certainly knew that Lot was not descended from Abraham. Perhaps it should have been the lot, as in all three, were descended, etc. Bildad certainly was a descendent of Abraham and Keturah, as the references clear, and Durham points out (Job 8).

show the devil a liar], and justify God, though on a dear experience to Job. God will have the trial of the faith of his own found unto praise (1 Pet. 1:7), himself found faithful, and Satan a calumniator, in all their trials.

The book has three parts. 1. A description of Job's prosperity (vs. 1-5). 2. Job's trial (1:6-42:7). 3. Job's <u>outgate</u> [*delivery*] and restoring (42:8ff).

In the first chapter we have, I. Job's prosperity (vs. 1-5). II. The change of it, in adversity; and so the first part of the trial (vs. 6-19). III. The effect this change had on Job, how he comforted himself under it, and bore it (vs. 20-22).

I. In the first of these, beside the designation of the place where Job dwelt, we have Job's prosperity described in these five things or steps.

1. That *he was a perfect and upright man*, not without sin, but as the dispute shows, sincere, no hypocrite; and *one that feared God and eschewed evil*; one that had real fruits of holiness and piety, grace [*appearing*] in his heart and conversation ([appearing] by these two, inward reverencing of God, and outward watchfulness in all his carriage to eschew evil).

2. A second step of his happiness was in his children. He had *seven sons and three daughters*, which was above riches; and he had not simply children, but obedient children to him, and agreeing well among themselves, and in all appearance gracious, not addicted to the world.

3. A third step is his *great substance* (1:3), and both this, and the former are observed to set out the greatness of Job's trial when denuded of all these so suddenly.

4. A fourth step is Job's care of his family and children, fearing they should sin, even in that sinless way of mutual entertainment.

(1) *He sent and sanctified them*, i.e. used a ceremonial way of fitting them rightly to go about such a work (as Ex. 19:10; Lev. 1:3), but especially by prayer, warnings, and such like; giving them warning that they dishonored not God in their mirth (and that he *sent* to do this, shows his care even when they were out of his sight, and his sparing no pains to prevent sin.)

(2) He rises up early, and offers in order for them all, commending them to God, and offers particularly for them one by one, an offering

for every child (he thought it not enough to mind them together, and to offer for all his children, but particularly he will go through them by name).

(3) In the reason he gives for his so doing, his care appears. *It may be they have sinned and cursed God in their heart.* Not that he knew any particular out-breaking in them. It is not likely they would fall out in blasphemy, but he gives a disorderliness and raging of the heart from God this name. He puts the worst sort of name on the least sin, so to speak, to tell that God heightens sin even in nearest relations, and is suspicious, but nature extenuates it. *and this Job did continually* (that is, every time, especially when they were together), because then temptation will then more readily prevail in company and cheerful fellowship, even of godly friends, than when they are more solitary.

Quest. *How could Job offer for the sin he knew not they were guilty of?*

Answ. [1] He knew there was sin in them in the root, and that they had their own infirmities, and were in hazard to break out in sin; therefore he goes to Jesus Christ to prevent that, or if acted, to have it done away. And [2], though he knew no particular sin, yet he (as it is commendable in David, Psa. 119, and in all others) remembers secret sins, for which he and they need to be humbled. Folks would make use of Christ for doing away of these, though they know them not (there are many errands to Christ, our own sins, and children's, to pardon them, and prevent them, and for secret and open sins).

II. The great change follows, and the first part of his trial (vs. 6-19). Wherein, 1. The rise of it (vs. 6-12); and 2. The execration of it (vs. 13-19).

1. *Sons of God* (v. 6) are angels there, and the devil's coming unto God, is a figurative and borrowed speech, expressing God's dominion over angels, devils, and all creatures, and his commissioning them for his errands, and not as if the words were to be understood literally. For spirits need not use words to communicate their mind. But it is like that speech [in] 1 Kings 22:19, when God sends forth a lying spirit in the mouths of Ahab's false prophets; neither can there be going forth from God properly, as it is here expressed, but as superiors have their attendants, that do nothing but by orders from them, so God's sovereignty and dominion is such, that devils and men do nothing but as he gives them commission.

The particulars the story holds out are: (1) God's dominion, who sits on his throne of majesty, having angels, good and evil, at his command, and who are liable to his court (as these are amongst men; who in sign thereof do at certain times appear) and particularly devils are taken notice of, because folks are ready to think they have more scouth [*opportunity*] and liberty, and can do more than other creatures, as if God's dominion did not so reach them. Verse 8. I come, says Satan, from going to and fro, and walking up and down, which shows the restlessness, maliciousness, and roving and vanity of that evil spirit (his punishment and his malice.)

(2) To let us see the Lord's observing and delighting in Job's carriage. Hast thou considered my servant Job? The Lord has a love of complacency [*complacent love for*] and delight in his own, and their sincere walking.

(3) Satan's opposition to this testimony: Does Job fear God for nought? (v. 9). Satan [*can*] least abide the man that God loves, but calumniates, slanders and curses that man above any. In Satan's answer we have: [1] His calumniating of Job, alleging he served God for hire (when he cannot deny his carriage, then he traduces his end, as if he were not single [*sincere*], but selfish in all his piety.) [2] His slender probation of it (v. 10). He is but a time-server, serving God so long as he is well done to, and he will do no longer [than] he is fatted with temporal blessings. [3] Because the proof is weak, he desires a new trial, and prophesies impudently (v. 11) the apostasy of this sincere believer. And God, not to please the devil, but to prove the reality of his own grace, Satan to be the liar, and himself to be faithful, gives him a commission to light on [*touch*] all he had, for he durst not stir the least feather of a fowl belonging to him till then; yet the commission is with a limitation (God gives no commission concerning his [people], but with limitation, as in this, and the following commission also, though they come far) not to touch his person (v. 12). This is the rise of Job's trial, to clear whether God or the devil lies (to speak with reverence to Him.)

2. The execution of the trial is from 1:13 to 1:19. (1) And as Satan got power over all that Job had, so he leaves him nothing, except one messenger at every stroke to bring the tidings, that in respect of Job had [been] better had they gone [been destroyed] with the rest. If Satan got his will he would not leave the believer a cock to crow day.

(2) He [be]wails the time for the stroke, when his sons and daughters were feasting in their eldest brother's house, that they might seem to be taken away in their sin, to make the poor man heavier.

(3) The heaviest trial is hindmost, and every one at the end of another, that Job gets no leave to draw his breath after one to make for another.

(4) He takes not one away but many, makes use of several instruments of wicked men on earth, of fire from heaven, of the wind ruling the air and making heaven and earth, God and men seem to conspire against him. And the last stroke on his children, is to intimate that as Job feared they had forgotten God, that he had plagued them, and 'take up your praying and sacrificing now' (would he say) 'a sad trial' [i.e. for his praying and sacrificing Job got a sore trial].

III. The last part of the chapter is Job's carriage. 1. He is not senseless, but rises, rents his mantle, etc., using a form suitable to that time. It becomes [*agrees with*] folks in their outward carriage and posture to be suitable to God's dealings with them. 2. His carriage in respect of his words or government of his tongue is good Naked came I into the world, and naked shall I return, etc. 'I had neither goods nor children when I came into the world, and I can take none with me,' and blest be his name 'who hath both given and taken, for none of these could make me eternally happy.' It is a notable point of heavenly wisdom, a rare practice to use the world as not abusing it (1 Cor. 7:30-31). If Job's heart had been in his gear [*possessions*], as many a man's is, he had said otherwise. The Spirit of God gives approbation to his carriage in this trial, as if he had said, 'The devil has once gotten the foil. He said he would garr [*make*] Job sin, and he is beguiled.' In all this Job sinned not, etc. A right eye on God in any trial, brings submission to God and a good outgate [*finish*].

OBSERVATIONS more explicit.

On the first part observe: 1. It is the greatest commendation of a man, and part of his happiness to be perfect, upright and sincere before God. That perfection will go to the grave with him; other things cannot. Blessed are the dead who die in the Lord (Rev. 14:13). Therefore it is set down in the first place; neither Satan nor Sabeans can take this from Job. They may take a man's gear, but they cannot take peace of mind from the sincere man.

2. Where this perfection is, a man will be fruitful, fear God and eschew evil; careful to prevent sin in his own person, family and others, when he wins in to get peace with God, through Christ.

3. It is no idle thing to be perfect and sincere, but it will be a daily task, what one's self, what to their family, which it puts together.

On the second part observe: 1. That for as great hatred as the devil has at God's children, he nor none of his instruments can stir a tail of any of their beasts without God's permission.

2. Where there is much grace, God often sends sharpest trials. There was none like Job among the children of the east, and none is so tried. God will not boast of every man's grace, though he carry through the weakest. Let these that have grace be humble; if they have much, they will get as much ado with it.

3. Grace, yea God's approbation of grace will not keep folks from sharpest trials; so live as resolute through many afflictions, to enter into heaven. You think much of quartering and plundering,[2] but what would you think to have the devil master of all you have? Mistake not trials. A time of trial is not the worst time, nor is God then less tender, or more rigid.

On the third part, Job's carriage, observe: 1. There is nothing [which] evidences folks' grace more [*than*] a right carriage under affliction. The devil said Job is but a fair-weather man. Now he is found a liar, when in all this Job sinned not.

2. Steadfastness and integrity is best known under a heavy strait and trial. Folks' love to the world is then known when they are called to part with it.

---

2 Note this is written during Cromwell's occupation of Scotland.

2

In the former chapter Job's trial began; in this it goes on. And there are three steps added to the former, which are the parts of the chapter.

I. The first part is that whereby his body is stricken with boils from the sole of his foot to the crown of the head. The devil getting leave to smite his body, chooses this as the most loathsome disease and violent pain; and we have this step of the trial, with the cause and effect (vs. 1-8).

II. The second step or part is that between Job and his wife. When the devil has thus gotten Job low, loathsome, and in pain, he is angry that he will not speak as he would have had him. Therefore he brings in his wife, and gets her to take his part, and by her instigation seeks to obtain his point; but Job refutes her calmly, and stops her mouth (vs. 9-10).

III. The third part, Job's three friends came to him, and instead of comforting, they sit down beside him, and are dumb for seven days, and (as we will hear) they become a vexation to him, worse than any he had yet met with (vs. 11-13).

I. In the first part we have four things: 1. The causes instrumental in Job's trial, or the occasion and rise of it (vs. 1-5). 2. The commission that Satan gets (v. 6). 3. Satan's executing the commission (v. 7). 4. Job's carriage under it (v. 8).

1. This appearing of the sons of God or angels, and Satan before God, is not to be taken literally, as if there were any day more special [than] another, or a coming into or going forth from God. But it is a figurative speech or resemblance, to show and set out the Lord's sovereignty over all creatures, and the sovereignty he has over, and immediate hand he has in all the afflictions of his people. The particular steps of it are to set out the thing as we are able to take it up. Angels wait for his commands, and run his errands; devils must wait for orders from him ere they can execute their malice. Therefore

ere Satan go forth he must have a commission, and God questions Satan, and he makes answer to tell [*show*] he must give account to God.

In the third verse we have God's taking special notice of Job's shaming the devil for all that is done to him. 'Behold he is not the man thou called him, notwithstanding thou movedst me against him;' not that God is moved to anything which is not decreed of him. But (1) To [*show*] that what is aforetime decreed is in time executed. (2) That though God only executes his purpose in afflicting his people by Satan and wicked men, yet he can and will charge them with their affliction, as if he had not a hand in it. (3) To let us see the difference between God's hand and theirs in his people's affliction. It is not out of hatred and malice, but from love, holy wisdom, goodness and kindness, that God afflicts, not always out of respect to sin, but to vindicate his own grace in them, and to make it shine, as here in Job. But Satan and wicked men afflict out of hatred and malice, and to drive them off their feet, and blacken God's work in them.

In the fourth verse Satan's answer, *Skin for skin*, etc. This answer is set down to let us see the nature of Satan, that he is shamelessly impudent, so that grace will never be that palpable, but he will contradict it and traduce it. Therefore here he cries down God's testimony the second time. The word which he uses seems to be a proverb used in these times. The meaning is, 'A man will bear other burdens better as long as his skin is kept healthy; intimating the more personal that afflictions are, the trial is the sharper, and the worse to be borne.

2. We have the commission Satan gets (v. 6). God gives Satan a new sey [*assay; trial*] of Job, and liberty to execute his purpose, yet limits him.

3. Satan executes his commission in doing what he desired, which his going out imports, and he smites Job in all the parts of his body with boils (v. 7).

4. We have Job's carriage under all this (v. 8), *He took him a potsherd*, etc. It is likely his wife and servants loathed him, and would not come near him (as chapter 19:15-17), his breath being stinking and corrupt, and when scarce any can know a nail on him, he sits *down among the ashes*, and takes a piece of an old broken *potsherd to scrape himself withal*. And though he has poverty without, and pain both without and within, yet he is silent, and will not open his mouth to fret and repine against God.

Quest. What can be the reason that Satan gets leave to add this affliction, and yet God says it is not a chastisement for sin?

Answ. These reasons vindicate the justice and wisdom of God in it. 1. God's sovereignty and absolute dominion over the creature. It is enough that he does it. *Who can say, What dost thou? the potter hath power over the clay* (Rom. 9:21). It is enough that God thinks good to inflict it. 2. That he may leave the pattern of patience complete to all posterity. 3. He will show how low he can bring these he loves dearly. 4. To let us see that a gracious heart will not cast out [*fall out*] with God for crosses, or judge the worst of his love for all that; therefore he will have Job come to the height of the trial, and yet [*show*], it is not out of respect to sin. 5. That God may get glory in a real proof and demonstration of his own grace that is often traduced, as here it was in Job. 6. It is also for the advantage of his people to vindicate them from the aspersions, reproaches, and calumnies of wicked men. 7. That the mouths of the wicked may be stopped, who said, 'They would go the wrong way, if they were tried, and they were all but hypocrites.'

But how is it that the devil gets power over Job's body? For Satan to get power over the bodies of God's dearest children, to inflict sickness on them, or to pull down the house on them and [*smother*] them, it is no argument of hatred, but may well consist with God's love. It is all one to him whether their sickness or death is wakened up by any humor in their body, and they die in their bed, or suffer a more violent death by Satan and wicked men; as when wicked Cain slew just Abel, and in the Jews' crucifying of Christ. The covenant stands sure, and God has a care of the soul even when Satan gets power over the body. The devil but executes God's purpose.

II. The second step of the trial and part of the chapter (v. 9), and his carriage under it (v. 10). When for all this Job will not blaspheme God, the devil is angry, and yokes his wife to him. The word may be rendered, *Dost thou still retain thine integrity, blessing God and dying?* The Hebrews abhorring to speak the phrase according to the meaning, express it by the contrary, or otherwise, that is, *blessing God* for *cursing*. Should then the words be read as they are here? No question Job's wife sinned in this expression, for Job's reproof speaks that much; therefore it is the less matter which of the ways they be read. But the words may be as well read, Bless God, and die. And the meaning is in a scorning way, casting up his religion to him. She says, 'Will you ever bless God? Will you go to your grave that way? See if your blessing of God, and all your prayers, be of much worth now, when he has given you such a loathsome skin. Better leave off that way, and confess your hypocrisy.'

The reason why we think this to be the meaning is: 1. Because it is not likely she would tempt Job to so gross an action, as flatly in even-down terms to curse God. 2. Because Satan and Job's friends' shot [*aim*] is to bear in on Job, and make him take with it [*agree; own up*], that he was a hypocrite , and that he would take all that is come upon him as a fruit of God's wrath therefore, and so be discouraged and fret. And this being the drift of the dispute afterward, it is likely Satan begins it here, and by his wife bears it on him that it were better he should take with his hypocrisy in time. But both expositions prove it was a temptation to sin, and to prove Job is not sound by the hard things he had met with, and Job's answer (v. 10.) confirms it. Thou speakest as one of the foolish women, 'and not as one that has lived in my family.'[1] Shall we receive good at the hand of God, and shall we not receive evil, as having indignation at her words? 'Shall we limit God to one way of dealing? Shall not we that have had a long life of honor, riches, and ease, be content to take a little contempt, poverty, and pain too? It would be better reasoning, that after long prosperity we should contentedly bear a cross.' And then the Spirit of God gives Job a second testimony of the victory, that whatever wrestling was within his heart, yet, as it bursts not out, he sinned not with his lips as afterwards.

III. The third step and part of the trial is from his friends. What they were we will not dispute. Though they were good men, yet they mistook Job; therefore God accepts a sacrifice for them in the last chapter, after he reproves them. They come to visit Job in his affliction as friends should do, and when they see Job they lift up their voice and weep; and, according to the custom of these times, rent their clothes, and put ashes on their heads, and sit down silent for seven days and seven nights.

Quest. What should be the reason they sat so long silent?

Answ. 1. God having a mind to complete Job's trial, he will let him get comfort from none; yea, they shall rather be matter of stumbling to him. 2. They could not conceive his sorrow half so great ere they

---

1   Durham: As [in] Psa. 73:22, *So foolish was I and ignorant*, etc.; speaking of his giving way to the like temptation — this folly is in men naturally, counting that way most approved of God, which is in outward things most countenanced; and that way or person [not] loved of God, which in outward things is crossed. Which way of reasoning Job rejects in his answer, as afterward in his friends, as an argument proceeding from ignorance and unacquaintedness with God's way.

came; and the good thoughts they had of Job before, as if a holy man, wearies out upon the beholding of his stroke, and they know not what to say to him. Yea, in as far as they let the temptation work in begetting a prejudice at him, they are wrong and prove hurtful to him.

OBSERVATIONS.

From God's sovereignty observe: 1. The Holy Ghost would have God eyed in all men's trials and afflictions. Therefore is the sovereignty of God prefixed to the second trial, to teach us that it is not devils nor men that guide the world, but it is God who sits on his throne, and gives them commission, limits them, and calls them to account — a thing the people of God would have much in their eye, and behold God now as immediately governing affairs, as if he were on a throne, and all opposers were called before his bench or court.

2. There is no part of a man's religion pleases God better, and honors God more [than] uprightness under a trial, and then to keep still his integrity. This is it God boasts of (to speak with reverence) [in] Rev. 2:13 and 3:10, because God's credit is more engaged in folks' carriage under a trial; for it is whether grace be true in such a body or not, and a right carriage then is (so to speak) a saving of the Lord's credit, which cannot in the least be in hazard; yet, before men it honors him, whose name might otherwise be blasphemed. This is it that God puts us now to, and we would so much the more take notice of it.

3. One foil will not put away the devil, but after he is foiled he will set on again. He is like a roaring lion, walking about seeking whom he may devour (1 Pet. 5:8). And when he gets not the soul destroyed, he gets not his end, and is not at rest, therefore he still rages the more he is resisted. There is one part of our trial by, but be not secure; for our strait is but beginning, and if God prevents not, and keep us not watchful, we will go down the wind [*go to decay and ruin*].

4. God sometimes for his own glory and the good of his people will bring [them] under trial, when it is causeless in respect of sin, as here in Job. To apply it: There has been a great reproach lying on the people of God in Scotland, as favorers of sectaries,[2] and it's likely he

---

2 *Sectaries*: Those against an established national church, who ranged from just left of the more or less reformed Independents to radical groups such as the Fifth Monarchy Men. Most of Durham's ministry took place in the 1650s, during Cromwell's control of England and Scotland. This was also the period in which the

may put them to a trial to wipe away that reproach, to evidence his grace in them, and to give a malignant and profane temporizing generation the lie, and this will be worth all that we can suffer.

On the second part observe: 1. That oftentimes the sharpest trials come from such as are nearest friends, and these that are in nearest natural relations are often greatest temptations. Therefore Satan leaves Job's wife behind the former, for a sorer affliction and temptation, and most able to prevail.

2. It's a hard matter when folks in near relations live peaceably together till affliction comes, and then to be instruments of one another's grief, and serve the devil's turn by irritating and provoking expressions. Therefore wives, and all in a near relation take warning from Job's wife's example, to beware of such a carriage.

3. From Job's answer to her, observe that long-sparing mercy and forbearance may well abide a whiles trial. They that have had much good, may well bear a whiles ill; we that have had long peace, have reason to take in good part a time of trouble.

4. The Spirit of God puts a new mark of the victory on Job, He sinned not with his lips. Observe, where sin is kept in, and comes not out to a height and open out-breaking in his people, God often counts it no sin, but that they are victorious when they set [themselves] honestly against sin.

From the last part of the chapter observe: 1. That often that which folks expect comfort from, proves comfortless. We hear not a word of Job's wife being a comfort to him in all the story. His friends, who intended to comfort him, turn [out] his greatest cross; for Job's trial must be complete, therefore a word of comfort is spoken by none to him.

2. It is good to have friends and Christian fellowship, but we would die to them, and learn to make up our consolation in God. If we depend on the creature, it will go dry when we have most ado

---

Scottish Kirk was troubled by the Resolutioner/Protester schism. Durham shared the sentiments of the Protesters, but spent most of his efforts trying to restore unity to the church. His efforts failed. He wrote his classic book, *A Treatise Concerning Scandal* as a dying plea for church unity (Published by Naphtali Press, 1990). Because the Protester's were favored by Cromwell, it is possible the Resolutioners were accusing them of 'favoring sectaries' or at least their principles. When the severe trial of the "killing times" came to Scotland, it was mostly those who followed the Protesters (the Covenanters) who suffered for not conforming.

with it. When Job's friends cast him off, he had fallen in the mire if he had not had a sure ground to lean on for his comfort.

3

W e heard how wonderfully Job has borne through his former trials, when his wife and friends and all had forsaken him. Now that which has been for many days kept in, breaks out. Job after long silence in the bitterness of his spirit expresses himself in a sad complaint and expostulation. And the scope of the chapter is to show how out of the misery and anguish he was under, he expostulates these four ways.

I. Wishing he had *never been born*, or if born, that he had been taken away without suck (vs. 1-12). [*These*] expressions of cursings are not needful to be insisted on, being ordinary in scripture. As [in] Jer. 14, wherein the saints in anguish show the greatness and excessiveness of their grief, and therefore turn to curse all the means of their help, the womb, the knees, the breasts, etc., in a rhetorical way, expressing how vehemently they desired that they had never been [born]. Therefore Job to show the excessiveness of his grief, through the misery that was on him, would have the day of his birth marked as a cursed day, and scraped out from among the number of days, and all that cursed any day cursing it, especially the mourning women that used to curse sad accidents, he would have them turning about and cursing that day. Words of passion long kept up, now overflowing and keeping no bounds.

II. He gives reasons of his wish in the same way (vs. 13-19). All the good he had gotten before and the principle he had laid down are forgotten, and he prefers his being dead to his present being, and says had he died when newly born, great men and he had been all alike, for there is no disparity in death. He had been as great as any of them, whereas now he is under much misery and reproach. *There the wicked cease from troubling.* There are no robbers such as the Sabeans and Chaldeans in death, and there *the weary have rest*, the servant and the master is alike there. And so [he] goes on in the same rhetorical way, to tell how he preferred a never being, or a soon dying, to his being.

III. He is angry that ever the benefit of life was allowed to him (vs. 20-22); as if he said, 'The thing I would <u>fainest</u> [*most joyfully*] have is death, and it is my misery that I cannot get it. A man would never have had a golden mineral [*to rejoice in*], [*than*] I would have death; why would such a one live.'

IV. He crowns all with a sad expostulation, that God is against him, which Jeremiah (Lam. 3) looks on as a sad evidence of anger (vs. 23-26). And having expostulated this, he proves it by three instances:

1. Because no means of consolation can do him good; he is not the better of meat and drink; it has no relish to him, and his roaring flows out like a stream from a fountain that has no drying up. 2. Had he [*chosen*] a sad condition, that which he feared is come; he feared a condition of extremity, and it is carved out to him. 3. That notwithstanding he was not secure, but watchful and worshipping God; yet God had broken through all his prayers and sacrifices. 'In my duty [he] has lighted on me.' And this most affected him, that God was contending and he saw no cause; he knew not wherefore. This is the saddest word and the greatest part of his sin, and seems to be the rise of the debate that follows.

That we may know the better how to look on this scripture, I shall shortly answer some questions.

Quest. 1. *How shall we judge of Job's carriage here, and how shall we take up [understand] his sin in it?*

Answ. [*These*] are expressions of sinful infirmity without doubt, and the Lord's reproving Job clears it fully. As for the sins here they may be drawn to three heads:

First, there is his limiting the wisdom and sovereignty of God; his finding fault with God's government, as if God had done him wrong that he was born, or had given him a being and life. He is reproved by the Lord for this (40:2): 'Do you think Job that you should instruct me when you should be born, or taken off the world;' *in this ye have been foolish.*

Secondly, though he defends a just thesis against his friends, to wit, that a just man such as he was might be *hardly* [*harshly*] afflicted. Yet in this he sinned: in his fretting that he in particular should be so dealt with, especially he being in his duty. His failing here was in application of the general thesis to himself; therefore (40:8), the Lord says to him, *Wilt thou condemn me, that thou may'st be righteous?* or as the first word of the verse is, *Wilt thou disannul my judgment?* As if he had said, 'Is there no way to justify your own innocency, but by finding fault with me?'

Thirdly, there is a rashness in his expressions, though in maintaining a good cause; in his expressions, rubbing on the majesty of God, and not riding marches [*clearing the boarders*] well for vindicating the Lord. Therefore it is the first of God's challenge (38:2). Who is this that darkens counsel by words without knowledge; and he leaves not Job till he takes with this [*confesses this*] (42:3), and acknowledges that he has spoken words which he understood not. In the heat of his passion he was led to expressions that his friends take advantage of; therefore Elihu on this ground pleads that he failed in his expressions, especially in application to himself (as 37:11-12).

Quest. 2. Seeing [*these*] are great sins, and corruption venting itself strikes at the root of God's sovereignty, got not Satan here his purpose? and if so how can God absolve Job?

I answer in these three: 1. Consider Job's infirmities, and look on them as having grace going along with them. The great debate between God and Satan was not whether Job had sin in him, but whether he was a hypocrite, and whether he had grace or not? And though many things break out, yet he keeps the main ground of his interest in God clear, and will not cast out with him; maintaining a just cause, and keeping clear his interest. The shining of grace in him justifies God, and makes Satan a liar.

2. Consider the case he was in, the great temptation he was under, all sorts of hardship, trysting [*meeting*] on him from without, and terror within. It is no great marvel that under such a heat his pot cast a scum. Put the best [of men] in Job's case, they would have other expressions; and the Lord comparing his expressions with his case, thinks it a victory he has gotten.

3. Consider Job in [*these*] infirmities in a kind of roving [*raving*], as it were one in the height of a fever, whereas in other parts of this book we will find far sounder divinity in Job, laying his hand on his mouth and submitting to God. And God never justifies a man's grace by fits [*irregular intervals*], but by the tract of his way, and the event of his business. Therefore we may both let Job be faulty wherein his corruption kyths [*appears*], and yet keep up [*maintain*] what God has spoken of his perfection.

Quest. 3. But might not God have kept Job from [*these*] infirmities? and would it not have been more for God's honor?

Answ. God works his end in Job's trial more by letting his infirmities [*appear*]. 1. Because the more Job's infirmities [*appear*], and that like a spate or flood of waters, the more [*appears*] his grace in Job that is not drowned with it. The messenger of Satan is sent to buffet Paul (2 Cor. 12:7), and his weakness must kyth, that God's grace over passion is more than if his passion had not broken out. 2. The Lord gains his end better, because as he had one end before him, to stop Satan's mouth, so he had this end, to let Job and all his children know what they hold of him, and how he will have them in his reverence. Therefore the best of the saints with Jacob have a halt [*limp*], that they may know the strength whereby they stand, and to whom they are obliged for the victory. 3. God's end was not only that Job may have the victory being tried, but that he might be a pattern to these that should come after, and therefore he will have his infirmities to kyth, and yet do them away, and give him the victory: bring him to the brink of despair, and yet uphold him, and give him an outgate [*deliverance*], that other saints may not be discouraged nor despair though their condition should be like his. And often Job's infirmities [*appearing*], have proven as comfortable to the people of God as his patience and other graces.

OBSERVATIONS.

1. First from the general drift of the chapter observe, that the greatest measure of grace when it is put to a trial, will be found to have much corruption going along with it. Under strongest faith will unbelief there be found lurking; under the strongest zeal, lukewarmness; under meekness, passion. This heart brings out much dross, which none would have thought had been in Job, and it is ordinary for God to discover corruption under the graces that are most eminent in his children. Patience is eminent in Job, yet here impatience [*appears*]. In Abraham faith is eminent, yet (Gen. 20) a fit of unbelief takes hold of him. The Lord will blot out all faces, that all may be watchful, and none may despair. What if many of us were put to the half of that which Job was tried with, what fretting and cursing in another kind would there be. Therefore be very humble, and not conceited nor vain, because of any little bit of grace you have gotten, when so much lurks at the root of the height of grace that Job had.

2. Observe when God reckons the grace of his children, he reckons it with a large allowance. Therefore this man is highly commended of God for all his infirmity, and (James 5) set out for a

pattern of patience. The best gold has need of allowance, and so has grace, and gets it here. David had many foul slips, yet he is called a man after God's own heart, and was perfect without turning aside either to the right hand or the left, except in the matter of Uriah, all his other faults are past over [by] the Holy Ghost. So also Asa. He persecutes the prophet, oppresses the people, seeks to the physicians, etc.; yet his heart was perfect with the Lord all his days (Cf. 1 Kings 15; 2 Chron. 16:10). And this is a notable consolation when we reckon our own condition to know how God reckons it. 2. It is also a good direction to us in reckoning the condition of others, not to follow any or our own, but count as God counts here.

3. Observe that if believers get their own will under their trials, they would never do well. Job would do nothing but die, if he had gotten his will. But God is wiser then we. We often meddle with things too wonderful for us; O what impatience and fretting and rubbing on the sovereignty of God does often [*appear*] in our fits of passion.

4. Whenever folks rub on the majesty of God, it is to their own prejudice; therefore Job is reproved for this. Give God his will, and justify him, and <u>stoop</u> [*bow*] before him.

5. Job under both the former trials and this, had peace with God and a good conscience. But now he finds God to look angry like, and [*can*] not endure that. Observe there's nothing so terrible as the wrath of God, when it looks a soul in the face. This made David roar. And if God is so terrible to his children in the way of trial, how terrible will he be to the wicked when he shall not only hound out one devil, but all the devils in hell, and that without any limitation upon them, and they shall have no peace, nor good conscience as Job had? When the little thing that Job felt is so terrible, what will it be when the wrath of the great and living God, and an unreconciled sinner meet? Fear to meet God, and have the cup of his wrath to drink. When a small drop of the brim is so bitter, what will the dregs be? when they shall be wrung out, and all the wicked of the earth shall be made to drink them, and they shall cry out for hills and mountains to cover them, and shall not get them. And though they would give all the world for one tear that fell from Job to wet their tongue, it shall not be granted them. Consider that word (Psa. 90:11), Who knows the power of thy wrath? For according to thy fear, so is thy wrath; and therefore pray, So teach us to number our days, as we may apply our hearts to wisdom.

4

There is (as you would think) a great part of Job's trial past, yet there follows as sharp, piercing, and sifting a part of it as any of the former. The great contest between God and Satan is whether Job was a hypocrite, or not? And when this is brought out by any of the former trials, Satan wakens up a new debate by Job's friends, and gets them to further his end, and to impugn that thesis that there was any real grace in Job (to chapter 32). And in this dispute, he defending, and they impugning, they go thrice about, except Zophar who speaks but twice. Then Elihu speaks from chapter 32 to chapter 38. And last the Lord himself comes in to decide the dispute, and first reproves Job, and then his friends, and vindicates Job, and puts him to make their peace, from chapter 38 to the end.

Ere we come to this chapter in particular, take some generals for clearing the whole dispute.

I. The great end of this trial is one with the former, that is, to bring Job's righteousness to light, and to make it evident he is no hypocrite; yea, he must be made a complete pattern of patience. Therefore, three able, learned, and good men, must seem to combine together to bear him down, and God carries him through, and makes his grace shine the brighter. But Satan's shot [aim] is the contrary, to get Job quitting his thesis, and to get him made a hypocrite out of his own mouth, and God condemned.

II. Job's friends' end is not to be subservient to Satan in his design, but: 1. To vindicate God and justify him, and to rub off these aspersions which Job's expressions seemed to put upon him. 2. Their purpose is not to cast off Job; but as it is 4:19, and 5:8, and often through this dispute, to humble, restore, and comfort Job; good intentions, but miscarrying in their way of dealing with him. 3. Their carriage and manner of proceeding both in this chapter, and in the most part of the grounds they go upon through the dispute, is drawn from God's justice and sovereignty, and experiences of God's dealing, that are in themselves sound, and being rightly taken up, may yield solid doctrines. But they fail: (1) In [their] mistaking Job's condition, [by] judging of his state from his infirmities in the height of his passion, as if grace could not stand with such expressions. And mistaking the disease, they misapply the cure. Therefore (2), looking to the extraordinary stroke which was befallen him, they fall upon the hypothesis going from the thesis itself, stretching the justice of God beyond, and drawing conclusions from the premises which they will not bear; from a temporary judgment, concluding eternal cutting off. (3) They misapply the most clear visions and sound truths to obtain their point, to have Job down and taking with it [*agreeing*], that he was a hypocrite, that he might be humbled and lay a new foundation. (4) They carry on this with rough and uncharitable expressions toward Job, who should have been more tenderly dealt with.

In this chapter Eliphaz, mistaking Job's condition, makes way to mollify what he is to speak by prefacing in the first two verses, yet tells a necessity lay on him to censure his expressions. *Who can withhold himself from speaking.* But his fault is that he goes from his expressions, to condemn his state; although supposing Job's condition to be that which he took it to be, he is right.

In the rest of the chapter he lays down three grounds to prove that Job in respect of his state is not right; but none of them will bear it.

I. The first is from Job's impatience under the cross (vs. 1-6). [It's] as if he said, 'If grace in you had been real, it would have borne out in adversity as well as prosperity.' And he proves Job to succumb in adversity, because the comfort he had given to others, he is not now able to take it to himself, but he faints and frets under his affliction, which indeed inferred that Job was in a distemper, but not that he had no grace. *Is not this thy fear*, etc. That is, 'By this you may see what kind of religion you had. You boasted meikle [*much*] of God's protection before trouble came, and all was well with you, but where is it all now? You seemed to be an upright man, and to have faith in God, but now it is seen to be nothing.'

II. The second ground (vs. 7-11), he proves Job could not be really gracious, because of the sad dispensations he was fallen under. And this ground he follows two ways.

1. He bids him consider, if *ever a righteous man perished*. Take it totally, and eternally, the argument holds true; but it will not hold in respect of temporal judgment, and Job is not yet cut off nor perished.

So he draws a wrong conclusion from a true ground, and misapplies it to Job (v. 7).

2. The second way how he follows out this argument, is by bringing in his own experience in observing the judgment of God that had in his time befallen the wicked before his eyes (vs. 8-11). *I have seen*, he says, *they who plow iniquity, and sow wickedness, reap the same*; as they have hewed to themselves, and as they served God hypocritically, so the judgment of God came on them (v. 8). This argument he amplifies (v. 9). *By the blast of God they perish*, etc. That is, the wicked man's portion is an evident sign of his wrath; yea, the height of it. For let the wicked man be as strong as he will, like *a lion*, he shall *be broken* (v. 10). The best of them all, when they have lived never so long, fall down, and their posterity shall be scattered (v. 11).

Now there are sundry deceits in this argument: (1) That from a temporal judgment he concludes Job to be a wicked man. (2) That he alleges all wicked men are so dealt with, because some are so handled. (3) He is wrong in his application to Job, for Job is not yet cut off.

III. The third ground propounded is from a particular and immediate revelation, wherein there is first the circumstances (vs. 12-16), whereby he prepares Job to hear, and from v. 17 holds forth the revelation or thing revealed to him. The scripture then not being written, God spoke to holy men immediately, and Eliphaz not knowing well how to answer Job, he tells how God taught him what to say. His insisting to tell how it came to him, is not only to prepare Job to receive it, but to persuade him it was no counterfeit thing, but some divine majesty of God [which] was let out upon him to fit him to receive the vision. [He] then shows what the word was that was revealed to him by that vision (v 17). *Shall mortal man be more just than God?* A word that might have done Job good if rightly applied and made use of, for Elihu and God run almost on the same grounds. But Eliphaz held not at the condemning of some expressions and actions in Job, but runs in on the state of his person, and from his harsh expressions would bear upon him that he made himself more than God. This always holds true, that there is no man when he speaks with God but he shall have cause to justify him; and it is most absurd to think the creature wiser in his way [than] the Creator.

This general doctrine he amplifies from the more to the less (v. 18). If angels contend with God, he will find folly in them. If we look on angels' purity and compare it with God's, they are infinitely inferior to him in purity. Or suppose angels would contend with God, they would not be found pure. *How much less man* (v. 19). The argument is followed in two or three instances or steps:

1. If angels must not stand by their own strength, but God will find folly in them, if they should go to plead with God without acknowledging their dependence on him, how much less they that dwell in houses of clay. 'The angels in heaven would be charged with folly if they took such a way as you take, and how can you or any man, that is but a silly bit, like a worm crawling among the ashes, and as easy to be crushed as a moth, begin to contend with God.'

2. The argument is followed in a step further (v. 20). Angels are not subject to dying, but man is here the day and away the morrow; therefore much less can he be justified if he shall contend with God.

3. And a third step (v. 21). Man that thinks much of himself when in health or strength, but a brash or fit of sickness takes him, and he and all his excellency is gone; he minds not his frailty till death come on him, and then he gets not time to mind it as he ought. So he concludes if angels cannot be justified, much less man in contending with God; therefore Job cannot be right in taking such a way. And the argument will bear this much, but not that Job has no grace.

OBSERVATIONS.

1. In general observe, that in the Lord's righteous judgment and wisdom, Satan may oftentimes prevail so far with good and able men as to make use of them to serve his point and advance his end unawares. [*These*] men, without knowing of it, do so here. Therefore beware of being swayed with good intentions in yourself, or with grace in good men to that which is not good in itself.

2. Satan prevails much, and thinks he gets great advantage when he gets use made of good men to drive his design. Paul and Barnabas were men full of the Holy Ghost, yet contention falls in, that sets them by the ears [*at variance*].

3. When good me fall by the ears in a debate, readily and ordinarily they exceed. Paul and Barnabas waxed sharp in the contention; and if we look to this dispute, these show the height of the contention. (1) The rubbing expressions and reflections that the one has on the other. (2) Harsh judging one of another. (3) The more they dispute, the more each is confirmed in his own opinion, and are the more confident — a rife [*common*] and ordinary evil. (4) There is no taking away or closing of the dispute, nay not by Elihu, till the Lord himself

comes in, and yokes one of them to pray for another, a thing that should humble and make all to fear to enter on contentious disputing when such effects follow on it.

4. There is no temptation whereby Satan gains his point more, neither any affliction more bitter to the people of God, [*than*] when good men are yoked against good men in dispute. Therefore this comes in as Job's last trial when [*these*] men take their part against him. (1) It says such a thing may be, especially when a people or person is low. (2) That it is a most prevailing temptation. (3) And very sharp and piercing (Acts 15:39). All Paul's suffering and dying at Jerusalem was not so burdensome as when good men would divert him from his duty (Acts 21:31). Think it not <u>uncouth</u> [*strange*] to meet with opposition from good men, but by all means labor to eschew it.

From the general drift of this chapter observe:

1. If a man maintain one mistake, an hundred will follow upon it; therefore take heed what ground we lay. To maintain a wrong <u>ground</u> [*premise*] will have many bad conclusions.

2. When a man has laid a wrong ground, he is given to use all the arguments he brings to maintain it. He will misapply right grounds to that end. As when a man takes a wrong rule to measure by, he will more readily cast the right rule [*away*] than hold by it.

3. The most clear truth, though it were revealed by vision from God, may be misunderstood and wrested to a wrong end, when a man who is <u>prejudged</u> [*prejudiced*] acts. It is like [when] the Spirit said to these disciples, 'Paul would be bound;' but they misapply it. Use truths soberly; drink them in sincerely. Truth spoken from heaven will be wrested if prejudices get place. That is a good word (2 Pet. 1:19), *We have a more sure word of prophecy whereunto ye ought to take heed,* etc. (1) Be sober in searching for light. (2) Be wary how you apply the mind of God in anything made known, that you draw not conclusions from it that God never intended, as is too often found in men that God gives gifts to in any measure by ordinary.

4. However they misapply, this will hold good: It will *be well with the righteous, and ill with the wicked.* It will be well with them that worship God, and a curse will pursue them that do not.

5

We heard of Eliphaz's scope in the former chapter, and the strain and way he took to bring it about. He had not a mind to destroy Job, but to bring him near God, and conceiving him to be a hypocrite, on that supposition he deals with him, seeking first to humble him, to prepare him to make his peace with God. But as his arguments brought for this purpose in the former chapter were not sure, no more are they in this.

The chapter has three parts. I. There is a new argument brought in to convince Job of his hypocrisy before God, and the want [*lack*] of an interest in God (vs. 1-7). II. An exhortation or direction to Job how to carry himself, to betake himself to God rather than fret as he does (vs. 8-16). III. An exhortation to Job to bear well God's chastisement (vs. 17-26). Verse 27 is the close of Eliphaz's dispute for this part, pressing on Job the right use of what he has said to him.

I. In the first part, the argument he brings to convince Job of hypocrisy has two parts or grounds whereupon it goes. 1. 'Never [a] saint carried himself as you do; therefore you are no believer.' This is no sure arguing, for we are not to count our interest in God according to patterns that have gone before us, for the first believer had not a pattern before him. Besides it strains the sovereignty of God, who takes liberty to exercise his people as pleases him. *Call now if there be any that will answer*, etc. As if he said, 'You are in an afflicted condition, but carry not yourself as believers did before you; therefore you are none of that number.' Or knit [*these*] words to the former chapter, the scope is clear; 'look both to the angels and to righteous men that have gone before you, and see if any of them have had signal strokes as you have gotten, or if they fretted against God as you have done.' Or knit the words to these that follow, the scope is one and the same, to prove Job's disconformity to the saints and conformity to the wicked, both in his strokes and carriage under them. The wisest of the Papists themselves lay by this place for being a ground for invocation of saints, as inconsistent with the scope and their own principles. He proves Job is not like a saint, but like a wicked man in his carriage, because none other will so canker and fret against God, but a foolish envious silly man (v. 2). Eliphaz by this might have proven Job to be infirm, but every fit of folly proves not a man to be wicked.

2. A second proof of his conformity to the wicked is the dispensation he was fallen under, which he follows forth in two or three particulars. (1) 'The wicked have flourished for a time, as the only happy men, but within a little they have been made patterns of God's curse' (v. 3), 'and so has it been with you.' (2) 'The wicked have had many children but they have not been suffered to live long; yea, many of them have come to be crushed in the gate' (that is, made examples of judgment), 'and so have yours' (v. 4). And (3) 'Wicked men may have many cattle, great substance, sow much, have a great harvest, and never shear it, but the robber comes and swallows up his substance. Yea, if any little pickle is left behind the rest, that is taken from him, and look how like this is to your condition' (v. 5).

But there is a deceit in this reasoning. (1) In restricting his chastisement to the judgment that comes on the wicked. (2) In applying the experience of some wicked men to all. (3) And in concluding there was none other so dealt with but wicked men. He does not reason that no ill can come to a righteous man, and no good to a wicked man, but the judgment that was come on Job was so signal and rare, he could not think that such a stroke could befall a good man: 'A godly man could not be so afflicted.' This argument he confirms: (1) From the supreme cause (v. 6). That *though robbers take away a man's substance, yet it is from the just hand of God.* (2) From the fountain or meritorious cause (v. 7). *Man is born to trouble as the sparks fly upward.* Troubles flow from sinful men as sparks from a fired peat. 'Now, seeing extraordinary crosses are on you, and they are not come by guess, but have a cause, and the efficient cause goes [*always*] with the meritorious cause; consider if this is not your condition, Job.' There is a good in this reasoning in so far as it exalts the sovereignty of God, attributing all dispensations to that, and that afflictions come for [*because of*] sin. But it is no good reasoning to say, 'Therefore they come [*always*] for sin.'

II. In the second part there is an exhortation to turn to God, for his own example; although had he been in Job's case it is likely he would not have been so well. There is much solid and sound divinity here, but look upon it with [*these*] caveats. 1. To beware of Eliphaz's [*aim*] in it, of bearing in on Job that he was a hypocrite. 2. We would not [*expound*] [*these*] temporal premises according to the letter, but stretch them in the application to spiritual peace, as that wherein they mainly have their accomplishment to believers, though in the primitive times, even temporal blessings and benefits followed a righteous way of living, and temporal curses and judgments a sinful life. The exhortation is to seek unto God, to lay down his cause before God, and not to dispute with him. This is laid down (v. 8), and then backed with five reasons:

(1) It is from the greatness of God, who can do great things, and there is no limiting of his power (v. 9). And he might readily restore Job if he would take this course (Eph. 3:20): *He can do abundantly above all that we can ask or think.*

(2) It is from God's common goodness, in the giving of rain (v. 10), which is an encouragement to folks to seek spiritual [goodness]. And he enumerates two other common mercies (v. 11). He gives evidence of his desire to do good by helping poor folk in their need, and that should encourage to seek him (Acts 17:26, 27). Common mercies well improved may encourage to seek spiritual [mercies].

(3) It is from the severity of God against them that take another way (v. 12-14). Let men take never so crafty a way to gain their point, if they turn not unto God, they shall not prosper. God shall disappoint them. Yea, so far are they from carrying through their design that they are snared therein; they are still the further in the mire that they take a crooked way to be out of it. And when they know not God in the clearest cause, they shall go wild.

(4) It is from the suitableness between God's goodness and Job's poor condition (vs. 15-16). The argument is laid down (v. 15), and a conclusion drawn from it (v. 16). That *to the poor there is hope*, expectation of through-bearing, and hope of <u>outgate</u> [*delivery*]; but the man that takes another way, and laughs at the poor that trust in God, shall be brought down, and *his mouth stopped* to his shame.

III. In the third part, is the last exhortation (vs. 17-27), to teach Job to bear the cross well and stay him from fretting. And this he does by showing him how good a thing it is to get correction, and a lesson with it from God (Psa. 94:12). Otherwise the cross considered is a fruit of the curse. *Therefore despise not thou*; the word is, *Reprobate not thou the chastening of the Almighty.* Labor rather for the blessing of it, [*than*] to cast it; and this he presses on Job by many reasons.

1. From the benefits of God's delivering him from the miseries he was under (vs. 18-20). He should heal his wounds, give him plenty,

etc; either take his present troubles from him, or sanctify and sweeten them, and take the sting out of them, that they shall not hurt him.

2. From God's preserving him from new troubles, particularly, *From the scourge of tongues,* a great evil (v. 21).

3. A third is from the sold peace and confidence that men have by taking this way (v. 22); nothing shall trouble their peace: (Psa. 112:7). *They shall not be afraid of evil tidings.*

4. A fourth argument is from the covenant that he shall be in with the creatures, so that they shall not hurt him, but work God's point and his good (v. 23).

5. A fifth argument is from being made master of his own house; yea, *He shall visit his tabernacle, and not sin.* For a man that is not at peace with God sins in looking on anything he enjoys, both because he is an usurper, and idolizer of what he has. But he that is at peace with God, gets a lawful and refreshful use of the creatures, and sins not.

6. The last argument is (vs. 25-26), *Thou shalt come to thy grave in a full age,* etc. Not cut down ere it is ripe, but taken ripe to heaven. And as he began with a preface, so he closes with a word of warning, that he would consider this truth and make use of it for his own good (v. 27).

OBSERVATIONS.

Eliphaz begins where he ended, to shake Job's interest. Observe: 1. It is an ordinary temptation of the devil to shake folks' interest in God (Matt. 4:3-6). *If thou be the Son of God,* etc. The reason is: (1) Because Satan can get the believer tempted to no ill turn, till he gets God and him casten out [*to have a falling out*], or him to question his interest in God. (2) Because when he gets him casting his interest in God, he gets him to rub on the image of God within him, as he is given to do. (3) Because he cannot get God and the believer separate, he labors to torment the believer with this temptation. (4) The devil's drift in this to Job, is to get it proven out of Job's own mouth, that he has no grace.

2. As this is no new temptation, so it is no little thing; but gives Satan exceeding great advantage to cast or question our interest in God. Many have it in a trick [*many are deceived*], as if it were a thing pleasant to God [for them] to question their interest; but what

advantage [do] you think had Satan gotten of Job, if he had been of that religion?

3. Satan often represents folks' condition to them, as if never [a] one's case that believed in God before had been like theirs. He will suggest, 'Never was anyone handled as you are.' (Psa. 22:4. with 6). *Our fathers trusted in thee*, etc. *But I am a worm and no man*, etc. It is a mercy that God has left the book of Job to stop the mouth of this temptation. We have here a pattern of many crosses, and of wrath on a man's spirit, and infirmities [*showing*] under crosses, etc; therefore think it not <u>uncouth</u> [*strange*] to be so handled.

4. The rise of affliction is not rightly taken up till it is seen to flow from original corruption, as sparks fly from the fire.

5. There is no solid <u>outgate</u> [*delivery*] from under affliction, till God is acknowledged in it, he sought unto, and ourselves and cause submitted to him.

6. Many folks may be stouter of their grace when the day is far off, [*than*] when they are tried; men may appear humble, patient, etc., till they get a [*trial*], and then the contrary [*appears*]. Eliphaz says he would have done better [*than*] Job, and it is likely he would not have done so well.

7. The cross is no ill thing when folks can make a right use of it; it is a blest thing to be corrected, and get a lesson with it (v. 17). It is folks' corruption and carnal carriage that makes it a curse.

8. From the word of warning wherewith he closes, observe it is not enough for folks to hear much sound doctrine, if they fall not about the practice of it (Matt. 13:23; 7:24). Many are like these hearers [in] James 1:23. Turn over [*these*] exhortations to yourself, as if they were spoken to you in particular, and follow them in practice. That is right hearing.

6

Eliphaz in his own name, and in name of his friends, has laid a sad charge on Job, wherein there were two main faults: 1. That he misconstructed Job in judging him to be a hypocrite, which he drew from grounds that would not bear any such thing. 2. That for the making out of this prejudice, that he and the rest of Job's friends had taken up against Job, he falls to maintain an unsound thesis. In this chapter Job speaks mainly to the first, that is, to remove these mistakes that Eliphaz and the rest grounded their misconstruction of him upon, as if they saw such rottenness in his carriage as proved he had nothing of the grace of God. I. He insists to remove three grounds from which they seemed to draw their conclusion, and after he has removed these grounds which unjustly they imputed to him, he subjoins to every one of them a sad reproof for dealing so with him (vs. 1-27). II. He has an exhortation to his friends to leave off that [way] of dealing with him, and closes with a more clear [proposing] of the question between him and them (vs. 28-30).

I. 1. For the first ground, he labors to remove and vindicate himself from the imputation fastened on him by Eliphaz (4:3, etc.); to wit, that Job was [a] comfort to others, and now he cannot comfort himself. He answers to this, and removes it, by holding out the extremity of weight that was lying on him (vs. 1-5). *O that my grief were throughly weighed* (he says), nothing would down-weigh it. 'Therefore you would not judge of me according to my expressions in it.' And this expostulation of his grief, he follows, telling it was *heavier than the sand of the sea*, and therefore they knew not his condition well that spoke of him. Yea, *his words were swallowed up*, that is, he would not express it, or as it is on the margin, *He wanted words to express it.* Whereby he grants that his words were not so well waled [*chosen*], nor so fully expressing his mind as need were; and (v. 4), touches upon the great burden that lay upon him, that weighted him more than the loss of kine [*cattle*], or sheep, or the boils that were on his body, to wit, that God was to him like a bowman, and he is as the butt or mark. [God] shot his arrows at him which never missed him, and these arrows were not common arrows, but invenomed, and *drank up his spirit.* Yea, God seemed to him as one mustering all his arrows, and drawing them up in ranks and battle array against him, a silly poor pained man; whereby he lets them and us see, he was not only under outward crosses but inward terrors at once [*as well*].

This he follows forth (v. 5), *Doth the wild ass bray when he hath grass? or loweth the ox over his fodder?* 'A beast will make [*noise*] when it wants meat [*lacks food*], and therefore wonder not when I am in this pinch, and under such a weight that I make din, and that my carriage is altered from what it was.' And (v. 6), *Can that which is unsavory be eaten without salt? or is there any taste in the white of an egg?* He applies this to his friends, as if he said, 'you have taken pains to comfort me, and mitigate my sorrow; but there is no more seasoning in your words, than there is taste in the white of an egg. Yea (v. 7), *The things I refused to touch are as my sorrowful meat,* or 'as the sorrows or sickness of my meat.' That is, 'That which you would have me taking, mars my comfort. For to call me a hypocrite (as you would have me to do) would turn my best comfort to sorrow; that would put me clean over the brae [*hill*].'

2. He labors to remove a second ground or mistake, and does not remove it so well as the former (vs. 8-23). He removes the first mistake soundly, by showing that his carriage inferred no such conclusion as they put upon it. But when he comes to remove the second, which was the desperate wish which they challenged him for, he says, *O that I had my request,* etc. His scope is to show he had reason for that wish, and he counts himself not only rash in such a wish, but shows it is the thing he would [*most*] have (vs. 8-9), as if he said, 'O that he would utterly take me from the world, and not pine [*afflict*] me piece and piece. O that he would once make an end of me.' And he shows some reasons for it, whereby he would insinuate he was not so desperate as they took him to be, in so wishing. He says (v. 10) for then *I should yet have comfort, and would harden myself against sorrow.* That is, 'the hope of death being near would make me bear this trouble the better. Therefore *let him not spare,* for I have a testimony within me, I have not concealed his words, or hid them' (as it is, Psa. 40:10; Rom. 1:18, *who hold the truth in unrighteousness*). The meaning is, 'I have no challenge for suppressing any light that God has given me, or for being deficient in any known duty; therefore I am not desperate in seeking death, as you would make me to be.'

A second reason of his wish is that he had no hope to live (vs. 11-12). Yea, that it was impossible his body would long sustain that pain it was under. *What is my strength that I should hope?* That is, 'I have no strength that I should hope to win through this pain.' *And what is my end, that I should prolong my life?* That is, 'It is but a short time that I have to live, for there is more upon me [*than*] would slay an hundred; yea, if I were made of stone or brass, there is as much on me as would undo me.' This mistake (as we said) Job does not remove so fully and well, for though he is right in comforting himself from the life to come, and in thinking the strength he had was but small to bear the weight that was lying upon him, yet he is wrong in limiting God, and in prescribing God a way out of anxiety.

A third reason is (v. 13), *Is not my help in me?* In the original it is, *Is not there that which sustains me in me?* that is the being and essence of sincerity. 'And do you think that the being and essence which once I had of a sincere man is now away?' This interrogation has the force of a negation, that he is not the man they took him to be, a hypocrite, and a man void of spiritual wisdom such as became a sincere man to have; but that he is sincere and spiritually wise. So in this verse he directly contradicts their assertion which they had of him.

Then he follows out a reproof to them, in showing (vs. 12-23):

(1) What should be the duty of friends to friends in the day of affliction, and how unlike their practice and carriage to him was unto that. *To him that is afflicted pity should be shown* — 'a friend should sympathize with his friend in trouble, and if you were friendly you would do so to me, and comfort such a man as I am.' *But he forsakes the fear of the Almighty* — in the third person checking Eliphaz, who had added a burden to his weight. Then in comparison he shows what was his friends carriage towards him. 'My friends when they came to comfort me,' *they have dealt deceitfully with me.* And he shows how they have been like a brook that in winter is full of water, but in summer is dry and has nothing in it to refresh the weary traveler, when he has most need of a drink. 'So have my friends been to me; they have cast by their old friendship when I have most need of it,' importing that a friend should be a friend and friendly at all times.

(2) It holds out the disappointment that honest hearts may meet with from friends. And when he has applied the similitude to them (v. 21) he aggreges [*enlarges on*] their unfriendly dealing (v. 22-23). As if he said, 'I might in this my poverty, have sought some of your substance, and your help against the enemy that robbed me, and you were bound to have done it, as Abraham did Lot (Gen. 14). But did

I seek this of you? I did not. I would bear the [*lack*] of goods and wrongs from enemies, and not seek a revenge, and when I have sought so little of you, you might well have bestowed a comfortable word upon me, and not have added to my wound.'

3. The third ground or mistake they went upon, and which he labors to remove, is a wresting of some of Job's words in the end of chapter 3, as if Job had denied God's justice. Which Job denies he did, and speaks of God's justice as well as they did (vs. 24-27). And first, shows how willing he is to be taught, and take instruction in that wherein he has been wrong (v. 24). And that he will not tenaciously stick to words; for right words are forcible, but their arguing reproachfully, and captiously snatching at words would never convince him. A second fault is that they left the substance of the matter, and stuck too much to words, and it was not [the] time, when he was lying under such a heavy burden, to stick upon words, especially when he was not abiding by any words that were wrong. Therefore, he says, 'it were better that you should leave words, and take yourself to the matter' (v. 26). 'But you are so far from this, *that ye dig a pit for me,* your friend, by bearing upon me that I am a hypocrite, instead of doing me good.'

II. In the second part of the chapter (v. 28-30), he has a double exhortation, backed with a reason. As if he said, 'I exhort you, since you do me no good by this sort of reasoning, leave it off. *Be content* with what is said, insist not in taking notice of words; I allow not myself in them; rather consider my case as it is, and *Return,* come to yourself again, and insist [*continue*] not in your guilt, after I have given you warning, for that will be a double sin to you.' Or 'think not that these expressions you chop [*bandy*] so much at, will bear so much, as if there were nothing but iniquity in me.' The words will bear both. *My righteousness is in it.* 'It concerns me nearly, whether I am a hypocrite or sincere man; therefore lay by such a way of reasoning, for I cannot admit of it.' Then he closes with proposing a ground which he intends to follow forth in the next chapter. 'The main cause is not iniquity, for I have gotten as much from God to discern what is right, and what is wrong; and therefore seeing it concerns me so nearly, stick not to the sentence you passed upon me.'

OBSERVATIONS.

From Job's way wherein it is commendable, observe: 1. That it is a part of a friendly duty when folks have mistakes, to endeavor in a friendly way to remove them. Though friends should count and call us hypocrites, not to be angry at them for that, but labor in a friendly manner to remove the mistake. Selfish pride [*can*] not abide any more talking, if once folks' sincerity is questioned. Job teaches more humility, and therefore labors, (1) To remove this personal prejudice his friends had at him, ere he dispute the main thesis; for till [then], disputation is to no purpose. (2) More particularly, whatever is his miscarriage, he has high thoughts of God, and this puts a luster on all his expressions. When true piety is well planted in the heart, high thoughts of God, and reverent expressions of God will not soon wear out.

2. He counts more of the terror of God, [*than*] of all his other afflictions that he suffered; and indeed, where the terror of God is let forth on the spirit of a creature, it is the greatest weight. There is no affliction [compared] to that; *A wounded spirit who can bear?* It is the greatest happiness to have God to be our friend, and the greatest misery to have him to be our enemy.

3. For as hard expressions and vehement temptations as came from his friends, and for all that sense and suggestion concurring with them can say, *he will not cast his integrity.* To digest that, was as poison to him. His practice is a pattern worthy of imitation, and evidences the strength of his faith; his soul refuses whatever may weaken his confidence in God. Any of you that have any soundness, quit it not; but having taken up your condition aright, and having cleared your interest in God, stick by it. But little knows many of you what it is to maintain a conflict on this account as he did, and the less evidence have you that matters are right between God and you.

4. From that wherein Job miscarries, observe: (1) That it is a right hard thing when once a good man has vented himself in an evil <u>tent</u> [*purpose*], to draw him off it. When Job has wished for death, he renews his wish, and comes ere all be done to defend himself that he is right in so doing. Jonah says, *I do well to be angry.* So says Job in substance.

Quest. But how does Job, in this his sinful wish, entertain the peace and quietness of a good conscience?

Answ. Certainly there was sin in Job's words, and something in him that makes him think he had peace, but he looked not rightly on his distemper. He leaned so to the bygone experience of God's favor, that he took no notice of intervening sin, which he is made to [*acknowledge*] (chapter 40 and 42). The example of Job and his friends here may give us this word of warning, to give more charity one of us to another in debatable matters. In our hearing and speaking of, and to one another, let us give some more grains of allowance one of us to another, and stick not captiously to words, else our dispute will [*disappear*] in words without profit. For [*wrangling*] about words serves to no purpose, but for subverting the hearers.

7

Job having begun to answer Eliphaz in the former chapter, he here goes on, and having some way excused the bitterness of his expression, he sticks to one thing he seemed to [*misunderstand*] in his reproof, to wit, his vehement desire of death (6:8-9). Wherein having reproved his friends of their uncharitableness in judging him, he now justifies his desire, and gives reasons why he should vehemently desire death rather than life. And this he goes on in (vs. 1-16). And secondly (vs. 17-21), he some way mitigates his peremptoriness in desiring death, by turning it over into a more moderate suit to God, for a little ease and breathing, and that God would forgive him his sin. This is the scope and sum of this chapter: Job laying out his complaint before God, supplicates for some ease, if it were for never so short a breathing time before death, that it may be known he is not the man he is judged to be.

I. In the first part of the chapter he lays down three grounds to maintain his vehement desire of dying, and every one of them grows to a greater height.

1. The first ground is from the equity of the thing, which he lays down by way of comparison taken from a thing which is general to all men. Every man has a task given him of God, and there is a time set to every man's labor and burden, so must there be to mine (v. 1). And the servant that is hired to a hard work may long for the shadow in the heat of the day to rest in, and may look for his reward at the end of his labor, and so may I (v. 2). 'But I am delayed in obtaining the end of my task; yea, whereas servants get some ease in the night, I get none; and not only days and nights, but *months of vanity* are measured out to me. Therefore I have much more reason to desire death, than the servant has to desire the shadow or end of his labor' (v. 3). [This] he aggreges [*enlarges on*] in the next two verses: 'I no sooner set myself for ease in the night, but I think long for day, and *I am full of tossings too and fro;*' that is, 'neither night nor day get I rest, but am tossed to and fro, both by night and by day, and so my

condition is worse than a hired servant' (v. 4). 'And for the condition of my body, this skin of mine is *broken*, my *flesh is clothed with worms;'* that is, running out filthy matter, where it is very likely worms have bred. *And with clods of dust*, that is, scabs like clods of dust; or it is likely, he being sitting among the ashes, lumps of the dust did stick to his sores. And by reason of this broken skin, '*I am become loathsome* to myself, and much more to others; therefore no wonder I wish to be <u>away</u> [*dead*]' (v. 5). Now this comparison, and his reasoning from it, in some things holds good, as (1) That God has appointed to every man his task and burden. (2) And a time and an end to every man's task. (3) But In this is Job's fault, that he strains the argument in setting God a time to his task and end of his work.

2. The second ground is from the certainty of death coming so swiftly: why may he not wish and long for it? This argument he follows out from vs. 6-11. 'I am,' he says, 'fast wearing near an end; the spool runs no faster through the web, [*than*] I <u>post</u> [*haste*] toward death, and there is no hope of my recovery' (v. 6). And therefore [he] turns to God in a particular way, and says, *O remember that this life I have is but like a puff of wind*, 'and I expect no more good here away;' drawing a conclusion from sense, or from what sense and temptation spoke, and in this he failed (v. 7). This argument he enlarges, '*The eye that hath seen me*, and thought something of me, *shall see me no more. I am not for the world any more; thine eyes are upon me, and I am not*; when thou looks angry like upon me, it puts me from having any being' (v. 8). Then he uses a new similitude to set out the suddenness of his dying, and the impossibility of his returning to a present world, *as the cloud is consumed and vanishes away*, that is, 'a cloud when it rises, seems something, but incontinent, it [*disappears*]; so am I, and all men' (v. 9). *He shall return no more to his house.* That is, though man while he lived, seemed to have been dwelling, and enjoying the pleasures of a present time at his will, yet when death comes, his house shall wear out of acquaintance with him, and he with it, and he shall have no more pleasure in it (v. 10). And his <u>shot</u> [*aim*] being to show what put him to this peremptoriness in his wish, therefore he says (v. 11), he will take the more liberty to open his mouth and give vent to the bitterness of his spirit. But he fails: (1) In mistaking his condition, as if there were no possibility for him to live. Thus it fares with him, and may fare, when the grounds of sense are more weighed than the grounds of faith, and submission to God. (2) In making the shortness of his time a ground for liberty to speak the more freely, and to vent his nature and sense, and that he has a kind of indulgence to natural reason and passion.

3. The third ground is from the necessity of his dying. He must, and behooved to die, and therefore might choose and vehemently desire it. This he sets out in a more expostulating and passionate way than the former (v. 12-16). *Am I a sea, or a whale, that thou sets a watch over me?* that is, 'What am I to be thus beset with the iron soldiers of God's indignation to wait upon me? Am I a senseless creature like the sea? or like a whale? I [*can*] not abide this trouble. It would destroy any creature.' Wherein he shows his infirmity could not abide such hard dealing (v. 12). *When I say, my bed shall comfort me,* etc., that is, 'when I use many shifts for ease and rest, and lay down in my bed for a little sleep, I am nothing the better,' *for thou scarrest me with dreams,* looking to God as his supreme cause, *and terrifiest me with visions.* That is, 'when I look for ease by sleep, I get none; for thou affrights me by ugly representations in my sleep, that I have no more rest in sleep, [*than*] if I were waking, but rather less' (vs. 13-14). And he repeats the conclusion (v. 15), *so that my soul chooses strangling, and death rather than life.* That is, 'ere I were in this life, I would rather be hanged. It were better for me to abide any violent death than be in this condition.' A horrible word — *I loath this life,* 'and abominate it.' *Let me alone,* 'let me even die, give me even leave to die. I would not have this life though it were offered to me; *for my days are vanity,* and why should I be in more trouble' (v.16). [This] lets us see how when passion gets vent, it <u>heightens</u> [*grows*] in them in whom it prevails, and <u>rubs</u> [*reflects*] on God. All Job's mercies are now forgotten, as if they had not been.

II. In the second part of the chapter, because it is likely Job could not justify himself in [*these*] words, he therefore mitigates both his peremptoriness in his suit, and his expressions, and that by way of removing or answering two objections.

1. God is not always angry when he exercises; but where most graces are, he often if not ordinarily exercises most, and magnifies his grace by sustaining under affliction. He answers (vs. 17-18), 'I know that to be true, God will magnify men by taking pains on them by affliction, and his own grace in sustaining men under affliction by his power.' *But what is man that he should be thus magnified?* 'Is man a party to God? or can man hold out and bear up in such a hard exercise? He cannot.' *And what is man, that thou shouldest set thy heart upon him?* that is, 'What is man that God should choose him out from among other creatures, that he may visit him, and bring him under some chastisement for his good; and that God should do this with delight, and continue such a constant course of exercise with him? Man is such a <u>feckless</u> [*helpless*] thing, that he [*can*] not bear such

dealing.' So he grants in the general that God may love them whom he exercises hardly; and that God in exercising magnifies men, and makes their *faith to be found unto praise* (1 Pet. 1:7). But he had rather [*lack*] the good as have the trouble of such an exercise; or fearing not to be borne through the exercise, he had rather want it, and get leave to lie in the condition he was in ere the exercise came, [*than*] have such a straitening [*way*] as that. Therefore he closes (v. 19), *How long wilt thou not depart from me?* that is, 'How long shall this heavy and sad exercise last, *let me alone till I swallow down my spittle;* I get not leave to draw my breath.' He quarrels not so much God's exercising him here, as the continuance of it, that man was not able to endure.

2. Is there not cause for all this exercise, and for the continuance of it also? Is there sin in Job? His sense answered the former objection, and he makes faith answer this. 'I grant,' he says, 'it is true, *I have sinned,* but will this hard exercise, or my suffering, take away my sin?' *What shall I do unto thee, O thou preserver of men?* that is, 'O thou that saves these whom thou savest freely, and hast appointed salvation to me on another score than by their suffering to satisfy thy justice, *why then am I set as a mark against thee?* seeing my suffering cannot satisfy thy justice, why am I so hardly handled? *so that I am a burden to myself,* much more may I be so to others' (v. 20). *Why dost thou not pardon my transgression, and take away mine iniquity?* 'It were better for thee to take away my sin freely, and why then takest thou this way with me; seeing thou takest it with no other? for whom thou pardonest, thou pardonest freely; and thou must deal so with me also; for if thou go on thus with me, *I shall sleep in the dust,* I shall soon wear away, and shall not be found again. *Thou shall seek me in the morning, but I shall not be.* I shall never be to set out thy praise any more in this generation.' And [*these*] last words are the main argument whereby he deals with God for a little breathing, even that he may vindicate himself from the aspersion put upon him, and glorify God in the land of the living.

So in the chapter we find Job in a too bitter way expostulating his condition; yet with a mixture of faith, to let us see there was some awe and fear of God, and faith in God, in the heart of the gracious man in the midst of his bitterest cup, and most tart expressions.

OBSERVATIONS.

1. When hard exercises lie upon, they will strain much infirmity and weakness out of the best, that folks would hardly have thought had been in them. And much grace will also [*appear*], that lurked

before; neither this faith and patience in Job had shined so brightly, neither this fretting and daring way of expostulating with God, had he not been thus tried. A thing that vindicates God, and should lay [low] the pride of the creature. Never [was there] a trial in Scotland[1] but it has discovered more steadfastness in some, and rottenness in others; therefore let none be proud, but *he that stands take heed lest he fall.*

2. When straits are straitening, it is best to round [*smooth*] over our case between God and us; not that it is excusable thus to expostulate with God in a carnal way; but it is better complaining to God than of God to any other, and it owns nature more, and he can answer our objections best. Besides that, it is most childish and wife-like, so to speak.

3. Observe from the grounds he lays, or arguments he brings: (1) How feckless [*weak*] man's life is, *it is like a weaver's shuttle, like a cloud, a puff of wind* for vanity and brevity. (2) And how feckless the persons of men are, though you had a sound skin as Job's, and though it were the skin both of a honorable man and pious, how soon may it grow loathsome to yourself and others, full of holes and worms. (3) When sense gets leave to judge of God and his way, it judges [*always*] rashly and hardly of him. This is from the last ground.

Use 1. Never look at our skin, but be humble, and make ready for death, for our days will soon wear away.

Use 2. Never let sense be judge of God and his way, for the sense of the best is a rash and corrupt judge.

4. Folks often seek and think to find satisfaction in creature comforts, in their bed and board, and such like, as Job did, but find them blasted when they come to them. Creature-comforts are disappointing; when we seek help in the creatures and means, God lets us find them broken cisterns. Our bed cannot ease us. Seek rest in him where only it is to be found.

5. Small temporal mercies ought to be esteemed great mercies, and if we were put on the rack as Job was, we would think more of one night's rest, without scary dreams and ugly visions, [*than*] now we do of many. Liberty to draw the breath or swallow down the spittle was a thing he could not win to. We have leave to lie down and rise, go out and come in, in peace, and know not what it is to prize [*these*] mercies. How this does demonstrate our ingratitude.

---

1   See previous footnote, pp. 11-12.

When to get leave to breath, to swallow our spittle, not to have our life loathsome to us, not to be made an object, not to be wondered at; [*these*] should be counted [a] mercy.

6. From the last part of the chapter, we find Job to be wrong in suffering sense to draw bad conclusions from true and good premises. He grants God magnifies man in taking pains to correct him, rather than to suffer him to go on in sin; but he had rather [*lack*] the good of affliction ere he had the trouble of it. Observe: (1) There is none who judge of trials right, but they will see something of God's love in them. (2) When God takes pains on man to correct him, it is his magnifying of man; it is his hewing and dressing of him as a workman does a piece of work; and so when God uses many means to reclaim Capernaum, it is lifted up to heaven in this respect. But great misery follows the abuse of great mercy. (3) See how irrational is sense where it gets way; though faith says a trial is good, yet sense will say, better [to] have strangling or violent death. (4) Believers are not [*outside*] the reach of temptations even to strangling; temptations of this kind may be incident to them that are precious to God, and it is no extraordinary thing to see it. (5) However folks deal with God under a trial, and however they are to take with sin [*acknowledge their sin*], they should never quit pleading for pardon, on the grounds of free grace. Job fails in some expressions, and confesses sin, yet he will not quite the hope of pardon, but pleads for it. And when folks separate any of [*these*] two, they will come behind; that is, when folks take not with sin, and are not weighted with it, but take them to mercy; or stick in the sense of sin, and come not to mercy. The right [*way*] is to join both.

8

We heard in the beginning of the dispute, the scope of Job's friends. They have a good [*goal*] to bring Job by repentance to a happy condition; but they mistake Job's case, looking on Job's temporal affliction as a fruit of wrath, and evidence of his hypocrisy, not considering God's sovereign way of dealing. Therefore they deal with him as one that never had any of the grace of God; and by the wisdom of God so over-ruling, for the completing of Job's trial, they are instrumental in furthering Satan's design, though they knew nothing of it.

When Job had put by one assault [from] Eliphaz, [he] hereby encounters with another by Bildad the Shuhite, so called because come of Shauh, born of Keturah (Gen. 25:1-2), whose children were sent to the East country, and lived there not far from Job. He sets on to deal with Job, and falls upon the same strain with the other friend. Mistaking some of Job's expressions in expostulating with God, he takes advantage, and thinks to cast all that Job had said as wind, and therefore says (v. 2), *How long wilt thou speak these things, and the words of thy mouth be as strong wind?* That is, 'How long will it be before you leave off challenging God as unrighteous in afflicting you?' or, 'before all that has been spoken convince you that you do not know God?' 'Another purpose would set you better' (even that which he [*proposes*] hereafter, v. 5.) The meaning is, 'How long Job, will you make much [*noise*] with empty talk that can neither profit you, nor hurt God's justice, more than a wind can hurt a strong rock; it were better you should justify God's justice, and [*admit*] your own unrighteousness.' This he lays down in general words (v. 3) that it may be the better digested, and leaves Job to apply it to himself, opposing God's justice and Job's expressions, as if Job did justify himself, and rub on God's justice, and Job's state, and the temporal judgments he was lying under, as if God could not so heavily afflict an upright man. As if he said, 'Job, either God or you must be in the wrong, *Doth God pervert judgment? Will he lay on strokes* where there is no just cause? That cannot be.' Or, '*Doth the Almighty pervert justice?*

Can God be swayed with bye respects to do anything that is wrong? That is impossible; therefore God is just, and you are unjust.'

The ground he lays is good, but he was wrong in opposing Job's expressions as if [they] alleged any such thing as he supposes, and from Job's temporal suffering concluding him to be a wicked man. This is the great fallacy in all this dispute, to argue from Job's temporal affliction that he was a hypocrite. He goes on to apply both to Job.

1. In the instance of God's taking away his children in the way they were removed (v. 4). 'God has taken away your children in the hand of their transgression; therefore there is just cause for what he has done.' [While] he [*proposes*] this by way of supposition to make him digest it the better; the words bear [the meaning], 'seeing they have sinned, God has taken them away in their transgression.'

2. He proves the second part, that Job is unrighteous, in the following verses, which he prepares by way of advice, that Job may the better digest it; and to show his scope is to humble Job, and bring him to repentance. As if he said, 'If you were righteous, God had not done with you as he has done. But if you would yet [*admit*] your sin, and timeously seek unto God, and not stand to the justifying of your own integrity; and if you would do this sincerely, as [if] all your bygone service had not been, all these strokes should not have come on you, if you had been sincere, so the strokes that are lying on you should be taken off you if yet you would seek God sincerely. Yea, the happiness that you have had should be little to that you should receive' (vs. 5-7). Good motives when rightly taken and applied, but unsound to convince Job that he had no sincerity.

Because he thought Job would hardly digest this doctrine, he confirms it by antiquity (v. 8-19). 'I grant,' he says, 'we are but young folks. We live not so long as these who went before us, and cannot have so much knowledge and insight in matters. But look to all the ancients that were before you, and see, if they are not of our mind.' Even as Eliphaz (chapter 5) appealed to antiquity, so does Bildad. 'You may think that we speak out of passion and prejudice, but look back and hear what they say who lived long since, and they will speak words out of their heart, and you may take the words off their hand, though you will not take it off ours.' And the doctrine he insists on is this, that whatever the hypocrite had, it was taken from him; and how high so ever he was lifted up, he came down wonderfully, even as it went with Job; and the righteous never suffered as he did.

And this he illustrates by three similitudes. 1. The first is to this purpose (vs. 10-13): 'Bushes will be green where there is water enough about them, but as soon as the water dries up, they wither before any other herbs; so is it with them that forget God. Hypocrites may flourish for a time, while things go well with them and theirs; but when a change comes, they are suddenly blasted and gone; and look if it is not so with you.' And he clears what he means by the hypocrite: It is such a one that forgets God, that minds not the honor of God, and aims not at the power of godliness; but minds himself, and rests on a form of religion.

2. The second similitude is taken from the [*spiders*] in windows, and their webs (vs. 14-15). As the [*spider*] when it has taken pains to weave a web, and [*build*] a house to itself in the window, and a [*broom*] comes and sweeps it away, so is it with the hypocrite. He builds a house and gets many common mercies, and thinks something of himself, and to enjoy rest and quietness. But when he thinks on rest; it is taken from him; he leans to his house, but it falls. All that he has fails him, and he seeks to hold fast his gathered comforts, but they are blown upon and [*vanish*].

3. The third similitude (vs. 16-18): 'The hypocrite may be like a tree that takes root and grows green, and shoots forth branches, yea, like a tree whose roots spring beside the fountain, whose *root is wrapped about the heap,* and so are flattened and look sicker-like [*securer*], *and seeth the place at stones.* That is, difficulties do not move him more than a stone does a tree. 'But if God comes to destroy the hypocrite, as he has done you; even as when a tree is cut down, it is not known such a thing was there.' And he applies this to the prosperity of the wicked (v. 19). All the wicked man's or hypocrite's joy is no more solid nor lasting, [*than these*] similitudes or comparisons hold forth. *And out of the earth shall others grow,* that is, others that were scarce known shall get his place, and in all this he secretly hints at Job's case.

Then (v. 20) he reports the conclusion, and applies it in an use to Job (v. 21-22). *Behold, God will not cast away a perfect man,* none that is upright will be rejected of God. *Neither will he help the ill doer.* He will not take him by the hand, as the word is. However he may flourish for a time; therefore 'look upon the advice that I have given you as the best; repent and seek unto God, and you shall get a comfortable outgate [*outcome; deliverance*]. Yea, this is the way to get an upper hand over all your enemies.' *And the dwelling place of the wicked shall come to nought,* which he repeats to fear Job from lying in the condition he supposed him to be in. He had seen his dwelling come soon down, and if he went on in the way he was in, it would be yet worse with him.

OBSERVATIONS.

1. In general. One good man may soon mistake the condition of another good man, and judge too hardly of him, and this was the fault of Job's friends.

Use. Beware of constructing hardly of one another from particular slips or infirmities. Seek to have a more solid ground of comfort to lean to, than the estimation and judgment of others. If Job had not a better proof of his sincerity, his comfort had been to seek [*questionable*] in the day of his distress.

2. Nothing will make folks more readily miscarry in rash judging of other men's state, than the judging of it by dispensations either outward or inward. Especially outward dispensations are not the rule of trial of ourselves or others, but the promises, and evidences of God's grace. Dispensations thus looked upon, are the great ground whereupon Satan gets advantage to mud [*cloud*] folks' condition, [such] as [when] you pray, and God does not hear you; you read, and get no comfort. Therefore beware of walking by this rule.

3. When once Satan and temptations enter, and get way to question a man's state, he will not be soon put from it; the temptation will not be easily repelled. Job's wife began the temptation, Eliphaz holds on, and Job resists both. Yet here he meets with a new onset, and more follows. Therefore think not this temptation soon put by, and weary not under it, but *resist steadfast in the faith.*

4. Oft-times men are given to count little of anything said against them by other men, and much of anything they say or is said for them. Job had said much to vindicate himself, yet Bildad casts all his words as vain. It is a thing incident to men in debates and disputes to stumble on an ill [*chosen*] word, and to [*mistake*] the main purpose and truth of the matter. Job's friends had sooner come to the knowledge of the truth, if this ill had not prevailed with them.

5. The first language of temptation is to persuade men that disputation and reasoning for clearing truth is needless, and that without any reason to quite it. Therefore Bildad (v. 2) says, *How long wilt thou speak?* 'you must quit it, and lay it by; your hypocrisy will

be discovered.' There is the like language injected on souls, when fainting and heartlessness comes in. 'You have nothing ado with grace. There is nothing sound in you; the promise belongs not to you. Therefore quit it and give over.'

6. From the third verse observe: (1) That when such temptations get way, they readily press to oppose God, and the person, as if their calling themselves upright and just did reflect on God and his righteousness. There is no more common temptation. God is just, and that is true; but the shot [*aim*] of the temptation, is not to humble, but to cast the soul out and at distance with God. (2) Whether God takes a way of justice or mercy with souls, he cannot pervert judgment; he can do no wrong in either of them (Deut. 32:4). *A God of truth and without iniquity, just and right is he.* Therefore give God the carrying on both of your private, and of the public work without a hink [*hesitation*].

7. Observe (v. 4), when the devil cannot win in upon men to question their state, he will seek to trouble them about the state of their children. 'Your children are taken away to hell in their sin, and what do you think of that?' He leaves no wind unsailed to gain his point with the soul whom he minds to tempt, to weaken their peace, to breed ill thoughts in them concerning these they desire to have good thoughts of.

8. Observe (vs. 5-7): (1) That when events fall out cross[wise] to folks' prayers, temptation is ready to say, God is angry at them and their prayers, that they have no interest in God, and are but hypocrites, and must take another way of seeking God, if they would be heard. For Bildad insinuates if Job had prayed right before, it had not been thus with him; therefore limit not God in prayer, and judge not of your state by the answers of your prayers.

(2) Take the words in a right sense, and they give this lesson, that right seeking of God has these three branches: [1] That it be timeously and earnest. [2] With humility, or humble supplicating of God as a party found in the chalk [*within the mark*] and guilty. [3] That it be with purity and uprightness; that the person be sincere, and walking after a right rule. *If I regard iniquity in my heart, the Lord will not hear my prayer.* Many lean to their prayers, and go to hell, because they never study for purity of heart. Hence Christ will say to many that cry, '*Lord, Lord,*' *Depart from me, ye workers of iniquity, I know you not.*

9. In the rest of the chapter observe: (1) That in folks' conferring and debating of questions, it is a gaining [*self-serving*] way not to lay

much weight on folks' own judgment, but that they seek to add weight to that they maintain rather from some other thing. Tenaciousness is an evil thing. (2) God's ordinary way of dealing with his people rightly taken up, is a good means of settling, and when it is mistaken, it proves a prejudice. (3) Hypocrisy and formality in religion never come well to, nor shall ever come well to, nor profit a person. The joy of the hypocrite shall perish; this is the scope of [these] similitudes. The hypocrite have what he will, is an unhappy man. Take it therefore as a known truth, and place your happiness in God's favor, and [in] dealing sincere before him, and not in an outward flourishing condition in the world. (4) Old hypocrites have access to God's mercy, if they will seek it in time. Job is supposed to be such a man, yet has an offer of mercy. So broad is mercy; God bars the door of mercy on none, nay not on hypocrites. It is not the hypocrite as such, but continuing such, that puts him from mercy. (5) All sharpness in threatenings and challenges should have the commending of mercy for their shot and end, and the commending of mercy is the way to cause challenges [to] work. Bildad is right in not shooting Job away by challenges, though Satan had another design. (6) From all [these] things God would teach us to take a right way to fix and settle ourselves against a storm. If we make not the foundation sure, as Job did, we will be soon shaken.

9

W e heard in the former chapter the way how Bildad proceeded with Job, and the sum of his procedure runs on these two: 1. In vindicating God, whom he thought Job in his free expressions rubbed upon, and that he intended to justify himself. 2. In the conclusion which Bildad draws from that general ground, *viz.* that God was just in punishing Job so oddly and extraordinarily, and inflicting such judgments on his children, and refusing to hear his prayers, and hence that Job was not a just man but a hypocrite; otherwise he had not undergone such hard and extraordinary trials. In this chapter Job answers to both these, and in the next chapter returns and vents his mind to God.

He answers to the first, granting the general ground laid down; that is, that God was just, and could not pervert judgment. I. He illustrates this and he clears his purpose (vs. 14-22), that he intended not to justify himself, and reflect upon the justice of God, and therefore, that [Bildad] was mistaken; and he lays by this as an uncontroverted conclusion. But the question stands on the conclusion which he drew from that, as if God could afflict no man as he was, with such extraordinary temporal judgment, but wicked men; and this he denies. Therefore he says (v. 22), *This is one thing, therefore I said it, he destroys the perfect and the wicked.* That is, in reference to temporal judgments, godly and wicked share alike. II. This question so stated, he clears [it], vindicating himself from the aspersions his friends put upon him to the end of the chapter (vs. 23-35).

I. Job asserts and yields to the same truth which Bildad held forth (8:31). *I know it is so of a truth.* 'I contradict not that truth, that God does not pervert judgment.' And he uses an asseveration the more to press his belief of it. *How can man be just with God?* Man is from a root that signifies mourning or misery. How can silly frail man be just with God? If he shall take upon him to plead with him, he would not be able to answer; foolish man would win nothing of that bargain, and therefore, 'I was not such a fool as you took me to be, to take that [*way*]' (vs. 1-3). He gives a ground for this (v. 4). God orders his way and working with men so wisely, that no spot is to be found upon it. It has no defect or <u>inlake</u> [*deficiency*], and he is so mighty in strength that there is no wrestling, nor striving with him. And this he repeats by way of [a] question. *Who hath hardened himself against him, and prospered?* 'Who ever took this [*way*] of contesting with God, that did win on it?' And he calls this gate a man's hardening of himself against God, as if no man would take such a course, but such a man as is without any awe or fear of God.

He illustrates God's power and might, and his wisdom in ordering matters (vs. 4-13). His power (vs. 4-9), is most spoken to, though his wisdom also is mixed with it. 1. In works of creation and providence, and the greatest things that are in the world. *He removes the mountains and overturns them in his anger.* If God is angry, he can [*make*] the mountains, that are of a greater strength than man, skip like rams. 2. He can [*make*] a little thing shake the whole universe; send an earthquake and make it reel to and fro. Is it then a wise thing for a man to dispute with him? 3. The sun is a more glorious creature than man, and yet when he commands, it rises not; he can send an eclipse, when he pleases, and with a cloud can seal or lock up the stars. 4. It is a great matter to spread out the vast curtain of the heaven, and yet that is God's singular property to have superiority over the heaven as well as the earth. *He alone spreads out the heaven, and treads upon*, or stills that raging and reasonless creature, *the sea.*

He gives a more particular instance of God's sovereignty (v. 9); *which maketh Arcturus, Orion and Pleiades, and the chambers of the South.* An instance of God's sovereignty, that to man's judgment has a more immediate influence in times and seasons and second causes, that God may be known to be the ruler of the effects, and of the causes of these effects.

Next he comes to illustrate God's wisdom, and speaks of it as inexpressible (v. 10); *which doth great things past finding out.* The things of God are [*outside*] the reach of man and any creature. Yea the things of God are wonderful in themselves, and in the way he carries them on; and they are without number, to point out both the greatness and excellency of the wisdom of God in his works. And he instances this in his particular dealing with him (v. 11). *Lo, he goeth by me, and I see him not; he passeth on also, and I perceive him not.* 'Certainly God has a particular hand in dealing with me; he is not far off, for he goes by me. But he is so supreme that I cannot [understand] the reasons of his dealing, so as to reconcile his dealing in all the parts of it.' [This] intimates that he did see God, but he got not that accurate sight that he was able to express what God was doing, and to give the reasons of it.

He then concludes this general doctrine (v. 12): *Behold he taketh away, who can hinder him? who will say unto him, what doest thou?* 'When God will take a way of his own to do what pleases him, who is able to hinder him, or who has right to hinder him?' And (v. 13), *if God will not withdraw his anger, the proud helpers will stoop under him.* If any helps of pride, as the word is, or proud nature in men, will stand in his way, he can crush them. And thus, 1. He vindicates himself, that he is as free as Bildad of rubbing on God's justice by his expressions. 2. He vindicates also his practice by a number of arguments:

(1) He shows he was not that foolish to take that way with God before whom no creature could stand (v. 14), and so goes on to clear his purpose (to v. 22), as if he said, 'Do you think that I would take that way with God, that I know no creature can take and come speed in [*succeed in*]. Think it not. If no creature can stand before God in such a [*way*], how much less I, in such a condition as I am in? Do you think that I would attempt such a thing, as if I could be able by reason to overcome him and bring him to my judgment.'

(2.) 'Nay, I am so far from that, that *though I were* more *righteous* than I am, *I would not answer.*' 'I would not answer him on these terms, *but I would make supplication to my judge.*' That is, 'I would rather submit to him, and seek pardon of him, [*than*] debate with him.'

(3) And he has a third argument (vs. 16-18), as if he said, 'I am so far from provoking God to that way of pleading, that I am rather on the extremity of fainting, than upon such a way of presuming. For if God had been pleased to hear me, and give me an evidence of some respect, I would scarcely have believed that he had done it, that he would have bestowed any ordinary favor upon the like of me.' The reason is (vs. 17-18), *He breaketh me with a tempest,* etc. That is, 'God's way is so terrible to me, and bitter to sense, that faith gets no footing to give him credit; I cannot be believing of that which I have warrant from him to expect.'

(4) A fourth argument is (v. 19), *If I speak of strength, lo he is strong; and of judgment, who will set me a time to plead?* As if he said, 'If I dealt with God as you suppose me to do, I behooved to deal with him either by the strong hand, or by law. But neither of these ways can I plead with God; for if I speak of strength, he is stronger than I, and

will overcome me; and if I would plead with him in law, who would set me a time for law? who could give me out summons to call God to the bar?'

(5) And a fifth argument is (v. 20), *If I should justify myself, my own mouth should condemn me.* 'If I were taking that course, my own mouth that has confessed I am a sinner before, should condemn me. *And if I should say, I am perfect, it should prove me perverse.* There needed no better argument to prove my perverseness [*than*] my saying I was righteous.' It is a word like that [in] 1 John 1:18, *If we say we have no sin, we deceive ourselves, and the truth is not in us.*

He closes this part of the chapter (v. 22), saying, *Though I were perfect, yet would I not know my soul; I would despise my life.* That is, 'Though I were come to a good measure of righteousness, I would not count of it before God, nor allow myself in the thoughts of such a thing; but I would be as denied to it as if I had never known such a thing to be in me. Any fruits of righteousness, I would despise.'

II. And having done with the first part, he comes to the second, to prove that the conclusion of Bildad will not hold (from the premises of God's justice, and his sinfulness, and plaguing him with temporal judgments), that he was a hypocrite and a wicked man. And he removes two doubts or aspersions that Bildad cast upon him. But secondly, he states the question, *This is one thing, therefore I have said it;* as if he said, 'It is not the question, If God be righteous and I a sinner. That I have granted. But [it is], whether [*these*] trials I lie under are an evidence of my hypocrisy and wickedness.' He proves the negative:

1. Because in God's ordinary way of dispensation in outward things, godly and wicked share alike. The perfect and righteous man, and the wicked man, may lie both under one rod; a temporal scourge without difference slays both bad and good together. *And he will laugh at the trial of the innocent;* for though one and the same scourge is a judgment to wicked folks, it is a trial to the righteous. And though he delights not in punishing his own, yet he delights to have them tried, that their *faith may be found unto praise at the appearing of Christ* (1 Pet. 1:7), and looks on their trial, as if he cared not much for it, because of the good he is making out of it (vs. 22-23). Yea, ordinarily wicked men get the earth for their portion; therefore it will not follow that good men have always outward prosperity, and are freed from temporal plagues, but rather the contrary. *And he covereth the faces of the judges thereof.* God makes wicked men masters of the earth, and promotes them to dignity, and tramps on them when he has done.

He lets the wicked tread upon just men for a time, and takes course with them therefore in due time. *If not, where and who is he?* that is, 'If it is not so that just men are often chastised and cast down, and wicked men are often lifted up and in prosperity, tell me where, or who is he, that has a large portion of the world, but wicked men. Produce me an instance to the contrary if you can; not that it is so always, but ordinarily, and for the most part it is so' (v. 24). And he opposes this sort of dealing to God's dealing with him (v. 25). *My days are swifter than a post,* etc. That is, 'It is true God's dealing with me is otherwise,' and he sets out the tossingness of his prosperity by three similitudes: (1) Of a post. (2) Of a ship. (3) Of an eagle; to let us see how evanishing [*fleeting*] a prosperous condition is; especially to good men. But (Psa. 73), the wicked often live long, and there are no bands in their death, and they have water of a full cup wrung out to them (vs. 25-26).

2. Then he comes to answer a second argument Bildad brought against him (8:5-6), the force whereof was this: 'If you were righteous Job, God would have heard your prayers? but he has not heard, nor does he hear your prayers; therefore you are not righteous.' He argues and vindicates himself from the dint [*force*] of this argument two ways:

(1) By telling that it is ill reasoning to conclude he was not righteous, because he got no return of his prayers; because it is not the effect of his endeavors, but the endeavors themselves that are a mark of his being righteous (vs. 27-28). As if he said, 'I have some endeavor to cheer up myself in God, yet I win not to it; God's sorrows so effect me for the time.' *And I know that thou will not hold me innocent.* In this he turns himself to God, telling the sense of God's afflicting him so discouraged him, that he believed the sense of God's terror, or listened to what it spoke more than any warrant he had to believe. That in respect of any outward evidences of God's answering him, he thought God would deal with him as with a guilty man. He was that hopeless to get God's way changed. But this is not in respect of Job's ultimate decision of the matter, but in respect of what sense said, and of his not coming-speed [*lack of success*] with God. Therefore (v. 29), *If I be wicked, why then labor I in vain?* that is, 'My laboring over so many difficulties, and continuing to hang upon God, and to pray to him, proves me to be an upright man and no hypocrite. For (27:10), *Will the hypocrite call always upon God?* If I were a wicked man, I would not be thus carried through in such a hard exercise in praying to God; therefore if I am wicked, as you take me to be, why do I labor thus? It were indeed vain to me so to do, if it were with me as you think.'

(2) And a second reason whereby he vindicates himself from being a hypocrite, notwithstanding he got not a present answer of his prayers, is taken from God's sovereignty. As if he said, 'I may pray, and it becomes me so to do, but shall we limit God as we would do the creature? Is he a man to be limited? It becomes us rather to acknowledge God's sovereign way that he takes.' This is the scope (vs. 30-34). 'For if I should endeavor by legal washings as well as by sacrifices to wash myself, God for all this in his sovereign way, to the appearance of man, might plunge me in outward misery, and make me loathsome to myself, as well as to others, *for he is not a man as I am that I should answer him.* He must not be limited for that; we must not tie him to laws as we do one another, *that we should come together in judgment. Neither is there any days-man between us, that might lay his hand upon us both.* He is more sovereign than to have law above him, or a judge to answer before, or to have any arbitrator to call us both to desist and hear him discern; therefore you wrong God's sovereignty in limiting his answering of prayer to the lifting off of a temporal rod.'

In the last two verses he returns to his expostulation, which he prosecutes, and goes on in, in the tenth chapter, 'If God takes this sovereign way no man can speak with him,' *But let him take his rod from me, and let not his fear terrify me; then would I speak, and not fear him.* 'If he will come to me in a way of grace, I will not be afraid to speak to him; and if he would take away his terror from me, I could be content to lay out my cause before him rather than before you.' And he closes with this word, *But it is not so with me.* 'He takes not that gentle way with me, but such a rough way as seems to confirm you in your opinion of me.'

OBSERVATIONS.

Upon the first part in general observe: It is the part of a perfect and righteous man to vindicate himself from the hardest reproaches that are put upon him, especially when they are put on him by good men. Bildad laid much to Job's charge, yet Job startles not, but at length labors to remove his mistakes. Mistakes soon grow, and getting foot do often continue long, and this is one of the causes of it, that there is not a humbling of men's selves, and a yielding to vindicate themselves from these mistakes. But this would be much endeavored when mistakes enter among them, that [they] should comfort and confirm one another.

2. Job calls a man's contending with God, a man's hardening himself against God (v. 4). Observe [that] to deal without the sense of our righteousness, and without the due acknowledgment of his righteousness alone, is the greatest token of a hardened condition that can be; and much of folks' pleading with God, not being ordinarily mixed with the sense of our own unrighteousness before God, and not coming with a stopped mouth before him, but often in the clean contrary temper, does evidence much of this condition to be in us.

3. The next Job vindicates is his practice, that he did not debate with God in such terms (vs. 14-15). *How much less shall I answer him,* etc., words that set out his low estimation of himself beneath any other. Observe [that] the more perfect a man is before God, and the more sincere, the more low thoughts he will have of himself. We will find a threefold soberness of spirit in him that is worthy of our imitation, and which, if it were in more vigor in us, it would lay [*put down*] many of our debates. (1) Comparatively he is less than any other man, *how much less I?* (2) He has a high estimation of God, *shall I answer him?* 'or choose out words to reason with such a sovereign Lord? That will I never [do].' (3) He abases himself, and has much sensibleness of his own infirmity in reference to himself. *Though I were more righteous than I am, I would not answer,* but humbly supplicate: three notable companions to go along with us, both in our dealing with God and with one another.

4. Observe (vs. 16-17): (1) That folks often give more credit to sense than to faith. The sense he had of the terror of God, had more weight with him, and got more credit than any warrant he had for believing. Folks especially in temptation are more ready to draw conclusions from sense than from the grounds of faith. (2) God may oft-times hear folks' prayers when they will not believe he does it, or when folks give credit to sense, they may mistrust God when he is hearing them and not think he is doing it; when God gently uses folks, and they will not [*trust*] a good word of God towards them but [*trust*] dispensation's language more than God, and take no heed to his mind toward them in the dispensation.

5. On the last part of the chapter (vs. 22-35), observe: (1) That the just and wise God can do no wrong, whomsoever he strikes or spares; and he will often exercise his wisdom and justice in the trial of his people when he is wroth at them for sin. *He laughs at the trial of the innocent,* even then he is dealing with them as with innocent, sin sways him not in putting that trial on them, and there (so to

speak) is a kind of mirth to him, though he has no passion as the creature has. And if God thinks good to make himself merry with the trials of Scotland, and this place [*Glasgow*], what lose we? *My brethren, count it all joy when ye fall in divers temptations* (Jam. 1:2). When God is merry let not our hearts be sad; for our trials tend to the praise and glory of God, and of his grace in his children (1 Pet. 1:7), and to the praise of his truth, and wisdom, and goodness. And this is no cruelty in God, but the kindliness of a father. It is like a father laughing to see his child weep, when he is doing something that is to both their advantages.

(2) It is far safer and surer reasoning to draw evidences of interest in God from our endeavors, than from the effects of endeavors; from our continuing in prayer in difficulties, than from our answers, or God's hearing of us. The reason is (vs. 27-29) because endeavors are a fruit of God's grace in us, and flow from God's grace in the heart, as a native act of it; but answers to prayer, and effects of endeavors are acts of God's sovereignty. Endeavors and grace are never sundry [*apart*], whereas prayer, and the answer may [be]; for the answer of prayer may be suspended and kept up.

(3) When temptation challenges God, it is good to take God's part against temptation, to look on God's sovereignty and not to limit him. In all this debate, we find that Job ordinarily does this, and casts [*away*] human rules, and the rules of sense, though in a fit it gets way, for he knew God was not a man as he was. This is a solid way in temptation, to be giving God his own way, as being sovereign, and not to bound or limit him, knowing that grace in God has its sovereignty, as well as any other of his attributes.

10

In the former chapter, Job has been vindicating himself from Bildad's imputation; and as in his debate with Eliphaz, so here he leaves Bildad, and vents himself to God as the more equal judge, that he dares speak more freely to, and not fear to be mistaken. So this chapter is a discourse between the Lord and Job, or Job's discourse speaking to God, wherein, through the excessiveness of his grief, he has many <u>mints</u> [*threatened attempts*] to the venting and outbreaking of [the] flesh, and the endeavors of faith to subdue all the risings of it.

The rise of his discourse is (v. 1), *My soul is weary of my life.* Wherein he shows what made him take this freedom in speaking to God, and it is because the heaviness of his affliction was such, that he was wearied of living any longer. Whether we take the soul for the whole man, or the soul distinct from the body, it is all one; he was weary to live any longer. Then flesh breaks out in a purpose now to give way to sense, and no longer to wrestle against corruption: *I will leave my complaint upon myself.* He will cast loose the reins of sense, and give it leave to vent itself as it likes, which is more clear in the following words. *I will speak in the bitterness of my soul.* 'I will no longer [*choose*] my words, but vent the sense and passion that is in me.' Then he sets down the subject matter of his discourse as two queries or suits to God (v. 2). *I will say unto God, do not condemn me.* And here the spirit gets victory to qualify his former resolution. Sense said, God was either to cast him off eternally, or temporally to deal with him as a cast-off man, and so to ratify the imputation his friends put upon him. 'But I will say *do not condemn me,* cast me not off;' he would be from under all their reproaches. The meaning is not only that God would save him from eternal off-casting, but that he would vindicate him before men. His second suit is, *Show me wherefore thou contendest with me?* 'If there is any quarrel between us, let me know of it, discover it to me.' And here faith strengthens itself against the former suggestion of condemnation, intimating, such a man could not be cast off, and God not tell him wherefore.

In the rest of the chapter, he prosecutes these two. I. He labors to strengthen his faith in God, that God would not cast him off, nor condemn him (vs. 3-17). II. He closes with putting up a petition that God would give him some breathing time, some refreshment under his trouble, ere he should go to his grave (vs. 18-22).

I. In the first of these he goes upon three grounds, which he sums up (v. 3), [*proposing*] them by way of interrogation, which has the force of a negation: *Is it good unto thee, that thou shouldest oppress?* As if he said, 'It cannot be that thou wouldst condemn without a cause, and confirm the sentence that [*these*] men have passed upon me; for thou that commands others not to oppress, thou will not do it thyself.' 2. *That thou shouldest despise the work of thy hands*? that is, 'thou that hast taken so much pains in making me, will not reject me;' and we are to understand, that not only is the bodily creature to be taken in here, but the new creature. He means, that God will vindicate that ere he go off the world. And 3. *And shine upon the counsel of the wicked*? 'If you take me away this way, you would seem to shine upon the counsel of the wicked, that ordinarily lay this for a conclusion, that extraordinary temporary judgments [*always*] prove a wicked man.' For however [*these*] good men were fallen in this error as the prophet in a fit (Psa. 73), yet it is the ordinary tenet of wicked men, and 'Thou, Lord, wilt seem to confirm that tenet.' He thinks God more engaged than that he should need to fear such a thing.

1. He then follows forth [*these*] three grounds in order (vs. 4-7). The force of the reason is this: 'If thou be such a God as will do no wrong (as I know thou art), what needs all this torturing of me to find out my condition?' The argument is taken from a similitude of the manner of men, who make inquiry, and put to torture to find out a thing which they cannot win to by clear proof. 'Thou needest not take that [*way*]; and art not thou from eternity, and of infinite wisdom, understanding all things? Why then so exactly searches thou out my iniquity? Thou cannot be deceived, neither art thou ignorant as man; what needs thou then press me to confess?' As (v. 7): *Thou knowest that I am not wicked*; or 'It is in thy knowing,' or 'open in thy knowledge;' and so 'though man must take that [*way*], thou needs not take it.' *And there is none that can deliver out of thy hand*. And this is to confirm him in his sincerity in attesting God, as if he said, 'It were folly to me to appeal to thee on a wrong ground, for none can deliver from thee. Therefore my boldness in referring my cause to thee, is a testimony of my sincerity.'

2. He enlarges the second ground (vs. 8-13): *Thou wilt not despise the work of thy hand;* 'therefore thou wilt not despise me,' *For thy hands hath made me, and fashioned me together round about, yet thou doest destroy me.* That is, 'How comes it when thou hast made me for matter, and fashioned me for manner, so wonderfully, that thou seemest to destroy me: this seems inconsistent with thy wisdom.' *Remember, I beseech thee* (an emphatic petition) *that thou hast made me as clay, and wilt thou bring me to dust again?* 'I am made of clay, and dare not abide this hard dealing;' even as if God had forgotten whereof he was made. The interrogation, *Wilt thou bring me to dust again?* supposes a negation, that God will not do it.

Then in the following words he shows: (1) How God had made him, beginning at his conception (v. 10). *Hast thou not poured me out as milk, and curdled me as cheese?* 'My beginning was but mean, when at my conception I was but as milk, but thou went on in the work and curdled me, and made me draw to some faster substance.'

(2) *Thou hast clothed me with skin and flesh, and fenced me with bones and sinews;* words holding out the excellent workmanship of God in making man out of nothing, having everything so bright in order, the flesh and skin being as it were the coat of the vital spirits.

(3) Third step is (v. 12): 'When my body was a dead carcass, thou granted me mercy to live.'

(4) And a fourth step in the same verse: *Thy visitation hath preserved my spirit;* 'When I was born, thy gracious dealing and continual influence as so many fresh visits has preserved me, and shall all this be for nought? wilt thou now cast me off? Thou wilt not.'

Objection. But it seems from God's dispensation, all that is forgotten; clods of dust are upon him? Answ. He answers in faith (v. 13): *These things hast thou hid in thine heart; I know that this is with thee.* 'Though God seems to <u>keep up</u> [*hide; keep back*] the evidence of his care of me, and does not manifest it as formerly, yet he hath them in his heart; his purpose of love is one and the same, though his dispensation is altered. His intention of being gracious continues.'

3. He enlarges and explains the third ground that he pointed at (v. 3), that is, that God would not cast him off, lest he should seem to shine on the counsel of the wicked (v. 14-17).

(1) *If I sin then thou markest me, and thou wilt not acquit me from mine iniquity.* 'Seeing' (could he say) 'thou wilt not cast me off and shine on the counsel of wicked men, how stands [*these*] two together: thy

not rejecting of me, and yet marking my sin. Therefore though thou seem to mark my iniquity, it must not continue so;' or 'if I sin of infirmity, thou marks me, and will not acquit me from mine iniquity. Thou will not let me go without a temporal judgment, as if thou intended to condemn me, and in this I dispute not to excuse myself, but *if I be wicked,* as my friends call me, *woe unto me.* I lie justly under all this that is come upon me, and will not say anything against it.' *And if I be righteous, I will not lift up my head;* 'I will not prescribe a way to thee, to take away this rod;' or, 'I will not be vain or presumptuous to debate with thee; that is not my mind.' But I am lying under confusion and reproach, and thou seemest to take their part that plead against me; therefore look on me, and grant me a breathing time, and vindicate me from their reproach, that draw all their arguments from thy dispensation.' He could not abide this reproach. It was to him as it was to David (Psa. 42), *Like a sword in his bones.* Therefore he says, *I am full of confusion, see thou mine affliction.*

(2) He goes on in this suite (v. 16). *For it increaseth:* 'my confusion and affliction grows greater and greater, because thou cometh not in to decide the matter.' And he shows the causes of the increase of his confusion and affliction: *thou huntest me as a fierce lion.* 'I would care little for affliction, if thou seemed not to quit thy former tenderness, and did not hunt me as an enemy.' And again, *thou showest thyself marvelous upon me;* 'my afflictions are wonderful, and not common, and all that look upon me think I am cast off by thee. Some are common afflictions' (1 Cor. 10:13); 'but mine are not so.'

(3) A third particular is (v. 17): 'thou seemest to bear witness with them that are against me, by adding new strokes to former, which they make use of against me;' *and thou increaseth thy indignation upon me.* This made all heavy; he had indignation before, and God lets it grow. This makes his cup bitter, and [he] sums all up in two pithy words: *changes and war are against me.* 'It is not one or two trials that I am under, but multitudes of trials; and God draws up these trials like an army of men in a warlike posture upon me.'

II. In the words that follow he strengthens his faith, and petitions God for some breathing time in an expostulatory way. He expostulates (vs. 18-19), *Wherefore then hast thou brought me forth of the womb?* 'If this is my life, and if I go this way away, I will repent that ever I came into the world; yea, I wish I had rather never been;' for then *I should have been as though I had not been.* 'For if I had died soon, or had never been, I should have [*gone without*] all [*these*] reproaches;' choosing rather than that he should have endured all these trials, to have [*lacked*] the good [*which*] came by them; speaking out the language of sense. Yet [he] (v. 20). shows his shot [*point*], *Are not my days few? cease then, and let me alone, that I may take comfort a little.* That is, 'Cease Lord from adding new strokes, that I may get a little ease and comfort ere I go off the world.' And this petition he presses by several reasons (as vs. 21-22). *Before I go whence I shall not return;* that is, 'ere I go to death,' which he calls the land of darkness, because there men have no conversing with men, as they have on earth; and because as men die, so they are esteemed of, and he would not in death get himself vindicated before men of the reproaches cast upon him, for there is no light to clear truth after death; 'therefore let me have a breathing time before death to vindicate myself.'

OBSERVATIONS.

1. Observe: (1) That there is a difference between the soul and the life. The soul is another thing than the life, as corrupt men would make it. Job differences in these two. (2) From the rise of his difficulty (v. 1) observe, that if folks give way to themselves under temptation and affliction, nothing is so unreasonable but it will vent itself. Job has been restraining himself before, and gave not sense leave to vent itself, and now his loosing the reins gives vent to that which follows, to tell us, it is evil to give liberty to passion.

2. Observe (v. 2): (1) That under trials folks are ready to apprehend, or be in fear of God's condemning them. They are ready to be under hazard of that temptation, for his saying, *Do not condemn me*, is spoken in opposition to that which was borne in upon him by sense. (2) It is good going to God under those fears, and to make all our complaints of God to God. So does Job here, and often in this book. (3) It is a main thing to be studied under trials, to know God's controversy. 4. God may long contend, and not let folks know wherefore. *Show me wherefore thou contendest with me.*

3. Observe (vs. 3-7): (1) In general, it is a part of spiritual wisdom when temptation presses hard to rub on God, and rent from God, to strengthen faith, in opposition to whatsoever the temptation says. God will cast off; say, 'It cannot be that God will cast off,' etc.

(2) In general. It will be hard under sore exercises to get faith fastened that God will keep off condemnation. Therefore Job uses argument after argument to get his heart stayed against this temptation. It is a wonder to see how many are never put to dispute

this question, when such a holy man as Job is put so hardly to it to defend himself against it.

4. Observe (vs. 7-13): (1) That the more folks' sincerity is questioned, they should the more maintain it, if they have it. Therefore Job says, *Thou knowest that I am not wicked*, and (27:6), *My righteousness will I hold fast, and will not let it go; my heart shall not reproach me as long as I live.* Many are ready to maintain their sincerity when there is no cause, and others are ready to quit it when they should stick by it. (2) A right observing of God's dealing in our conception and birth, should be ground to quiet our faith in the hope and assurance of God's bearing [us] through any trial we are under. (3) It is matter of admiration to see God's bringing forth such a creature as man. (4) And we should mark God's goodness to us, that when he might have made us a beast or a stone, he has made us men or women.

5. Observe (v. 13), when nothing is seen to sense of God's love, faith should keep the conclusion fixed. *These things thou hast hid in thine heart*, 'I know it is with thee.' Under any hard trial, especially from what is sensible, we would look to what is in God's thoughts, look through dispensations to his bosom. *I know the thoughts that I have towards you, thoughts of peace*, etc. (Jer. 29:11).

6. Observe upon the other part of the chapter (v. 18-22): (1) That good men may fall over and over again in one and the same corruption. Job began to complain in the third chapter, then in the seventh chapter, and now in the tenth chapter he falls in the same fault. Therefore watch against corruptions of this nature. They are not soon mortified, but will vent themselves under hard exercises.

(2) Folks that get any breathing time under sore exercises, would think it a great mercy; Job would have thought it so. He would have thought it a mercy before to get leave to swallow down his spittle; and here to get but a little comfort. How much more should it be prized to have houses, children, friends, rest and sleep, not to be scared with night visions. It would greatly aggravate our guilt, that we have these, and make not use of them, nor are thankful for them. Look [that] it provoke not God to send a scattering from these mercies, because we have not studied to bless God for them, and make a right use of them, etc.

11

W e heard [how] three of Job's friends came to comfort him; two of them have spoken very unlike their errand. Now Zophar, the third, comes in and follows the same strain that the two former did (which was wisely ordered of God for Job's exercise and trial). He begins to cast down all Job's confidence, and to reprove him for misleared [*inappropriate*] expressions; yea, to shake the very foundation of his interest in God. I. [He] labors to put Job in thoughts that God is dealing with him as with a foal or wild ass colt, though the conclusion is not expressed (vs. 1-12). II. He has some exhortations backed with motives of promises on the one hand (vs. 13-20), and threatenings on the other, which are good in themselves, though unsuitable to Job's afflicted condition.

I. 1. In the first place he lays down the grounds whereon he will proceed: And (1) He shows that Job must not go without an answer, and breaks off with a sad reflection on him, that he was a man of many words and full of talk. 'Is it [*suitable*]' (would he say) 'that such a man should go without an answer?' or, 'that the truth should not be vindicated which he cries down with his talk?' (v. 2).

(2) A second reflection (v. 3) is: *Should thy lies make men hold their peace?* 'Because you go on maintaining your absurdities, should men hold their peace? That should not be.' (3) 'Is it meet that you should mock all God's dealing, and none come to convince you of it?' And on [*these*] three grounds he goes on to stop Job's mouth; having in the first place laid this down, that Job was an empty talker, a liar, and mocker.

2. In the second place, he states the question from Job's own words (v. 4). *Thou hast said, My doctrine is pure, and I am clean in thine eyes.* He grounds this challenge on two places before, the one (6:10), where Job had said, *He had not concealed the words of the holy One*, holding forth his sincerity in not keeping up [*holding back*] the truth of God committed to him, and this Zophar [*expounds*] to be a crying up of his own tenet. And the other is taken from where Job had said

to God (10:7), *Thou knowest that I am not wicked;* which Zophar [*expounds*], as if Job had said he was without sin. And from this he strives to prove Job to be an absurd man, that dares attest God, so audaciously and presumptuously. But Job's expressions will bear no such exposition, and so his stating of the question meets not with the point.

When Zophar has laid down this ground, he goes on to prove that Job in his conversation was not clean, as he alleges he pretended; and the great argument he brings (vs. 5-6), which he presses by way of [a] wish, is that God would come and convince Job. *Would God* (he says) — '*that the Lord would* come and speak to you, and *show thee the secrets of wisdom,*' or let you see the depth of his understanding, whereof he searches out that which men cannot see, nor find out; *that they are double to that which is.*' That is, that these secret sins which men see not, are double to these which are seen. 'Therefore Job you cannot be clean.' And hence he concludes, *Know therefore that God exacteth of thee less than thine iniquity deserveth.* That is, 'take with your hypocrisy, acknowledge your wickedness, and defend no more your integrity, which you plead so much for. You are more gross, corrupt and profane, [*than*] ought that appears does demonstrate, or, [*than*] anything appearing in your scourge; and if God dealt with you as your iniquities deserve, you might get twice so much.' And this is true; for there is more sin in the holiest man [*than*] he sees, and God exacts less of us than our iniquities deserve. But yet for all that, [it does not follow] that Job's sins were the controversy which God was pursuing him for, or that he was the greater sinner because so heavily afflicted.

He prosecutes this argument, that God saw many sins that men saw not, and the ground he gives to prove it is this: God was infinite in wisdom to find out many things that man sees not. He propounds it by way of question (v. 7). *Canst thou by searching find out God? Canst thou find out the Almighty unto perfection?* '[Do] you think an infinite God should be limited with your bit of knowledge? or can you find out God's wisdom in searching things? You cannot.' Then positively he lays it down (v. 8). *It is as high as heaven, what canst thou do? deeper than hell, what canst thou know?* And (v. 9) *The measure thereof is longer than the earth, and broader than the sea.* By comparing God with the highest and lowest, the broadest and longest of the creatures, he sets him out infinite and boundless in all his attributes, and excellent induction of the mass of the creation, to set out the infiniteness of the Creator beyond all these, which is a good lesson for us to think upon in looking on the creatures.

The second way he follows out this argument is in the application of it (v. 10). *If he cut off, or shut up, or gather together, who can hinder him?* 'If God is [so] great, then whatever he does with creatures, not only have folks no power, but they have no warrant to hinder him.' Expressions holding forth God's sovereignty to be such that none can challenge God, whatever way he is pleased to take in handling his creatures. The second way how he sets out God's sovereignty is in God's taking notice of man, and the wickedness in men (v. 11). *For he knoweth vain man; he seeth wickedness also: will he not consider it?* 'He knows what men are, and sees all their sins, and will not he that sees all their sins consider and call them to a reckoning?' And this insinuates a clear application to Job, that God has seen, and is now considering his wickedness, and calling him to a reckoning for it.

[He] closes this part of the chapter with a reason why God takes such notice and inspection or trial of men, and discovers their wickedness (v. 12). *For vain man would be wise, though he be born like a wild ass colt.* Man by nature is like a wild ass colt, untamed and undaunted; yet he thinks himself wise. Therefore God under affliction, or by affliction, discovers his emptiness and folly unto him, else he would die in the dark. So he insinuates the reason of God's dealing with him.

II. In the second part of the chapter, he discovers what Job should do, and what true repentance is (vs. 13-14), and presses the practice of it on Job (vs. 15-20).

1. The first step he presses on him, is to fix his heart: *If thou prepare,* or fix *thy heart;* which seems to be opposed to the vanity of the heart spoken of before. He would have him seeking to have his heart established by grace.

2. *And stretch out thy hands towards him,* i.e. 'if you make your prayer and supplications to him.' He would have him first to wash his heart, and then stretch out his hands in supplication.

3. *If iniquity be in thy hand, put it far away.* 'If there be any sin in your practice that God is chopping at [*striking at*], put that away, and mend your life.'

4. *And let not wickedness dwell in thy tabernacle.* He would have him not only reforming his heart, and practices, and taking course with bygones, but reforming his house, to let none be in the house with him that are wicked. Or his meaning is, 'Let no sin, nor fruit, nor effect of sin dwell with you. If there be anything of sin, anything

come [of] an evil and sinful [*way*] within thy doors, send it back again.' A good pattern of repentance under affliction.

Then the motives follow: 1. *Thou shalt lift up thy face without spot;* 'thou shalt lift up thy face before God, and not think shame' (v. 15).

2. 'You shall have your heart settled, and your prosperity shall not fall about your ears as before,' reflecting on Job's condition before the stroke came (3:25).

3. For (v. 16) *Thou shalt forget thy misery, and remember it as waters that pass away.* 'All your former misery shall soon be forgotten; the prosperity that shall come from God to you shall be so comfortable, that it shall drown the memory of this afflicted condition.

4. A fourth promise is (v. 17): *Thine age shall be clearer than the noon-day, and thou shalt shine forth as the morning.* 'Thy life and conversation, thy age and health, and all the accidents that accompany life, shall have no darkness in them, but shine as the morning light.'

5. A fifth promise is (v. 18): *Thou shalt be secure;* not carnally secure but spiritually. 'You shall have inward quietness of mind, and outward peace;' as if he said, 'If God is a friend to you, you shall have no enemies, nothing that can annoy you.' *Because there is hope.* There is ground of hope and peace to expect this in turning to God.

6. A sixth promise is: *Thou shalt dig about thee, and take thee rest in safety.* 'If you are pleased to build houses, and not flit from place to place, as many do, there shall be nothing to trouble you. And the first part of v. 19 clears the former promise (v. 18), *Thou shalt lie down, and none shall make thee afraid.* 'You shall get leave to sleep soundly in your bed, and shall have none to trouble you, as if you were fortified with walls.' And in the latter part of v. 19 is a new promise. *Many shall make suit unto thee.* That is, 'you shall have more reverence and respect than ever you had before.'

In the last verse he sums up all his motives in a threatening (v. 20), to let Job see the necessity of following the way he has prescribed. As if he said, 'Job, you have need to repent, for I have shown you great good will follow the doing of it. And now I tell you of much evil to come on you, if you do it not.' *The eyes of the wicked shall fail.* The expectation of any comfort to a wicked man shall fail, and he shall not escape God's judgment, and any hope he has shall perish.

All [*these*] motives are good, being well understood and applied; but they would not be restricted to temporal things, as if outward prosperity did always follow true repentance, and always immediately upon the back of repentance. That will not follow. But one way or other, at one time or other, the penitent have all [*these*] promises made good.

OBSERVATIONS.

1. From the current of this chapter, with what goes before, observe: That when once a temptation and trial begins, where the Lord has a mind to exercise, he will add more witnesses than one or two to complete the trial. Therefore after two have spoken, a third comes in, and confirms what the former said is an undeniable truth. There are many more ways than one, that folks' integrity will be pursued, when it is brought on the stage; for we are not only to look on this as a dispute with Job, but as a temptation and trial to put a sey [*test*] to Job's faith.

2. From Zophar's beginning, and breaking off with sad reflections at the broad-side on Job, observe: A good man engaged in a debate, readily miscarries in coming over the debate to passionate expressions, and sad reflections. Inward prejudices, and sinister thoughts miscarry passion to a reflecting on the person. Long ere such words as [*these*] convince Job, yet they must [come] out, ere he fall upon the matter itself.

3. From Zophar's stating the question, upon the mistaking of Job's expressions observe: That oft-times the greatest debates among God's people, will be found to flow from their mistakes in circumstances of expressions in one another, rather than from the matter itself about which [the] debate is. This is clear here, and through[out] this dispute. Job (Job 9) disclaimed this which Zophar alleges on him. He did never plead he was without sin, yet they will speak to the circumstance of expression, and are kept off the main matter. Guard against mistakes of this kind.

4. From Zophar's way of prosecuting his argument observe: That God sees many things in folks that they observe not themselves. He sees many things that they see not. Therefore though we see nothing, we have no cause to be proud, but [are to] have an eye upon secret faults, that God may call us to reckoning for [them] (Psa. 19:12)

5. He wishes God to come in, and reprove Job; and when God came, he decided the just contrary to what Zophar expected. Observe that good men will sometimes be too confident in their

opinion, that they are right when they are wrong, and too soon attest God in cases which will not bear out.

6. Take it in opposition to the temptation, or that which the temptation bears in upon Job, and observe that temptation will, yea, uses to represent [*commonly represents*] God as an adversary to folks, when their state and integrity is questioned. It represents men's pleading, as if God himself were pleading against the man.

7. Observe: Let men speak as they will, and bring argument after argument to convince of an evil; there is no convincing of sin till God does it.

8. From his setting out of God in his attributes, by comparing him with the creation: Learn to do the like, to make use of the creatures for the end God has made them, even to exalt God; and let it shame us that have so many means, besides the work of creation, and yet carry so slender an impression of the majesty of God.

9. Observe (v. 12) that man is one of the emptiest, and yet one of the proudest things in the world. The proudest man is the toomest [*most futile*] and emptiest man, and the most empty man is the most proud man. The consideration whereof would be a good guard against pride.

From the second part of the chapter observe: There is no better [*way*], or rather no other [*way*] to true happiness, but repentance, turning to God, cleansing and fixing of the heart, supplication to God, reformation of practice in our own person, and in our families, and all that follow us to commend this [*way*]. If we would seek a way of making up our peace with God in Jesus Christ. (1) Let the heart be prepared to seek God. (2) Let the hand be stretched out in external duties. (3) Let iniquity be quit, and put away. (4) Let every evil thing be put out of the tabernacle. Till this is done, it is likely God's controversy may grow, and if it shall continue, we look upon folks not stooping to God, and not humbling of themselves before God, as the main cause of it. This was Zaccheus's repentance (Luke 19:1-10).

12

We heard of Zophar's sharp accusation to Job. Job's answer is in this and the two following chapters. In his answer, he: 1. Meets with Zophar's particular challenging of him, or with what he had spoken, in as far as concerned him, and vindicates himself (vs. 12:1-13:19). 2. In the rest of chapter 13 and all [of] chapter 14, he turns himself to speak to God immediately, as [before].

In this chapter he checks Zophar, and in him the rest of his friends, for his rough and uncharitable dealing. And at the back of every check, he adds a confutation of that wherewith they charged him, and wherefore he checks them, giving reasons wherefore he checked them (vs. 1-5).

I. His first check is for their too great estimation of their own judgment, which appeared in their tenaciousness, and sticking to their own tenets, notwithstanding he had spoken sufficiently against them, and this he [*proposes*] by way of irony (v. 2). 'You think yourselves the only wise men and speak as if none understood anything but you; I confess you are wise men.' But (v. 3) *I have understanding as well as you*. 'I know something in the matters of God, and in these truths you have been speaking of, as well as you do.' *I am not inferior to you*, or, as the word is, *I fall not before you*; that is, *I succumb not in dispute*. 'I am not as yet overcome by you in dispute; yea, who [doesn't] know such things as these? are not these common truths that you have insisted upon, that are known by all that know God. You have been in your discourse wading in the common and known attributes of God, as if I denied them, or were ignorant of them; but there is none that has any knowledge of God, but they will grant and know these things.'

This is the first check. And if it is asked, How it is that Job meets so saltily with them; I answer: He compares not his person with theirs, but it is in respect of the cause he maintained, wherein he will not yield to them in an hair-breadth. Even as Paul (1 Cor. 4:10): *We are fools for Christ's sake, but ye are wise in Christ; we are weak but ye are strong*; intimating that though they thought themselves so, yet they were not so indeed; and sometimes he is put to compare because of false teachers. So we are to construct of Job here, albeit in the heat of the dispute, somewhat of [the] flesh possibly has stolen in upon him.

II. His second check is for their gross and uncharitable dealing with him (v. 4). *I am as one mocked of his neighbor.* 'I am a man that is near the grave, and yet I am so far from being comforted, that they take their pastime of me. And it is not enemies that do this, but neighbors, and that not of the more common sort put professors of the same religion with me. It is not by a man that [*lacks*] religion, but by him that *calls upon God, and he answers*; by a man that prays to God, and gets a hearing in reference to his outward condition' (as v. 5. clears), 'and has an easy life of it, in comparison of me.' And in this check, he flatly contradicts their ordinary assertion, that it was always well with just men. 'It is not so,' would he say, *The just and upright man is laughed to scorn.* That is, the most eminent upright men are often trod upon and ridiculed. And he gives the reason of this (v. 5), *He that is ready to slip with his feet, is as a lamp despised in the thought of him that is at ease.* The men that are likely to perish by reason of affliction, are ordinarily despised by them who are in a prosperous condition. They think no more of them than they do of a puff of a crusy [*candlestick*] that is dying out, and has an evil smell; and in [*these*] two verses he contradicts that which Zophar said (11:15-16), that godly men are always in prosperity.

The second thing that Job does, is his clearing of their mistake that wicked men are always roughly dealt with and plagued of God by temporal rods. 'That is not true,' would he say. For whether they are wicked in reference to the second table (*the tabernacle of robbers prosper*), or whether they are wicked atheists, in reference to the first table (*They that provoke God*) [which] wrongs him immediately, [*They that provoke God*] *are secure,* and God *brings to their hand abundantly,* and they [*lack*] nothing that their heart can wish. And from this, and the former, he concludes his friends had no reason to mock him, for wicked men are often otherwise dealt with, than they alleged.

III. He confirms what he has said before (vs. 7-9), wherein he includes a third check, as if he had said, 'If you were any better then beasts in this point, and made that use of God's common way of providence towards the creatures, there is not a creature, but they would witness this truth that I have asserted, that just men are often hardly handled; the wicked are in prosperity.' And he interrogates them thus: 1. To convince them of their stupidity and ignorance in such a known truth. 2. To bring them to some more solid knowledge of it. *Ask now the beasts,* etc. Or, 'Look to the beasts and fowls. The best of them are not best used in the world, but the innocent and harmless are preyed upon by the ravenous and savage. Doves are pursued by glads and hawks, sheep are pursued by wolves; therefore happiness here in respect of outward things. Honesty or sincerity go not [*always*] together.' And he repeats this (v. 9): *Who knows not that God has put things in this order,* 'that you, and all men, that look on his working and wise providence, may see and acknowledge this truth, and God to be wise and just in so dispensing.' He clears how it is so (vs. 10-25), by God's sovereignty, omnipotency and wisdom. *In whose hand is the soul of every living thing?* There is not a creature, but it holds its being and moving of God, and is maintained by him, and especially man. And seeing it is so, has not the potter power over the clay? How much more God to dispose of man at his pleasure.

IV. Whereupon he subjoins a fourth check, and then goes on in his purpose. *Doth not the ear try words,* etc. As if he said, 'I proposed this doctrine before to you, and how is it you are so ignorant? If you were not tenacious of your own opinion, your ear would try what solidness there is in the doctrine you have heard, as the mouth uses to taste and try meat.' And he enlarges this check (v. 12), *with the ancient is wisdom,* etc. 'It is true, there are men beyond me, and aged men are ordinarily men of understanding. How is it then, that you are ignorant of this truth that I have [*proposed*] to you, which none of any understanding are ignorant of?' Elihu goes upon the same ground (32:7; 34:2-3).

And having thus checked them, as we said, he goes on to hold out these three grounds of God's sovereignty, omnipotency, and infinite wisdom, to the end of the chapter, giving instances of these suitable to the debate he is upon. 'All your way of proceeding with me goes upon the ground of God's justice, as if God were to always give reasons of his proceeding. And therefore when he afflicts, you conclude that there is always sin as the cause. But God is more sovereign, omnipotent and wise than [that]. *With him is wisdom,* and he knows how to afflict for other reasons beside. *And with him is strength,* to cast down or uphold, and he has counsel and understanding, and none needs to give him direction, how to handle his creatures. You are but plain fools in your manner of pleading for God, and God is wise, and has a better [*way*] of guiding the world, than you can prescribe or hold out' (v. 13).

He gives instances of this thesis, that God does in his sovereignty, what pleases him, and the first instance is (v. 14): *He breaketh down, and it cannot be built up again, he shuts up,* etc. God is thus sovereign, that he dings down as well as builds up, and shuts up man in straits as well as enlarges him, and there is no standing in his [*way*].

A second instance (v. 15) is in the ordinary course of natural things. Such a time he will let a shower come, another time he will withhold rain, and send a drought to bring on famine; and again, he will loose the clouds and the fountains of the deep, and send forth waters as in the flood of Noah.

He (v. 16) repeats the proposition that he spoke of (v. 13), but the words here in the original differ, and serve to set out the wisdom and power of God more eminently, when he is coming to speak of the hand of God in civil and public things, and of his guiding of kings and kingdoms, and statesmen, as well as other creatures.

1. And the first instance of this is in these words, *The deceived and the deceiver are his.* In the original, *They are to him,* that is, they are both bounded, limited, directed and ordered of him, to work his point, and do no other thing than to serve his end. Rom. 11:36. *For of him, and through him, and to him are all things: to whom be glory for ever. Amen.*

2. A second instance is (v. 17): *He leads counselors,* that are much in estimation in the world, *away spoiled.* He takes them often in their own net, as men that have neither counsel nor strength, *and makes the judges fools,* that when they have laid their plots for their own standing, he breaks their necks, makes the plot misgive, and they bring forth a lie. He names these two sorts of persons, to let us see that God's sovereignty [*appears*] in ruling, and disposing of the wisest sorts of men in their plots and practices, as well as these who are more foolish.

3. A third instance is (v. 18) *he looseth the bond of kings.* That is, when he pleases, he looses the authority of kings, whereby they were able to bind others, that their subjects regard it not (Isa. 45:1). *And girded their loins with a girdle;* that is, he debases and puts them in the place of a servant. God is that sovereign, that he can put the highest from the throne when he likes.

4. A fourth instance is [in] v. 19. God's sovereignty is exercised on princes as well as any other, and the mighty are no more to him than mean folks.

5. A fifth instance is (v. 20): *He removeth the speech of the trusty, and taketh away the understanding of the aged.* If a man has a man that he lippens to [*trusts*] for advice and counsel, who is worthy of credit, he will sometimes in his secret wisdom remove such, in so far that he shall not have a word of advice and counsel to give. He can make aged men that should know things best, twice fools, or like bairns [*children*]. So [as in] Isaiah 3, the threatening goes forth against all sorts of persons, high and low, the mighty man, and the man of war, the prophet and prudent, etc. God's sovereignty extends to all.

6. A sixth instance is (v. 21) *he poureth contempt upon princes.* The word princes, is read *priests.* It is likely, having spoken of princes before, he speaks of priests here, taking in these who were employed in ecclesiastical affairs. [As in] Isa. 3, the prophet comes in among the rest. For when God pleases he can discover the emptiness of ministers, by suffering them to go out in their own strength, and then their weakness appears, or by letting their word have no weight among people, but to harden them the more as in Ezekiel's and Jeremiah's days, they were ridiculed as such as spake parables, and became the song of the drunkard. *And he weakeneth the strength of the mighty,* or looseth the girdle of the strong and makes feeble. As Amos 2:14-16: *The strong shall not strengthen his force, neither shall the mighty deliver himself; he that is courageous among the mighty shall flee away naked in that day, saith the Lord.*

7. *He discovereth hid things out of darkness, and bringeth out to light the shadow of death* (v. 22). Many things are hid from the world, but there is nothing hid from God; though things were as high and secret, as the shadow of death, he can bring them out to all the world.

8. *He increaseth the nations,* etc. (v. 23), which relates to God's sovereignty in respect of his power. Sometimes he enlarges nations, and gives them prosperity; he destroys and diminishes them.

9. *He takes away the heart,* etc. By the heart is understood all things in the heart, as if he said, 'Look wherefore any man is excellent, for place, power, or wisdom, he can make the best of men feeble and fools, and when their heart is taken away, or their gifts smitten, or they are left in confusion, they are like one in a wilderness, that knows not what to do, nor where to go.' And a second effect, *They grope in the dark without light;* they have no more wisdom than beasts, for as wise as they were before, and *they stagger like a drunken man.* They have no more pith nor power to do anything to purpose, [*than*] drunken men, when God befools the wisest of them. This is seen in many instances (take Nebuchadnezzar for one).

The scope of all these instances is twofold. 1. To confirm his checking of his friends, he will convince them that he had as good skill as they in reasoning. 2. To let them see out of God's attributes he could make a just contrary use to that which they made. They would from God's justice conclude him a wicked man. He concludes from God's sovereignty, that wicked men are often and better dealt with in outward things than the godly; for God does as he pleases, and there is reason he should do so, and not be limited.

OBSERVATIONS.

1. From that which Job implies to be in his friend's condition and carriage, observe: That folks too ordinarily esteem too much of what is their own judgment and expression of things, as if none had the like; though what they have is but common and <u>bauch</u> [*insubstantial*] like other men's, they are ready to think better of their own thoughts [*than*] of any other, and to be in conceit with their own errors, as if they were new lights.

2. Observe: Charity and humility should be so regulated, as folks never thereby wrong a good cause. Job has a twofold cause to maintain. (1) Against the devil, that he was no hypocrite. (2) He has God's sovereignty to defend, and he thinks it no charity nor humility to give way to his friends in wronging any of these. (1) Because it gives the devil advantage. (2) Because it wrongs truth to cede to others' judgment in that wherein we are right.

3. Observe: It is too ordinary a fault to them that are in ease, to be harsh in censuring others that are in trouble. It is easy to cry down men and their cause, were it never so good, when they are in adversity (vs. 4-5).

4. Observe: There is no sort of contest and opposition heavier to be borne in affliction, [than] that which is met with from honest men (vs. 4-5). This lay heaviest on Job here, and David regrets that it was his companion that had lift up his heel against him. It adds to his affliction, that such a one that had the name of honesty was the instrument of his trouble.

5. Observe: It is a shame for folks to be ignorant of the main and common principles of religion, especially these that concern God, and his attributes, his sovereignty, wisdom, power and providence. He attests the beasts — they were not in some sort ignorant of these — [that] among them will be found the knowledge of God's

attributes. If Job lived nowadays, he would find many ignorant folks that think they have knowledge.

6. Observe: The right knowledge and acknowledging of God in his attributes, especially in his sovereignty, is a way to loose many doubts both doctrinal and practical. It is as it were the common place Job makes use of against his friends, that it was God's part and place to guide and dispose of things, and not creatures; that it <u>became</u> [*suited*] creatures to submit, and not to plead with him (Rom. 9), *Who art thou that repliest against God, shall,* etc. The consideration whereof would teach men sobriety in the doctrine of providence, and would allay many curiosities, and be a means to settle much carnal fear and anxiety. To make a right use of the wisdom of God, and not to be out of hope when we see things confused; and of the power of God, knowing there is nothing too hard for him — and though we are at our wits end, and have no strength to believe, yet to quiet ourselves upon it. Wisdom and strength are his.

7. From the general context, observe that it belongs to God as a pearl of his crown, to have an immediate hand in the ordering of all things under the sun according to his pleasure. It is his unquestionable royal prerogative to lift up and put down, to make nations honorable one year, and half slaves another. *The deceiver and deceived are to him.*

8. Observe: However matters go, whether up or down, whether devils be let loose or [made] fast, wicked men prosper, or beat under, etc. God is always carrying on his design, which he laid down before the beginning of the world. Yea, even sinful instruments are in his hand, and he has a holy hand in their work, and is performing his own purpose and pleasure by them, as in the king of Assyria (Isa. 10). His counsels are always in execution, and whether good or ill angels, devils or men, as they are under his dominion, so they are working to his hand. It were good for us to drink in the knowledge of this in our practice, and to be established and stayed in the faith of such a point in such a reeling time as this is.

13

J ob continues his answer to Zophar's speech, and him to all his friends. The chapter has two parts: I. He speaks directly to them (vs. 1-19). II. He speaks immediately to God (vs. 20-28).

I. There are three parts of speech to them. 1. In the first two verses he confirms what he spoke before of God's greatness and sovereignty in doing all things, and not limiting him, to which his friends tied him, in doing good to godly men in temporal things, and inflicting judgments on wicked men. *Lo, mine eye hath seen all this.* 'I have seen such a thing to be true; therefore I say it over again. *Mine ear hath heard and understand it.* 'I have learned of others what I saw not myself, and drunken in this doctrine of God's sovereignty solely. *I know what ye know, and am not inferior to you,* in the knowledge of this truth, and have no cause to cast my words as vain.'

2. He goes on to a reproof, mixed with an advice, which he backs with reasons (vs. 3-12). He begins with a desire to speak to God, not out of a fretting humor, nor to justify himself; but in his cause that he was a sincere man. He here opposes himself to Eliphaz (5:8), and wishes for God to speak unto, to commit his cause to him as well as he; so it holds out Job's standing by his sincerity. But the meaning seems to be this: 'Though I would speak to God, and do not fear to commit any cause to him, yet I have little cause to speak to you.' And the words following clear this to be his scope. 'But *ye are forgers of lies,*' that is, of doctrinal lies (as the apostle says, *speaking lies in hypocrisy,* 1 Tim. 4:2), which is applicable to the thesis they maintained, that God does always punish wicked men in this life, and reward the godly. And to be forgers of lies is more than to be venters of lies; to be forgers of lies is to put them in mold and shape, and set them well together, a word borrowed from these whose proper work it is to forge things.

The second part of his challenge [is], *Ye are physicians of no value;* which is applicable to their mistake of his condition, they taking him to be a hypocrite, and their way of dealing with him. He means they were miserable comforters to him, and he speaks here to them both with respect to the general thesis, and as they applied it to him.

In the fifth verse he gives them his advice. *O that ye would altogether hold your peace, and it should be your wisdom.* That is, 'it would be better you should hold your peace than insist on your mistake, and oppose the words of truth that I have spoken.' This he backs with several reasons, repeating the conclusion (v. 13), as if he said:

'It is true you are aged and wise men, and know God indeed; but hearken to me. You take the wrong way to condemn me, that you may justify God, to the end you may condemn me, to limit God's sovereignty. In this you speak wickedly and deceitfully for God. For will you accept his person out of some by-respect to wrong truth, and will you have a respect to contending for him more than to the cause? [Do you] think that God will approve you, that out of a good intent to plead for him you should wrong me? Will you contend for God on [*these*] grounds? It would be far better for you to hold your tongue, than wickedly and deceitfully so to speak for God.' He condemns not their contending for God, but their contending for God on such grounds.

And a third reason he gives (vs. 9-10): 'Can you abide God's searching of you, and will you force him to call you to a reckoning? [Do you] think that he will be pleased with your words?' Or, 'Can you mock him as one silly poor man will mock another? No, he will surely reprove you. If you accept persons and your shifts in contending for God will not do your turn when you are partial, and wrong truth on the one side do the other.'

He does not charge them as if intentionally they mocked God, but because they were taken up in pleading for God's justice, which had a fair face to defend God, and did not regard how they wronged truth, and Job. He lets them see how apt a fair pretext is to lead them wrong. He urges them from God's excellency to hold their peace (v. 11); as if he said, 'Are you not afraid to father things on God that he will never own? Know you the justice and sovereignty that is in him, while you do so? Should not his dread rather scare you from such a course?'

This he amplifies (v. 12), by laying them before God. *Your remembrances are like unto ashes.* That is, 'Whatever makes you memorable, or whatever is excellent in you, it is but like ashes.' *Your bodies are bodies of clay*, or 'your heights are like bodies of clay, but God in his excellency is infinite, and how then dare you venture on that, [in which] God is concerned, in such a way?'

3. And [he] therefore repeats the conclusion (v. 13). *Hold your peace, and let me alone.* And withal proceeds to a third thing he is to say to his friends, which is the third part of his speech to them; and that is to vindicate himself in appealing to God, giving reasons of his sincerity in so doing (vs. 13-20).

Let me alone that I may speak, and let come on me what will. It is not a word of desperation, but he means this much: 'Hold you your tongue, and I will take my hazard to God.' This he clears by removing an objection (v. 14). 'You think me like a mad man in this; like a man that is tearing his own flesh. But I would ask you, wherefore do I hazard my life in venturing upon God? Dare I do it if I were a hypocrite? I dare not.'

Another evidence of his sincerity is (v. 15): 'I am so far from despairing that I judge not God by dispensations as you do. *Though he should slay me, I would trust in him,* and keep confidence in him.'

A third evidence, *I will maintain my own ways before him,* 'I will not maintain every step of my way. That for my course I have not been a hypocrite, this I will maintain.'

A fourth evidence is (v. 16): *He also shall be my salvation.* 'Though he should slay me, I am sure I will get another life.' He gives a reason of this. *For a hypocrite shall not come before him.* 'The hypocrite will not trust in God when he is angry at him, he dare not lay open his cause before God as I do, nor trust his soul to him when his breath is going out as I do.'

He repeats what he said (v. 6) to put them to observe his speech (v. 17), and gives the reason (v. 18), *I have ordered my cause.* 'I go upon good and solid grounds, and *I know that I shall be justified;* my confidence shall not be shaken. I am persuaded when God comes, he will decide in my favor.' And (v. 19), 'Seeing I have this testimony that God will justify me, who will come in my way to plead against me,' — a defiance to them all. In the courage of faith, he rises, and will maintain his integrity, and he gives a reason why he speaks so confidently. *If I hold my tongue, I should give up the ghost.* 'My grief is so heavy, and the pressure of the temptation so great, that it would put out my life, if I should not get a vent.' He thinks it not easy to vent his mind to God, and bear down unbelief, the more it would be up.

II. He speaks to God (vs. 20-28), and ere he speak he propounds two things to God humbly, not to carve out to, or limit God, and then he will speak to God, and these two things follow (v. 21).

1. The first is that God would take the present rod off him. 2. That he would not let his dread make him afraid; that is, that he would not deal roughly with him, or as in the way of the covenant of works, but as one in a covenant of grace. And if he will do so, then (v. 22) either *speak thou*, he says, *and I will answer, or let me speak, and answer thou me.*

Then (vs. 23-24) he [*proposes*] two grounds of complaint, insinuating confidence. The first is like that word (10:2), as if he said, 'I am not conscious to myself of any hid sin or wickedness, but if there be any hid sin, let me know of it.' And the second is, 'If I am not conscious to myself of any hid wickedness, why [do you] take such a severe course with me as to hide your face from me, and to deal with me as I were an enemy.' But there is in it a secret argument of faith that God will not deal so with him.

A second argument is (v. 25): *Wilt thou break a leaf driven to and fro,* etc. 'Am I a party to thee, who am like a withered leaf and dry stubble?' It supposes he is not a party to God, who is so feckless a creature. Then to the end of the chapter, he expresses some words holding forth some things that said God seemed to break him as a leaf and pursue him as stubble. As (1) *Thou writest bitter things against me,* as a man libeling up the process of another in court. (2) *Thou makest me possess the iniquities of my youth.* 'The sins I thought had been forgotten, do stare me in the face.' (3) *Thou puttest my feet in the stocks.* 'I am so straitened with temporal judgment, that I am like a man not only sentenced, but on whom the sentence is executed, as in a pair of stocks.' (4) *Thou lookest narrowly to all my paths.* 'Thou takest narrow notice of, and censures every circumstance of my walking.' (5) *Thou settest a print upon the heels of my feet.* 'Thou seemest so severe, as to mark every foot I lift.' And the last verse is a close of this chapter, but knits with the next. *And he as a rotten garment consumeth,* etc. 'I, a silly man under this sore trouble, am no better than a garment that is moth-eaten, and as a thing that is rotten and consumed.'

OBSERVATIONS.

1. He that [*proposes*] or defends anything for truth, had need to be well persuaded of the truth of it, that he may say with Job, *Mine eye*

hath seen it, mine ear hath heard it, and understood it (v. 1), and as 1 John 1:3, *That which we have heard,* etc.

2. It is an ease to a tempted soul to get leave to vent itself to God, otherwise it would burst (v. 3. with v. 19). This is a great advantage; believers have in all their difficulties a door open to God, *a new and living way* (Heb. 10).

3. Take it thus, 'I would speak to God, because you are forgers of lies.' Observe that it is a great advantage to them that deal with unreasonable men, that they have God as an equitable and reasonable judge. And this is our advantage; there is a time coming when God will admit of a second hearing.

4. Many folks may be sinning foully, wronging God and truth, when they intend to defend both. [*These*] men thought they were doing both, yet Job calls them forgers of lies, etc. (vs. 4-6).

5. A good intention will never justify an action that is not good in itself; we often take too much liberty to defend a good cause by unsuitable [means], and that is to speak wickedly for God. For there is nothing that God allows and calls for as a duty from us, but God has appointed a [*means*] suitable and lawful to come to it. He never carves out an end that can never be attained in a lawful way; therefore matters that concern the honor of God would be handled tenderly and soberly, and folks would not take liberty to speak or hold by words, as they tend to a good end, but see that the words are suitable to the end.

6. From his check and advice to hold their peace (v. 5), observe that it is far more wise to hold our peace in things wherein we are not thoroughly clear, than to undertake to speak when we are unclear, were our end never so good. *Even a fool when he holds his peace is counted wise, and he that shuts his lips is accounted a man of understanding* (Prov. 17:28). *Be swift to hear, slow to speak* (James 1:19). This would prevent many mistakes in our disputing and reasoning, if we were clear, ere we engaged, rather than to engage when unclear; and it may be when we have questioned a good while, know not well where we would be at. Better hold our peace than mar a good cause through our carnal way of handling it, as Job's friends here.

7. God will never accept as service to him that [which] wrongs our neighbor, or prejudges the duty we owe to our neighbors, whether it is in reasoning for God, or in the purchasing gear to bestow it for God. Love to God and our neighbor must never be separate, but go

hand and hand together. Therefore Job's friends are justly checked because they pretend and did indeed intend tenderness to the honor of God, but are not tender toward Job; *will you accept his person,* etc. (v. 8).

8. Observe (v. 11), that the most part of our mistakes and wrongs in practice flow from mean thoughts of the excellency of God, and not fearing his greatness. Therefore Job bears it on his friends that the excellency of God had not right weight with them. The excellency of God rightly thought of, would make folks tender and sober, and wary to pronounce sentence on these.

9. Observe (v. 12), that there is much of folks' selfishness and tenaciousness that proceeds from [*lack*] of right thoughts of themselves as well as of God. Or take it thus: Right thoughts of folks' self would move and induce us to walk tenderly before God, and charitably towards one another; mean thoughts of God, and big thoughts of bits of clay makes many of us miscarry. For Job's laying this before them from their selfish way and tenacious sticking to it, tells us that their forgetting of it made them fall in this fault.

10. From the same words learn that the best thing in men here away is but earthly and frail, having an earthly subject, which is but brickle [*brittle*] and will turn to dust again. These are right thoughts of ourselves, which are humbling thoughts. *Dust thou art, and unto dust thou shalt return* (Gen. 3:19).

11. *Though he should slay me, yet will I trust in him* (v. 15). Observe how bold and resolute faith is. 'All that is come on me,' Job says, 'shall not make me distrust him, nay, though he should do worse to me, it shall not make me quit my confidence.' Then strong faith will never quit grips of God. Or the stronger that faith is, the more stronger will it grip to God, especially when he seems to cast off. Or take it thus: Faith is not to and fro as it meets with difficulties and harsh dispensations, nor up and down as God seems angry or well pleased, for dispensations are not the object of faith, but the word of promise. And having that for its object, it rests on it, and will not quit it, and it is a good way to meet unbelief with the more strong faith, and to have faith resolved, clear and peremptory.

12. Observe (v. 18 compared with v. 15), that folks can never trust God too much, but the more faith trusts God, and lays its burden on him, it has the better ground to expect an outgate [*deliverance*], when he has said, 'I will trust in him, though he should slay me.' Then he comes to this, 'I have ordered my cause, I know that I shall be

justified.' So Paul (2 Tim. 1:12). *I know whom I have believed, and am persuaded that he is able to keep that which I have committed unto him against that day.* Too much cannot be laid on faith, or expected from it, because the ground of it is infinite, and it is a thriving way to learn to give God credit in difficulties. It has present peace, and there is no other way to peace. There is no way to be justified but this way, and there is no way to peace were the objects never so palpable and promising, till the heart comes to hazard on God, and give him credit.

14

In the close of the former chapter, Job has been pleading for man's fecklessness, that God would deal gently with him, who was so [*frail*] — like a leaf, the dry stubble, or moth-eaten garment. I. He goes on here amplifying and pressing the same request of God's forbearing him, and removing of the rod which he could not bear, being so [*frail*] a creature.

The first ground proposed to clear man's [*feebleness*] is, *his being born of a woman, having few days, and full of trouble* (v. 1). [This] is illustrated by a twofold comparison, one of a flower that soon fades, another of a shadow that flies away (v. 2), upon which the conclusion follows (v. 3): *Doest thou open thine eyes on such a one?* 'Is a man a party for thee, to deal withal, to look angry like upon' (as 7:12). 'That thou should bring me into judgment with thee, as I could stand before thee?' No, and he adds to the former two a third, as the greatest cause of all: 'Who can bring a clean thing out of an unclean?' Not one. 'Man that is come of an unclean stock cannot be clean himself, and is man then a [*suitable*] party to come in judgment with thee?' Which is not brought in to extenuate his guilt, or the guilt of any, but to prove man is feckless and sinful, that he is no party to stand in judgment with God.

A second ground is from a set time that every man has from God for such a piece of work. He lays down the ground (v. 5), draws his conclusion from it (v. 6), and backs it with reasons; *Seeing his days are determined,* etc. 'Seeing thou hast peremptorily carved out many days, and they are all numbered in thy decree, and thou knowest he has but a little time to live.' *Turn from him,* etc. 'Give him a breathing time to perform the work thou hast given him, because if he be removed, he cannot return to perfect the work.'

This he presses, 1. from a dissimilitude (vs. 7-10). 'Man is not like a tree, for (vs. 7-9) there is hope of a tree, that though it be cut down, it will grow again. But (v. 10) it is not so with man; he dies, wastes away, <u>dwines</u> [*fades; withers*], and wears to his last thread, and then gives up the ghost. And where is he? he is never seen to sprout here away again.'

2. From a second similitude (v. 11), he has the waters of the sea dry up (which is taken generally for any multitude of waters gathered together, that has streams running from them to the sea, yet not having a spring they die, because the sea is like their mother). The streams run out. So it is with man when his natural life is out. There is no more of him, till the heavens are no more. He is not raised from the sleep of death till the last day (v. 12).

II. The second part follows to the same purpose, but handled another way. *O that thou wouldst hide me in the grave* (v. 13). By the grave is not meant the place of the dead, but (as the words following clear) a hiding place, as these that are hid in the graves are free of calamities, so he desires some shelter of God, till his wrath (that is some effects of his wrath that were [*expounded*] so by his friends, and were in themselves fruits of anger) were past. As if he said, 'O that thou would suspend thine anger, or set a time for the lasting of it, and in the mean time grant me a shelter under it, that this thine anger last not forever; and having set the time, that thou would remember the time to give an <u>outgate</u> [*deliverance*].' For God's remembering Noah, and others, is for giving them an outgate from the strait they were in.

1. This suit for some rest here away, and for God's bounding his calamity, he presses (v. 14): *If a man die, shall he live again?* 'If I be taken away by death now, I cannot live here away again. There is no recovering of men who are once dead, to live in the world among other men.' And because this seems a sad word, he subjoins unto it a strong consolation; 'suppose it be so, that man once dead never lives a natural life any more, yet I will not fear death that much as to weaken my waiting for a better life. But all the days of my appointed time will I wait till my change by death from a miserable to a happy life comes.' The consolation follows (v. 15). *Thou shalt call, and I will answer.* That is, 'God shall call, and I will answer. In the great day he will seek account of a person that he began to work a good work in, and will not [*lack*] me.' The words being thus taken home, there is no difficulty in them. He means though he should be taken away by death now, God would call for him at the latter day. But if we take the words in a larger sense (as we may), as relating to Job's looking to a time when God should put an end to his outward trouble, then he means that he would wait till God's time of <u>outgate</u> [*delivery*] came, and he should bring him out to the fields, a delivered man.

They may also imply his waiting till death comes, that God takes his soul to himself. Neither of these can well be excluded.

2. A second ground of his desire of outgate: because God's way seemed to be exceeding strict towards him, so that he was not able to stand before God. *Thou numberest my steps.* 'I do not step a step, but thou tells them all.' *And watches over my sin.* 'Thou keeps it as a sentry, and presents it in a reckoning' (v. 16). 'Nay, My *transgression is sealed up in a bag,* not a miscarriage in me, but thou sews them up as in a purse, as folks sew up money, and seal it, that it may not be lost, or as folks sew up papers, and count that they may not be lost, so thou seemest to take strict notice of all my sins, to charge them upon me' (v. 17).

3. A third ground of the desire (v. 18) from the effect the former had upon him, *The mountain falling cometh to nought.* 'A mountain cannot endure such dealing, neither the hard rock, but it should be removed out of its place, if thou should show thyself angry.' This he clears (v. 19); 'the continual dropping of water will wear stones, and far more will thy anger wear away man. Thou canst make rains to fall, and the floods to overflow, and grass, and corn, and all is taken away, and man's hope is destroyed.' Then the particular application of this to man follows (v. 20). 'Thou prevailest forever against him, and he passeth; when mountains and rocks cannot abide thee, there is no hold again to thee in them; when thou art angry, no creature can stand in thy way, far less man. Thou soon changest his countenance, pale and wan.'

His state in the grave is described (v. 21). 'When he is gone to the grave, he is like a man that never was. Whether it will be well or ill with his children, he knows not, for all the pains he took of them.' And (v. 22) he amplifies this effect of God's wrath, that not only is man sent to death by it, but living men are made a burden to themselves, as if he said, 'Man has but two things to see to; his body and his soul.' He can pine the body with sickness and sores, and by a blink of his anger on the soul, he can make him mourn.' And therefore seeing he, nor [any] man else could be party to God, he passes the point, that God would take a kindly way of dealing with him, and remove his wrath and rod off him.

How can [*these*] things be motives to God? *Answ.* 1. Job is not so much pleading here to bind God with reason, or move God with arguments, for nothing from the creature can bind or move God. Rather he is bringing in some confirmations to his own faith from God's dealing, who breaks not the bruised reed, and quenches not the smoking flax. 2. We may look on [*these*] grounds as flowing from the heat of his spirit under hard exercise, wherein he does not order and guard things so well as need be; yet well understood they may have a good meaning.

OBSERVATIONS.

1. Man is a poor creature, and has a short and miserable life here away, which this book and much scripture clears. (1) It is a common truth, and should make us prepare for trouble, albeit everyone would be without it. (2) And it should make us seek to make sure another life that is without trouble, which will make us happy and satisfy us seeing this life cannot. Provide for a crown and kingdom that is incorruptible. Live every day as these who have few more to spend. We live as if eternity were here, and put death out of sight when it may be <u>hard by</u> [*close by*] us.

2. Observe (v. 4), man's misery is never well known till his original corruption is known, which shows the fountain cause that misery comes from.

3. The corruption of nature being seen, is the most humbling thing. There is nothing so abases man, and heightens God, nor puts man to make use of a Mediator, [*than*] the sense of that corruption of nature that man brings with him in the world. This humbled David (Psa. 51) and Paul (Rom. 7; Eph. 2). He lays out this to make the righteousness of Christ [to] be welcomed. And the reason of the pride of nature is the ignorance of folks' original condition; the want of the sense of our loathsomeness and uncleanness makes us so securely pass over our time, as if we could plead with God.

4. It is often folks' best temper when they are most sensible of their vileness, whether actual or original. When a man is in a most lively frame, and most intimate with God, he has the clearest sight of sin, and has the most sharp censure of it. Hence Paul says, 'I was a blasphemer,' etc. (1 Tim. 1:3) and David (2 Sam. 23:5), *Although my house be not so with God,* etc. We often mistake conditions, are ready to think a sight of sin a horrible condition; but when sin is kindly taken with, it has often greater respect to God's glory and others' good, and is more profitable for us, more conducive to the strengthening of faith, and the commending of Christ, than any other condition.

5. Observe from the second ground (v. 5), seeing his days are determined: (1) God has given every man a task, and a time to

perform it in. (2) When that time is ended, there is nothing beyond it (Acts 17:26). *He has determined the times before appointed, and the bounds of their habitations:* the day, year, and hour, as well as the place.

Use. Partly to remove our anxieties in this time wherein troubles abound. Think not that men have power to take lives, or pull men off the stage before their work is done. This will hold true of all men, especially of these that have any special work from God: their days and task are determined with him (Rev. 2). The two witnesses could not be prevailed over till their testimony was finished. Partly, to make men busy in the task committed to them, while they have time. Let all watch, and be found in their work, for they know not in what hour their Lord comes.

6. *If a man shall die, shall he live again?* etc. (v. 14) . He lays it down partly as a resolution in duty, partly as a consolation against that he was threatened with, that there was a set time for him, and he would wait for it. Observe: Folks should not limit God in his way and timing of things to them, but wait upon and submit to his carved out time. *All the days of my appointed time will I wait till my change come.* (1) He waits without fagging, persevering in waiting. It holds out his expectation, faith and confidence of an <u>outgate</u> [*deliverance*]. (2) A quieting himself on God and his word till it comes. (3) A continuance in quieting himself; this is a notable guard against crosses and temptations, and against God's hiding of his face.

7. Another thing on this verse is, that the hope of the change that is coming, and of God's renewing his mercy after all [*these*] days are by, is a consolation that ought to quiet believers. That there is a time coming when God who seems to forget now, yet (as it is, v. 15.) will call for his work, will not leave a grain of their dust in their grave, but raise it up again, because he made it and renewed it. There are many difficulties in man's life, and in our time, but there will be a time of the change of the condition of God's people, and of his enemies also. It is coming; wait for it, and comfort ourselves in it.

8. *Thou wilt have a desire to the work of thine hands* (v. 15). Observe: However God seems to neglect his work for a time, he will ask for it again; for it is upon a general ground that Job goes here. 'Thou wilt not neglect the work of thine hands, and so thou wilt not forget me in whom thou has begun a work.' Habbakuk (Hab. 3) on the same ground, prays to revive his work; his work is perfect, and he is a God of judgment, and where he begins he finishes. He knows how many souls he has together, and what length he has reformation to bring; and he will own his work, and carry it on to the last soul he has to

bring in. And it is a consolation to souls where there is <u>aught</u> [*anything*] of God begun. God has a desire to the work of his hands, be it little or meikle [*much*], he will not [*lack*] it.

15

We heard before of the state of the question between Job and his friends. They have all three spoken, and he has answered. Eliphaz who began first, begins the second time, and goes upon the same grounds, and has the same ends before him. He continues in his mistake, and prosecutes the end he had before him in his first speech, only being further engaged (though a good man) after debate, he is more irritated, and more sharp upon Job. I. He has a sharp reproof to Job (vs. 1-13), which is a preface to the debate following. II. He debates his old theses several ways (vs. 14-35).

I. 1. The first cause wherefore he reproves Job (vs. 2-3), is for speaking proud, vain, and windy words, having a show of wisdom and knowledge, but no substance. *Should a wise man utter vain knowledge?* etc. 'Wherefore serves all this discourse? No wise man, as you have been thought, should take this [*way*].' And he speaks by way of interrogation, to bear in his reproof more sharply on Job.

2. A second challenge is added as a further degree of the former (v. 4). *Yea, though thou castest off fear, and restrainest prayer before God.* 'This way of defending yourself is an evidence of your casting off fear, and your rejecting of our advice in making supplication to God. It evidences your restraint of prayer, and of pouring out your heart before God.' A sharp check, but built on a mistake of Job's expressions. Yea (v. 5), he charges him for not only casting off fear, and restraining prayer himself, but that by his doctrine he taught others to cast them off, and not to take with sin [*not to acknowledge their sin*]. And he proves it, *for thy mouth uttereth thine iniquity.* 'In your discourse you teach iniquity, and propagate it to others, to [*teach*] all men not to humble themselves before God.' *And thou choosest the tongue of the crafty.* Job confessed he was a sinner, but Eliphaz alleges that he had but craftily done this in the general to hide his wickedness. But he says (v. 6), *Thy own mouth condemns thee and not I.* And this he takes from Job's word (9:20). *If I justify myself, my own mouth shall condemn me. If I say I am perfect, it shall prove me perverse.*

3. The third charge or challenge he bears on Job, is for sticking to his own judgment, and rejecting [that of] his and his other two friends, which is followed forth in several verses following (v. 7). *Art thou the first man that was born?* '[Do] you think, Job, that you were the first man. It seems by your sticking by your own judgment, that you have been made before others, seeing you will not take counsel from us.'

Have ye been upon God's secret? (v. 8). 'Is there none that knows God's way of walking with men but you?' *What knowest thou that we know not?* (v. 9). 'Are you any wiser than we? We have had a long time and as much experience as you. And (v. 10) we are not alone in this cause, but *with us,* or upon our side, *are the aged or grey-headed,* men of experience, whom you should reverence.'

And (v. 11), *Are the consolations of God small with thee?* '[Do] you think little of all we have said, and will you take a [*way*] of your own?' *Is there any secret thing with thee?* 'Have you any secret revelation of any other thing, or [*way*] of serving God than others have revealed unto them, and if there be no [*way*] but that which is revealed, why do you take a [*way*] of your own? a way which your own passion and inclination leads you to. Why does your heart carry you away, to such a way?' *And what doth thine eye wink at?* 'Why will you mock our advice which from God we have given you?' *That thou turnest thy spirit against God:* 'Will you turn such a mocker, as to let loose your spirit not only against us, but against God? Your words reflect on God's justice, and you condemn him in justifying yourself.'

All [this] proceeds on a mistake, as if God's justice could not be defended, except Job [*agreed*] that he was a wicked man.

II. He goes on in the debate; and prosecutes his old thesis (vs. 14-35). 1. None can be clean or innocent, therefore not Job (vs. 14-16). 2. Then he applies the argument to Job, but in a secret way, giving a number of evidences of the wicked man, which he would have Job taking to him [*applying to himself*] [vs. 17-28]. 3. He gives some predictions, or threatenings of judgment, and closes with a reason why Job will perish in that way if he shall continue in it [vs. 29-35].

1. He proves from man's corruption (which Job had asserted before) that man cannot be righteous. 'What is corrupt man but an unclean branch, come off an unclean stock, therefore he cannot be righteous' (v. 14). A second argument to prove that man is not innocent, is by comparison from the less to the more (v. 15). *Behold he putteth no trust in his saints,* etc. God is so spotless pure, that holy

angels and the congregation of heaven, being compared with the infinite and independent holiness of God, are unclean. He trusts not in them, that is, he lippens [*trusts*] not to their standing to themselves, but by his power sustains them. And if they are unclean, how much more man? For they have never sinned actually as man, who (v. 16) drinks in sin, as the ox does water; as the beasts are set on their meat and drink, so is man on sin. The argument is a truth in the general, but it includes nothing against Job.

2.   He applies this to Job, and because it was a hard doctrine to bear on Job that he was a hypocrite, he prefaces (vs. 17-20): 'Take heed what I am going to tell you, even that which I have seen and heard, not of fools, but wise men, who have had it from their fathers' (vs. 17-18). 'And these the most renowned fathers' (v. 19); that is, 'these who lived after the flood' (it seems Noah's sons). 'It is a truth that all generations have received, *or unto whom alone the earth was given*, may point out the dignity of these fathers, that others of the world made judges, and they ruled so well, that they kept the earth from being overrun by strangers.' The former seems to be the more simple meaning of the words.

Then he gives marks whereby to know the hypocrite, and subjoins the sad dispensations he meets with, whereunto he knits his sins as causes of these dispensations.

(1) A wicked man is all his days in pain and misery. *The number of his years are hid to the oppressor* (v. 20). That is they are determined and appointed in God's secret counsel to the oppressor, as 'you are to be a prey to the Sabeans and Chaldeans.'

(2) A second evidence is (v. 21), he has [*ever*] the terror of God and an ill conscience pursuing him; and though he come to prosperity, he shall be destroyed, and get no rest; 'and it is so with you Job.'

(3) A third evidence (v. 22): A wicked man in a strait has no hope of recovery, trows [*trusts*] never to win out of it, but grows desperate in his poverty; and after poverty the sword comes. 'And such is your case.' Yea, a wicked man (v. 23) has [*nothing*] to entertain himself and his family, and he is so compassed with straits, that he wots [*knows*] not how to submit. 'And is it not so with you?'

And (v. 24) he amplifies the same evidence: Not only shall he be in straits, and hopeless of outgate [*deliverance*], but trouble and anguish shall overcome him, and all his stoutness shall be laid, and he shall turn impatient and be able to take no comfort (as chap. 4) to himself that used to comfort others. And these judgments shall come upon him as a king in battle. But either: [1] This is not truth; [these] things are not proper to all wicked men, for good men may meet with them sometimes. [2] Or it is not true that Job's was so afflicted for hypocrisy and wickedness.

The second part of this part of the chapter contains the second part of the wicked man's description, in his sinful carriage. (1) And he will not stand to enter in contest with God (v. 25); yea (v. 26), he is so far from yielding to God, that when God comes against him, he strengthens himself, like a mad man, and runs desperately on God, by not submitting to him. He gives a reason of this (v. 27). *Because he covers his face with fatness.* Because while he had prosperity, he was a man given to ease, and pleasure, and carnal delights. *Their face stands out with fatness* (Psa. 63:7). (2) A second cause is (v. 28): *He dwells in desolate houses.* That is, he builds ruinous and desolate cities and houses. He is [so] rich that he is able to buy and build them, or, [they are] cities and houses which by oppression he has made desolate and taken possession of. Upon this ground [he] scorns to submit to God; 'and this was your condition Job.'

3   The third part of the debate is, by threatenings and predictions of judgment, whereby he would terrify Job. The first is (v. 29), whatever that man does, he shall not continue rich, but God shall bring a curse on all that he has. We may win to a sort of perfection in riches, but he shall not prolong it. A second is (v. 30): *He shall not depart out of darkness.* When God has marred his prosperity, and bought him into the darkness of adversity and trouble, he shall keep him in it, and the judgment of God shall be like a fire to burn up his branches. Yea, by God's indignation, shall he pass away.

A third is by way of advice (v. 31). Seeing it is so, that he who thinks much of riches, which are but vanity, shall have a deceitful bargain, 'Let not such a man as you beguile yourself in trusting to them.' A good advice if well applied. A fourth (v. 32), which may be an aggravation of the former threatening from the suddenness of it: God's judgment shall take him away before the ordinary course of nature, and his children like the olive that casts the fruit ere the flower be off it (v. 33). 'And so has it been with you.'

And he closes with a general threatening that bears a challenge not obscurely against Job. 'As it is with you, so shall it be with all hypocrites. As they had families like congregations, and God scattered them, so has he done with you.' And in this challenge, bribery is laid to Job's charge (as 22:6). 'Yea, the wicked take much pains, and have little profit of it; they hatch sin, and bring forth a lie, and do neither good to themselves nor others (vs. 24-25); and so it is with you.'

But Eliphaz defends a wrong thesis, and mistakes the question. (1) For Job never called himself an innocent man, though he would not grant he was a hypocrite. (2) He goes on wrong grounds to prove Job a hypocrite from temporal judgments, because the godly and hypocrites partake alike in these. (3) He unwarrantably charges secret and great sins on Job, whereof he had no evidence, but because he was so afflicted, as in the following chapter. (4) He heightens a number of Job's expressions, that had infirmity in them, to the highest pitch, as evidences of unbroken nature.

OBSERVATIONS.

1. That such an approved and sincere man, one that was aiming at the honor of God, mistakes Job so far, and uses such hot expressions, that neither tended to the honor of God, nor the edification of Job, teaches us a holy soberness and Christian meekness and wisdom in our carriage, especially in our debates and contests with men of integrity. How may it humble folks to look on [*these*] men bearing out this dispute against Job, and yet honest in their aim, and following their light, and as confident of their own cause, as if all Job's expressions had been wind. Therefore seeing we are apt to go wrong, and to maintain our wrong, be sober and [*choose*] our steps at the entry.

2. That he says 'let not him that is deceived trust in vanity.' It is a good advice in itself, worthy to be laid to heart. We have gotten experience of the vanity of all things, of outward peace, of grandeur at home and abroad, of external ordinances when <u>dotted</u> [*over-loved; trusted in*], of armies of men, of wisdom and self-confidence, etc. Then let us not who are deceived trust any more to vanity; let us not fall foully in that fault over again, in making men our confidence, either to fear us from duty, or to shelter ourselves under them; but let us make God our fear and our dread, and we shall not need to fear man's fear.

16

The former chapter was a sharp challenge against Job, and contains very many long reproaches. In this and the following chapter Job returns his answer to what Eliphaz bares upon him. I. We have Job's reproof of his friends' unkindly way of dealing with him (vs. 1-5). II. More particularly, he answers to what Eliphaz said (16:6-17:16).

I. The grounds whereupon he reproves them are: 1. Their troublesome insisting on the same mistakes or grounds (v. 2). 'It is not the first time I have heard these things,' *Miserable comforters are ye all*. In the original it is, *Comforters of trouble are ye all*. Either 'you have no skill to comfort me,' or 'you vex me by renewing words that have no power nor strength, for the end you speak them for.'

2. A second is (v. 3), 'what need you repeat these things you have said before? They are but words of wind. What emboldens you to speak them over again; what encouragement have you gotten so to do? Did you so well to it, or got yourself any advantage?'

3. He shows them (vs. 4-5), that he would not have dealt so with them. He tells them he would not have spoken to them, as they did to him. He could have heaped up words against them, and shaken his head and laughed at them; but if they had been in his case, he would not have done so. He would have strengthened and comforted them, and would have been so far from aggravating their grief, that he would have mitigated it.

II. He goes on in answering Eliphaz (vs. 6-22), who in his discourse did run upon two grounds. 1. Comparing Job in his affliction to an afflicted wicked man. 2. Comparing him in his practices to wicked men, to whom he was like, as he alleged. To both these Job answers. 1. He answers to the first (vs. 6-14), that it is true he was afflicted as [*like*] a wicked man, but it will not follow that therefore he is wicked. 2. To the second he answers (vs. 15-16), that he denies that he dealt stubbornly with God in his practice [*like*] a wicked man. 3. He disclaims his conclusion that he suffered these hard things as a hypocrite, and confirms the negative by several arguments (vs 16-22).

1. He grants he was in trouble, and if he debated, he was not the better, and if he held his peace, he was not in ease, and (v. 7) shows wherein his trouble lay. *He hath made me weary.* That is, God. Meaning, so long as he is pleased to keep up [*hold back*] the blessing from the means, they will do no good. Whereupon he turns himself to God, and says, *Thou hast made desolate all my company.* That is, 'It is not men that I have to do with. It is not the Sabeans and Chaldeans that have scattered my family, and put us sundry [*apart*]; but it is thou. And beside that my prosperous condition is changed, this body of mine is filled with wrinkles, that commonly accompany old age and poverty, and these are a witness that God is angry with me' (as 10:17). 'And by these he seems to bear witness for my friends.' And this he repeats to the same purpose: *My leanness rising up, bears witness to my face.* 'If I should say my condition were not hard, my countenance should prove I lie. I deny not that.'

Therefore the second part of his condition (v. 9) he sets out in man's dealing with him. *He teareth me in his wrath, who hateth me, he gnasheth upon me,* etc. All expressions to point out how everyone that hated him got leave to take their will of him (as Psal. 37:12). [*Then*] the violent hatred of the wicked against the godly is set out under this expression, *He sharpeneth his eyes upon me.* It is a reviving to the light of his eye; he feeds on it. Or it is a fiery look, to point out the inward hatred of the wicked, and it may take in Job's friends as dealing roughly with him. Yea (v. 10): *They gaped upon me with their mouth,* as men that laugh and say, *Aha. They have smitten me upon the cheek reproachfully.* i.e. 'They have buffeted me with their ill tongues though they held off their hands.' *They have gathered themselves,* etc. 'Like as men combined to carry on my affliction,' *God hath delivered me unto the ungodly* (v. 11). 'All this is come upon me by God's providence. This I deny not. All my substance is devoured by the Sabeans, Chaldeans,' etc.

The third part of his condition is the saddest. He grants (v. 12) that God evidences his anger as an enemy. *I was at ease, but God has broken me asunder,* in respect of body, mind and family. *He hath also taken me by the neck, and shaken me to pieces.* 'He has done with me as a strong man that is angry with another.' *And set me up as his mark* or butt, at whom he shoots the arrows of his judgments. 'For he has so many judgments, and every one of them lights upon me, and sticks into me, as a dart, time about [*in turns*].' *He cleaves my reins,* etc. (v. 13, a similitude taken from the most vital part of the body), and he does not spare. *He poureth out my gall on the ground;* he seems to have no restraint till he have the life out. *He breaks me,* etc. (v. 14). He goes on upon or against me with new judgments, as if the former were not enough; *And makes breach upon breach,* or death upon death, [*lacking*] words to set out what he would say. 'Yea, he comes upon me, *like a giant,* for strength and terror, as if presently he would put out my life;' expressing what sense he had of God's dealings.

2. He answers to Eliphaz's second <u>alledgance</u> [*allegation*] (vs. 15-16), showing what his carriage was. *I have sewed sackcloth on my skin,* or 'to my skin;' that is, 'I did not contest with God as you said (15:25). 'And my garment stuck to my skin, *and I defiled my horn in the dust.* I laid down that which is excellent and eminent in man, and humbled myself before God.' Yea (v. 16), 'the foulness of my face that has dust and tears on it, tells that I am an humble man.' *And on my eyelids is the shadow of death;* 'my eyes are so hollow, that the picture of death is on my eye-lids.'

3. In the last place, he comes to disclaim his conclusion; that for all this it will not follow that he is an unjust and wicked man. Therefore (v. 17), he gives a flat denial to his conclusion; 'it is not for any injustice; be the cause what it will, it is not for the cause you say. It is for no injustice in respect of my state, for I am reconciled to God; nor is it for injustice in my practice — I am no violent oppressor nor briber. Also my profession is sound, and my prayer is pure in the kind. Though not without sin, my practice is sincere.' And because much of the weight of the debate lay on this, he confirms it by arguments.

(1) 'If I be an oppressor, then let not the earth cover my blood and oppression (v. 18). As the blood Cain shed cried for vengeance, so let mine' (as Isa. 26:21). 'If I be a wicked man as you call me, I attest the earth not to conceal, but disclose my wickedness.'

(2) *And let not my cry have place.* 'If I be the man you call me, let not God hear my prayer, and if I were not clear [of the charge], I would not attest God thus.' Yea (v. 19), 'I am sure to win the cause' — *my witness is in heaven.* 'I have a surer judge and witness than either you or my conscience; he is in heaven, who has all my actions recorded, and I [*trust*] to him.'

(3) A third argument (v. 20): *My friends scorn me.* 'You laugh at all this, and think nothing of my attesting God, but are ready to scorn me' (as some expressions [in] 15:7 seem to bear out). 'But when you

scorn, I betake myself to God.' *Mine eye poureth out tears to him* — 'I have a melting spirit, and there is a venting of it to God that gives me some ease.'

(4) A fourth argument (v. 22): *O that one might plead for a man with God,* etc. 'It is true' (would he say) 'God is [*outside*] our bounds, and man cannot plead with him; but O that it were so that a man might plead with God. For if it were thus, I <u>durst</u> [*would dare*] venture my cause upon him. *When a few years are come,* etc. [This] is subjoined as an amplification or aggravation of the former argument. 'You will not believe me now when I speak sincerely, but it will be but a short time till I come before God, where my cause will be cleared, though it should not be in this world. And when I am taken away, I will not return; there will be no making-up of what is behind then. Therefore, I dare not dissemble now.'

OBSERVATIONS.

1. In general, consider Job's way of answering. The longer the temptation continues, he never alters, but goes upon the same ground. Observe that the temptation of shaking one's state and interest in God renewing itself, and being often repeated, folks should by all means labor to keep their ground, and not give it way. If folks wrestle a while with such a temptation, and get no victory, if the temptation be reiterated, they are given to question victories, because the devil sets on again, and it may be more sharply. But you would remember not to quit your ground, *whom resist stedfast in the faith* (1. Pet. 5:9). Keep faith as your shield. The temptation being the same, stick to your ground.

2. Observe from Job's way of answering, in granting what is true and denying what is false, that in every temptation readily there are two things: (1) A true ground; (2) A false conclusion from it. Satan will say, 'You are in such a condition, therefore you are not a child of God.' Learn then with Job to grant the ground, but to deny the conclusion. See it also in the woman of Canaan. She is said to be [*outside*] the covenant, and called a dog; and she grants it is true, yet she pleads that there is some allowance for such. Therefore because something is true, do not believe all is true. It is suggested there is much unmortified sin in you; you have been so long under ordinances, and have not thrived. Yea, you are backslidden. It may be all this is true, yet the conclusion will not follow [that] therefore you have nothing ado with God.

3. On the terribleness of God to Job, observe that God may show himself terrible, and yet not be angry at the person. He may set you up as his <u>butt</u> [*target*], cleave your reins asunder, pour out your gall, run upon you like a lion or giant, and yet keep love. Therefore measure not God's love even by his spiritual dispensations, as if God loved not when he looks angry-like. Our senses are not good judges. It is not right reasoning to say, 'God lays his heavy hand upon me, therefore he will not look upon me.' What if Job reasoned so? (2) It should stir up folks to consider what God's terribleness will be, when he has no love, and comes to render vengeance to all that know him not. When the fierceness of his countenance shall make all the families of the earth to mourn, who believe God is a consuming fire (Heb. 12:29). What will he be to the wicked?

4. Job's sincerity bears him out in all this. Observe [that] the efficacy of sincerity, and an inward testimony of conscience can keep the soul quiet, and hold a grip of God in the greatest trouble, anxiety and grief. Therefore a good conscience is a rich reward and worth itself. The meek shall inherit the earth. If folks know the worth of this, they would study above all things to keep a good conscience before God and men.

5. The vehemency of Job's <u>asseverations</u> [*emphatic assertions*], and using them so frequently, and doubling them, is to let us see that it is holy wisdom, and no presumption, when temptation is so violent and presses violently for the soul, not to deny its interest in God, but to assert it the more confidently, and take in fair upon him the head and score of God's grace (so to speak) and in a sort to presume. I say not, presumption is lawful at any time; but because faith will then be presumption to sense, we would set ourselves to do that which seems presumption, to ride near on that side, when the wind blows to such a shore to ply against it; so strong is the way of believing, that the more it is borne down, it breaks the more out. God help us to keep the right <u>midst</u> [*midpoint; center*].

17

You remember the thing Job is defending, and the purpose; he speaks to two things Eliphaz insisted on [in] chapter 15. 1. To bear in on Job that he was a hypocrite, and a wicked man, because of the sad things which came on him. 2. He had an exhortation to Job, to turn to God with promises of an <u>outgate</u> [*deliverance*]. In this chapter Job speaks to both.

In the former chapter he answers their charge, and his answer runs upon two things. 1. That it was true he suffered these things, he grants. But 2. That he suffered them as a wicked man, he denies (vs. 1-16), and confirms it with vehement asseverations to the end.

In the beginning of this chapter (vs. 1-5), he shows the reasons why he was so vehement in his <u>asseverations</u> [*emphatic assertions*], and to interpose God to take the matter off their hands. That it was no presumption nor self-confidence, but the nearness he was unto the grave, put him to it, which he hinted at (16:16), and it is the same he is on here. *My breath is corrupt, my days are extinct, the graves are ready for me.* 'I am that near the grave, that the rottenness of my breath is not far off. I am as sure of it, as if it were made for me' (v. 1).

A second reason why he is so vehement in pressing God to judge the matter now depending, [is] because his friends made not earnest of it (v. 2). *Are there not mockers with me?* 'They mock me, and does not my eye continue,' or (as the word is), *lodge in their provocation?* Their mocking is their provocation, and his eye lodging in it, is his eye being always on it, to point out how vexing it was to him, like that word [in] Psa. 42:10. *As a sword in my bones, mine enemies reproach me, while they say continually unto me, Where is thy God?* He could not abide to have that cast up to him.

Therefore (v. 3) he resumes his speech in obscure words: *Lay down now, put me in surety with thee, who is he that will strike hands with me?* Take the words as spoken to God, the meaning is. 'Seeing it is so that these men are mockers, and have no understanding to decide the matter' (as in the following verse), 'lay down a pledge, and put me in surety with you; you will be law biding.' It is spoken after the manner of men. He is content [for] God himself [to] come and speak, and if God will deal with him, as one man with another, he will venture to plead his cause before God. But take the words as spoken to Eliphaz, and the rest, the meaning is, 'You take on you to dispute this cause, but see if you dare lay down a pledge, and find me a surety to plead it before God.' The scope is one, and expresses Job's desire [that] the cause may be taken off their hands.

He gives a reason (v. 4), which clears the exposition. *For thou hast hid their heart from understanding;* 'they take not the matter up right, for it is like thou hast deserted them, so as they cannot take it up.' And the following words, *therefore shalt thou not exalt them*, expresses Job's confidence to gain the cause, as if he said, 'I am sure if it come before God, he will not justify them, and send them away as victors.'

And v. 5. is an instance that his friends will lose the cause. *He that speaks flattery to his friends, even the eyes of his children shall fail.* In the 13th and 14th chapters, he charged them for speaking for an ill cause because their end was good in speaking for God. He shows here that that will be no reason for them so to plead, for God loves not that men should hide truth for feud or favor, were it even for the end to plead for God. The man that does so, God's curse will come on him and his. The words are a proverbial speech wherein he hints at their end in pleading against him; to wit, their minding of God's honor, seeing no way to justify God but by proving him a hypocrite. This he calls flatterery.

The second way how he answers them is this: that though it was for no injustice in him that he was so afflicted, yet he knew that God had good ends for it. Therefore (vs. 6-7) he repeats his misery, *I am become a byword,* 'and they make merry of me,' *who aforetime was a tabret*, that is, 'I was ridiculed behind backs in my prosperous condition, and much more now in my adversity.' *Mine eye also is dim by reason of sorrow, and all my members are as a shadow.* 'I am come to the shadow of a man.' And lest they should say, 'Are not these tokens of God's wrath upon you?' he answers (vs. 8-9), *Upright men shall be astonished at this*, etc.

'They will marvel how all this is come upon me, and will wonder at the deep draughts of God's sovereignty in this his dealing with me, and the wise ends he has in it in reference to his people; and the innocent shall stir up himself against the hypocrite. This shall be another use of God's dealing with me, the upright man that meets with many rubs in following the way of righteousness, shall have my affliction to beat down that opinion that the hypocrite is ever plagued, and the godly in prosperity. For he shall say, Job was a godly man, and yet his affliction was greater [*than*] mine; hypocrites draw their arguments from success to prove their cause, and reason thus: your cause has no success, therefore God loves you not. But the honest men shall have a ground to bear out himself by God's dealing with me (v. 9). *The righteous shall hold on his way.* The man that has a good cause by my example shall be encouraged to stick to it, and shall not stumble because he meets with affliction when he looks on me.'

And a fourth expression as the end of the former: *He that hath clean hands shall be stronger and stronger.* 'He that has a good cause and conscience shall be always more and more bold, and learn meekness, patience, and perseverance from God's dealing with me.' It is like God had given him some secret intimation what he was to make out of his affliction (as James 5:11).

When he has laid down his answers, he gives them his advice (v. 10). 'Leave this [*way*] you are on, for you are like fools not in the right way, like the prodigal out of your wit. Come to yourself again, for I have not found one wise man among you in this matter.'

He goes on to answer the [*feebleness*] of their motives (vs. 11-16), whereby they stirred him up to repentance. 1. *My days are past,* etc. 'You did not use these motives to me, my days are past, and I am at an end.' *My purposes are broken.* 'I had many lawful designs to improve my substance for the advantage of my children, but now these are broken; I am cut short of them; the occasion of them is taken away.' *Even the thoughts of my heart,* 'the thoughts that were in my mind, how to dispose of my family and children, I have nothing ado with them; my mind is off them now.'

2. *They change the night into day* (v. 12). They, that is, his afflictions, or friends, put him out of a condition of worldly comfort, for he gets no rest night nor day. *The light is short because of darkness,* 'when the day comes, my troubles make the day dark.'

3. The third answer (v. 13), which he follows out to the end [is]: *If I wait, the grave is mine house.* 'If I wait for aught what can I expect? The grave is the house I wait for, and to take up lodging in it ere it be long.' *I have made my bed in the darkness;* i.e. the grave, because folks that are in the grave are forgotten and out of mind.

This he illustrates (v. 14): *I have said to corruption, thou art my father.* Corruption is the witness that is in the grave, or the corrupt principle that is in the flesh, that turns folk into dust and rottenness. 'I have said that I came of such corruption; I claim so far kindred to it that it is my father. I came of it, and will go to it again.' *And to the worm, thou art my mother and sister.* 'I claim no kindred to noble folks, but as I have called corruption my father, so I say of the worms, they are as my mother and sisters. We will dwell in one house, and they will feed upon me ere long; and if it be so, where is now my hope? What [do you] think is my condition? Where is there any hope that I shall live? Is there any worldly hope in me that I shall come through this? Who shall see it?' i.e. none shall see it. 'They shall go down to the bars of the pit. Any poor grandeur I could expect shall be locked up in the grave with me; all my worldly contentments and comforts shall then be gone. Therefore these motives you have brought from these things, are but weak and vain.'

OBSERVATIONS.

1. He tenderly guides the matter. He began with corruption and ends with it. Observe that right and frequent thoughts of folks' frailty is a good <u>aweband</u> [*restraint*] against the outbreaking of corruption, pride, selfishness, idols, and worldly vanities. Job makes use of this meditation to keep him tender before God, humble in himself, and without reflecting on his friends. What makes folks proud, but either infrequent thoughts of their mortality, as if they had no <u>sibness</u> [*relationship*] to the worms, or that they will not be brought to account and reckoning. Think on it; Job was as noble as any of you, and at this time it would <u>lay</u> [*allay*] folks' anxiety and fretting, and put them to other thoughts if they were looking to the earth, and to the worms that will eat out their eyes ere long. It will not be long ere you and the worms will both dwell in a rotten chest together, and thy belly will be full of them, and the worm will think itself as gentile as any of the highest blood.

2. Observe from Job's vehement desire to be at God with his cause, that faith daily promises good to itself from God. Job thinks [*ever*] to win the cause when it shall come before Him, and this is a reason why strong faith gives glory to God, because it expects [*ever*] some noble thing from God. Little faith, limiting God, is derogatory to God; but strong faith, like Abraham's (Rom. 6) that dares hazard on God, especially in a strait, argues much estimation of God, and gives much honor to God.

3. From the second part of this answer, observe that there is scarcely any misery men can think of, but it may be incident to the

people of God, were it to be a proverb and mocking stock. There is no outward dispensation of God but it may befall the godly, which casts [*overthrows*] all the debate of his friends.

4. The end Job mentions for God's dispensation with him, not that he has a mind to censure sin; but, 1. To make men wonder at God's wisdom, and to lay [*reduce*] their pride. 2. To strengthen innocent folks, who are to succumb in affliction. Job tells that in afflicting him, [God] had a mind to strengthen their faith and patience. 3. To remove a stumbling block out of men's way, who are ready to be scared from a good turn by affliction; Job has ridden the ford before them, that they may not scare for that. 4. That folks may labor for clean hands, or a good conscience, and not stand upon what success they get, all which are [in] vs. 8-9, and show what use should be made of the affliction of God's people. Others have been afflicted to give us these lessons at a cheap rate.

5. He says (v. 10), he cannot find a wise man among them, because being engaged they were not fit to determine the case rightly. Observe oft-times folks engaged in debates run themselves out of breath, and put themselves out of capacity to judge of matters; therefore folks would be wary to engage where they are not clear.

6. Observe on the last part, when folks come to the grave, worldly contentments will have little comfort or relish with them. 'What is my hope?' or, 'What do I now expect from these things?' To teach us how far he was above these temporal contentments they propounded to him. While folks have health and strength, they will not think the world can have so little bulk with them; but when all folks' designs are broken and laid by, the worth of the world, and all that is in it will be seen. Therefore use the world as if you used it not. Be as pilgrims and stranger in it, and be not entangled with it. He that will be rich falls in many snares, and pierces himself through with many sorrows. It is a pest that destroys many, and leads far more souls to hell, than either malignancy or sectarianism.[1]

---

1 *Malignants* were those who sympathized with the royalist cause. *Sectaries* were those who formed separate religious groups from the established church, usually departing widely from Reformed doctrine.

18

These words contain Bildad's second onset on Job, who after he had heard Job's reply undertakes a new confutation. His scope is the same, and his manner of prosecuting it almost the same also; to bear in on Job, God's justice in smitting him, and his wickedness that procured it.

The chapter has two parts. I. He sharply censures Job (vs. 1-4), [who] stood it out, and was not convinced by all that he and his other friends had said. II. He follows out the same thesis of God's destroying the wicked as Job was, and secretly insinuates Job's wickedness to be the cause of his stroke (vs. 5-21).

I. His censure or reproof has three parts. The first part is for Job not mak[ing] an end of words (v. 2), and to show Job's folly [he] insinuates a secret check in his way of expression: *How long will it be ere you make an end of words?* As if many were with Job. Mark [*note*], *and after that we will speak.* That is, 'let us know when you have ended, and then we shall begin,' or, as the word will bear, 'make us understand what you say, and we will say on.' [It is] a common fault; folks are loath to bear a contradiction in opposition to their maintained opinion, and to think all said against them but words.

The second part of the reproof is (v. 3): 'We have given you many reproofs, and they have no more weight with you, [*than*] if we were beasts and not reasonable men.' They count his casting [aside] of their doctrine as if he counted them no better than beasts. So ready are men to count it a discredit when their opinion is not taken, and cannot endure to be contradicted.

A third part of his reproof (v. 4): *He tears himself in his anger.* 'Job you are like a mad man in passion. Shall all folks quit the world for you? And shall the rock be removed out of his place? Shall this sure truth of God, which we have asserted [*about*] God's punishing of wicked men, and showing kindness to good men, which is as sure as a rock, shall it be overturned at your pleasure?' [This is] another fault that follows contradiction. Men are then ready to reflect on mens' persons, to cast up senselessness and folly, even to them that have truth upon their side, and to grow stiffer in their own opinions.

II. In the second part of the chapter, in the main, he prosecutes the same thesis of God's destroying the wicked, as Job was, in four similitudes, wherein he lays out God's dealing with hypocrites, and plainly shows [that] he includes Job among them.

1. The first similitude is as if he said (vs. 5-6), 'a wicked man may have his candle of prosperity burning as clear as another man's, but all his comforts soon vanish, and so it is with you.'

2. [In] the second similitude (vs. 7-10), he compares wicked men or hypocrites to fowls that snares are laid for, as if he said, 'Let wicked men get their will, yet the way they take shall ruin them, for they are walking like birds, or beasts in the midst of snares, and their own feet shall carry them to the pit. They shall run headlong to ruin, [as though no one] would touch them. For that which he thinks [is] his surest way for safety shall be his ruin, and the robber or fowler shall catch him, and prevail against him. It is impossible he can escape, for the snare is above, beneath, and round about him; and such is your case Job.' And (v. 7. compared with the rest), 'as beasts or birds in a snare or net, the more struggle they make by the strong hand to rid themselves, they are faster fastened; so shall it be with you.'

3. The third similitude (vs. 11-15) is taken from the pursuing of criminals before earthly courts and judgment seats; as a guilty man is dealt with by the judge, so are hypocrites dealt with by God. There is a king of terrors, whether death or any eminent terror like death, it is to one purpose. And he has under him, other under-terrors, as so many officers or sergeants, and when the hypocrite is quiet in his house, these shall come upon him, and put him to his feet to run away. But he shall not get away. Plague upon plague, terror upon terror, and rumor upon rumor, shall pursue him (as it is [in] Ezek. 27:20). God's net shall be spread upon him (vs. 11-12), and if anything be strange or beautiful, and were no more but his skin, it shall be more full of holes 'than yours is;' and death's neighbor shall devour anything that is firm in him, and 'you are in the next bore' (v. 13). He may dwell a while in his house, and contest and struggle for a while with his executioners, these terrors or plagues; but they shall not leave him till they bring him to death — the king of terrors, wherein all earthly terrors end.

And hereby is meant not bodily death simply or only, but it includes the spiritual also, that terrible reckoning that comes after death, which [the] wicked meet with (v. 14). *It shall dwell in his tabernacle.* His conscience shall have no rest; he shall have terror within as well as without. *Brimstone shall be scattered on his habitation.* It shall be made like Sodom, marked with some evident mark of God's indignation, which shall be scattered or sown upon it as sowing with salt is sometimes used for this end. And the third comparison is used to show how eminently God's wrath shall pursue the wicked: *Because it is none of his.* That is, either because it is ill acquired, being gotten by oppression or falsehood, or because it is not sanctified to him of the Lord, because he [*lacks*] a spiritual right, though he have a civil right to it, and its not being sanctified by the word and prayer, *therefore it is none of his.*

4. A fourth similitude [is in] v. 16, wherein the wicked man is set out to be like a tree flourishing, but it has a worm within, as there was in Jonah's gourd, and it withers without, and rots within. A comparison that has been several times used before, and is frequent in scripture. The hypocrite is compared to a bay-tree (Psa. 37:35).

Then in more positive and plain terms he sets him out (v. 17). [Assertion 1.] He has been hunting for credit, but he shall die, and his name shall rot, and in the street where men used to speak and be spoken of, no word of him shall be heard but to his shame.

Assertion 2. He that thought to live long in prosperity and pleasure shall be driven to a most miserable and comfortless end, that he shall have no being in the world. It sets out a constant and violent pursuing of the wicked by wrath (v. 18).

Assertion 3. He has been taking great pains to build houses, and buy lands to his posterity, but none of his shall <u>brook</u> [*enjoy*] his conquest; he may have children, but he shall be like Jeconiah — none of his posterity shall sit on the throne. No patrimony he shall leave them shall do them good (v. 19).

A fourth assertion (v. 20); his judgment shall be so remarkable, that as he was a terror to them he lived among, so they that come after him shall tremble to see and hear of God's judgment on him.

And so the conclusion is drawn (v. 21): *Surely such are the dwellings of the wicked.* 'Job, would you know a wicked man? Here he is, as he has been set out to you.' And there is a secret application of it to him, as if he had said, 'See how all these things I have spoken of the wicked man agree to your condition, whom God has set out as a mark of his wrath in overturning your prosperity, removing your children, and making these girns [*traps*] and snares overtake you. And so he ends his second onset.

OBSERVATIONS.

From the first part, [Bildad's] sharp censuring of Job, mark some secret faults that folks' contradiction carries along. 1. Impatience. 2. Carping at everything as reflecting upon others. 3. To be more taken up with reflections than the thing itself about which the debate is.

For the second part, the scope contains many good truths, but his conclusion is unsound that Job is a hypocrite or wicked man. Observe:

1. There is no condition so terrible, and has more of the terror of God waiting upon it, than hypocrisy — to have a fair profession of godliness, and not to know God in our practice. Job never denies this general [truth]. This sin is one of the grounds of so many woes pronounced by Christ. *Use.* Because of a rotten profession, of having a name that you are living when you are dead, of taking on you a name of that which you make no conscience to be like. We scare not folks from a profession [of faith], seeing the Holy Ghost scares none from it, but from resting on a profession.

2. There is no consolation that a wicked man has which endures long. The most warm fire he kindles shall be put out, *and he shall lie down in sorrow* (Isa. 50:11). God has often been pointing at this in this [our] time, to [*teach*] us to be abstracted from creature comforts.

3. Whatever a wicked man possesses without a spiritual right, and acknowledging God in it, God will never count it his. There is a twofold right that men have to things. (1) One before men, and that is a civil right which mens' wickedness looses not. (2) A sanctified right which is obtained on the other right; therefore we are bidden pray, *Give us this day our daily bread.* It is called our bread, because we have right to it by our labor, but in seeking it of God, and acknowledging God in it we get a second right, and it were good we were not content with the first without the second. And it is a sore matter when folks are put out of their houses, because they had not a right to them before God.

4. Wicked men, and these that know not God, are put together. Observe [that] profanity and ignorance of God in God's reckoning go together, and are all one. Ignorance is often the root of profanity (2 Thes. 1:8). *He will come in flaming fire to take vengence on all that know*

not God, and obey not the gospel. Among other faults that God is angry at, ignorance is one, and this may have much influence on God's dispensations to the land and this place. Be exhorted to study to know God better, not only in light but in experience; that some impression of the majesty, wisdom, power, and terror of God may have more sway to keep in our humors, than anything to the contrary can have sway to bring us in a way that may provoke him.

19

We heard in the former chapter, Bildad's continuing of a challenge on Job, as a man now pointed at by God's judgments to have been but a hypocrite, and therefore had such a portion as they have.

In this chapter, Job replies with very much meekness, and by many reasons, to put him and the rest of his friends from that rigid way of censuring and misconstructing him, to a more kindly way of pitying him, which is the scope of this chapter, that they may be drawn from a rigid censuring of God's way with him to construct more moderately of him.

The chapter has three parts. I. A preface, wherein Job regrets their hard dealing with him (vs. 1-3). II. He has a large following forth of grounds (vs. 4-28), whereby he backs his complaint, both to show the groundlessness of their rigid censure, and the justness of his complaining. III. In the last two verses he has an exhortation to that which is his scope, backed with a threatening (vs. 28-29).

I. The first part of his regret, or complaint, is from the nature of the exercise their dispute had on him. It was a vexing of his soul, and a breaking of him in pieces with words, and he charges them for lengthening both. The meaning is, 'how long will you be instrumental to add one sorrow to another?'

The second part of his complaint is (v. 3): *These ten times* (a certain number for an uncertain) *have ye reproached me.* That is, 'it is not the first time you have done this, but a number of times you have renewed your reproaches, and scarce would a hypocrite bide that.' *Ye are not ashamed that ye make yourselves strange to me.* 'How is it that you are not ashamed, who should have lived friendly with me, and sometimes did so, to be thus strange in your carriage towards me?'

II. He gives some reasons or grounds of this his complaint, and first he meets with an objection. 'You have sinned, and are in an error,' might they say? Because it is so, he says: *That I have erred, mine error remaineth with myself.* 'It is between God and me, and not before the world, and it becomes not [*does not suit*] you to cast that up to me, that God has kept secret (v. 4). A second ground which he follows out largely (vs. 5-22) as if he had said, 'It is not time now to add one burden to another. God has smitten me, and you should not smite me also' (as Psal. 69:2). It is marked as a fault to persecute him whom God has smitten, and this argument he follows by laying down particular instances of God's smitting and breaking of him at large, and draws the conclusion (vs. 21-22).

The instances which he gives are first more general. 'My condition' (would he say) 'is more than ordinary; God, in an extraordinary way has made me a butt [*target*] to his arrows, and has wonderfully overthrown me, but it will not become [*suit*] you to take that liberty [which] God does. God is sovereign, and may afflict whom and when he will, but that therefore you may afflict also, it will not follow (vs. 5-6). Particular instances follow. 'I get many wrongs of Chaldeans and Sabean, and others, and I cry to God, and complain of these wrongs, but I get not an hearing. He was wont to delay, or refuse me a hearing, but now he keeps [*shuts*] up himself, as if there were not a throne for judgment (v. 7).

A second instance (v. 8): *He hath fenced up my way* 'that there is no outgate [*deliverance*] for me;' and this he proves in the following words, that he had none from his family, none from his servants, none from friends, and none from God. Therefore his grief was not ordinary; God had made him a pattern of wrath, the particulars whereof we shall run through shortly.

(1) 'I was once honorable, the greatest man in the East, but now my glory and authority is away, and he has brought shame as well as loss upon me.' It is often so with men, loss and contempt go together.

(2) A third instance, and a second reason, to prove the former, of his fencing in, and having no outgate [*deliverance*] (v. 10): 'I am now like a tree that has lost the sap, and is withering all round about. On every side I am destroyed, compassed with terrors, and I am a gone man, and any hope I have is like a tree whose roots are cast up.

(3) 'He has also kindled his wrath against me, and counts me as one of his enemies;' a sad aggravation, yea, the most sad of his affliction; as if he had said, 'I would not care for temporal wrath in externals, but to be counted as an enemy, and to pray and not be heard, and to have the sparks of his indignation kindled within me;

to have God, who has been, and is my good friend, carrying himself so to me, is most bitter and sore to endure.' The most unhappy condition is to be God's enemy; and to be for a time dealt with as his enemy, is a most sharp exercise. This is enlarged (v. 12). God is like a general commanding armies, and he draws up his troops, the Chaldeans, Sabeans, the devil, the wind from the wilderness, fire from heaven, wife, servants, and friends, as so many companies, and they are set as it were to encamp about [him]. Whereby intimating God's sovereignty and immediate acting in all second causes and instruments.

(4) *He hath put my brethren from me,* etc. 'He has left me neither friend, nor familiar to comfort me.' He looks to God as scattering his friends, and making them strange and dry to him (v. 13). 'These of my nearest blood have failed me, are turned like a brook to me, and as a broken cistern, and my familiar friends that hung upon me when I had wealth to bestow on them, have forgotten me now;' as it is ordinary to have many such in prosperity, that are cold comforters in adversity.

Moreover (v. 15): *These that dwell in my house,* 'and were brought up with me, and the maids that were servants, they might well wait on at meal time of day to eat up what is left, but they give me little of it, and they are disobedient to me.' He looks on this as a part of God's troops; yea, he calls for his servants, but they let not wit [*don't let on*] they hear him, even when he entreated them (v. 16). 'And I would not have thought much of such dealing from my servants, but my wife, that had wont to live comfortably with me when we had enough, my breath became strange to her, and she forgetting all conjugal bonds, is become to me as strange as the rest.' A sad ground of complaint (yet often found true), that adversities do break the greatest ties and relations, even these between man and wife, but so it will where they are not founded on grace. Yet Job is very fair in his carriage to her; he intreats her meekly, and she will not know him.

Young children, or as the word is, *wicked children despised me* (v. 18). The vilest persons did laugh at him, and mock, and taunt him, that one time would have run out of his [*way*] when they had seen him. *All my inward friends* (or as the words, *the men of my secret*), 'that I was intimate with, as with my wife, or brother, or sister, that lay in the belly with me, these friends that are made for the day of adversity are turned against me.' Though not intentionally, yet really, and upon the matter, and that these friends who were bound with him in the bonds of grace, deal thus with him, he counts it heavier to be borne than his wife's mistaking of him (as we see in David, Psal. 49:9).

But this is not all. If he had a whole skin it were something, but this he has not (v. 20). 'There is no flesh upon me; the skin cleaves to the bone where it is [*whole*], and there is no more [*whole*] of me, but that which is on the gums or lips, so much as gives me leave to speak, I am escaped with so much.' For it is likely when the devil smote him with boils, he left so much free, as he might speak without pain to blaspheme God; but God made use of it, that he might speak many good words to the edification of his church.

He draws the conclusion, and makes application of the argument (vs. 21-22). *Have pity upon me, O my friends*, etc. It is no time now to reckon hard with me, and to prove cruel to me, when God's hand is so heavy on me. God is sovereign, but you are bounded and limited, and must not take the liberty that God does.' *Why do ye then persecute me as God?* 'Why are you as cruel to me as he seems to be? Will not this satisfy you that my body is gone, but will you persecute my soul also by disputing my interest in God?' For (Psa. 42:10), it is like a sword in the bones when that is brangled [*shaken*].

A third ground of his complaint (vs. 23-27): 'You think me a man transported with passion, and like a mad man tearing his own flesh' (as 18:4). 'But I am speaking like one that must answer to God at the great day, and therefore I would to God, that this controversy between you and me, about God's sovereignty in afflicting whom he pleases, and of my integrity, notwithstanding of my affliction, were written and registered the most sure way that can be, that it were left upon record in lead, or stone' (upon which they used to engrave things).

For (v. 25), 'I know there is a day after this that I will get a hearing, and that makes me so confident. I know I have a Redeemer, and that he is living, and that he shall stand as King of all the world at the latter day on the earth, when he has put all his enemies under his feet, and made them his footstool, for he may fight a while, the time comes when he shall get the victory.'

And (v. 26), *Though after my skin worms destroy this body*, 'though I be now hopeless of my life, the skin being destroyed already, and though after the skin the worms should crawl out-through and in-through me, and consume me, yet in the flesh I shall see God manifested in the flesh some way as he is within the object of a bodily sight.' And this he enlarges and illustrates (v. 27). *Whom I shall see for myself, and mine eyes shall behold, and not another.* 'This same, I say, this same flesh and skin that is all holes, and these same eyes shall see him, and I shall see him for my advantage, as a friendly judge to absolve me, *though my reins be consumed within me.*' Or 'in my bosom,' or arms, as the word is. That is, 'though a whole tack should not <u>bide</u> [*remain*] together of me, yet I shall get the sight of my Redeemer, who will own me as his redeemed and bought servent, though you dare not.'

III. And having thus borne out this testimony, he comes in the last part of the chapter to the third thing, that is, an exhortation to his friends (vs. 28-29). 'Leave off this way of dealing with me, and reflect upon yourselves, for you should rather be censuring yourselves than thus rigidly censuring me,' which in effect is persecution. And he gives a reason why he would have them altering their way, *seeing the root of the matter is found in me.* 'Seeing after all this trial, it is not blades and leaves of a profession that I have, but the root of grace remains in me, else I had not bidden it out;' and he backs this exhortation with a sad warning or threatening: Be afraid of the sword. God will not let such persecution go away, and often the sword follows such a bloody sin; for wrath, passion, or malignancy, which is the fruit of wrath, brings the punishment of the sword, for sin ordinarily brings much woe and wrath upon men. And he adds a reason of God's dispensing of such a punishment to such a sin, that they may know there is a judgment. 'If God should let you go, and not censure you, you would think there was not a judgment, but your malignity, envy, and hatred against me, shall bring you under punishment, if you continue in it, that you may know God will not wink at such wrongs.

OBSERVATIONS.

1. Ordinarily when God's people are brought low, there is a multiplying of their rods. A gathering, and adding of one after another, within, without, and in public, in private, in the family, from heaven, the earth, the servants, the wife, friends, strangers, wrath [*appearing*] from all arts, so that they have no third, nor choice, nor <u>outgate</u> [*deliverance*], but God himself; so he deals with the land and with us.

2. There is no quieting under the rod till God is acknowledged in all the branches of it, not only God has given, and God has taken away. For we have many sad crosses, but as Job here, we must look on all the parts of our anxiety as from God: when the paths are made darkness, when shame and discredit comes, when a friend becomes

dry of whom we expected comfort, or when the estate is lost, and the man has not to give out, and the wife brawls and chides when the wealth is away, that [was] wont to hold her tongue when there was enough under her hand, and should be the more kindly to the husband under the cross. And it may be the servants give an ill answer, worse words than can be given them. The hand of God in this being seen and acknowledged, would stay passion, and help to find out a fault on our side. That is, little reverence and respect to God in us, does possibly provoke God to let them have little respect to us. We know not what branches of these may be your cross. May be some of you are poor widows, and have nothing to live upon, and you have poor children, etc. But labor to see and acknowledge the hand of God in all.

3. Where God's hand is very heavy in afflicting, folks would be very wary in harshly constructing of it, and be tender and prudent in bearing sins on folks. It would be done with such meekness, as our so doing becomes not a new part of their cross.

4. On the chapter, observe: (1) That it is one of the most notable consolations that [there] can be under the cross, to consider that there is a day of judgment, and that we shall then see our Redeemer, our Judge, and be absolved of him. It was Job's consolation, and should be ours. Leave the Lord's cause to him, and let us suspend the clearing of it till that day. It is hard to know when the difficulty we are in shall be loosed, but a day comes when these who have reproached us will stand before Christ's bar with us, and he will give out right judgment; and it may be consolation, and content to us, then to be cleared.

(2) Folks, in all their carriage, especially under all their crosses, would speak, and do, and so carry themselves in all things, as if it were to be written in a book, and presented before the Judge, for God will let it be seen all is written; and consider if you would have this and that hasty or passionate word written, if you dare take an iron pen, and engrave them in lead or stone, to be kept on record to that day, and if not, forbear and watch the better.

(3) It serves much for believers' consolation, and keeping fresh of their grace, to be serious in the thoughts of their particular and personal appearance before Christ in the great day; it will keep grace in vigor, and bear down passion. To consider it is I, this same vile body, this same flesh that is now eating and drinking, that will see Jesus Christ come again at the latter day, and give out sentence on all. A truth that is commonly received but slightly believed; but when

it is believed, it is a noble consolation, and spur to tender walking, to have as much experience of the truth and faithfulness of Jesus Christ, as confirms us that the resurrection is a truth.

5. On the last part of the chapter, observe: (1) That there is no sader persecution of God's people than that which is in words. Therefore he complains of this (vs. 2-3), and here over again (v. 22), calls it *persecution*. What word is <u>rifer</u> [*more common*] than hypocrite whore, and hypocrite thief, and grace is called no grace but hypocrisy. O what persecution is that! which will be counted for one day.

(2) This sort of persecution brings on the sword, and yet we read not much of their wrath or anger, but that they could not endure that he should maintain the truth against them.

(3) There is no sin [which] engages God more to punish, [*than*] wrath and indignation against his people. This is among the causes of Scotland's ruin: enmity against the people of God, and look it be not one of the causes of Glasgow's ruin. Hatred against godliness and the godly, engages God to plague any place or people. It has provoked God against you, and may be the cause of more ruin [*than*] yet is come. God will not fail to be avenged on that bitterness of spirit if it be continued in, and you may look for a sorer stroke [*than*] yet is <u>lighted</u> [*landed*] on you. Job's friends, though godly men, [would have] come under judgment for this sin, if Job had not prayed for them.

20

Job made a very pithy and sober reply to what Bildad had said in the former chapter, and closed with an exhortation to leave off their rigid way of censuring him, lest wrath come upon them, at which Zophar storms that he should check them as men sinning highly against God, and therefore in this chapter breaks [him] off abruptly. *Therefore do my thoughts cause me to answer.* Therefore, that is, 'for the check you have given us in the close of your last discourse, I can endure no longer, but must give you a present answer.'

The chapter has three parts. I. A short preface (vs. 1-3). II. A large setting down of wicked mens' and hypocrites' judgment and destruction (vs. 4-28), secretly insinuating such a judgment was come on Job, and therefore that he was a wicked man or a hypocrite, and strongly contradicting Job's assertion that a wicked man might flourish in the world as well as the godly man, which Job maintains in the following chapter, and opposes his assertion that a wicked man is always pursued with judgment in this life. III. He closes as Bildad did in the eighteenth chapter (vs. 29).

I. 'I have such an impression of your intolerable insolence, that when I have heard your reproach, I can bear it no longer, but must hasten to answer you (v. 2). For I am so sure to win the cause, and I am so well acquainted with this controversy, that I will break down all your arguments at once.' The reflection Job put on him and his own clearness to answer, puts him thus to express himself (v. 3).

II. The matter of his answer follows. *Knowest thou not?* 'This is no new doctrine, *that the triumphing of the wicked is for a short time*' (vs. 4-5). Job has prevailed thus far with them, that they must grant the wicked may be in prosperity, but they say it cannot be long, and he names the hypocrite after the wicked man, lest Job having purged himself of wickedness before, should also do so of hypocrisy, and therefore if he will not grant that he is a wicked man, he will bind on him that he is a hypocrite.

Though his excellency mount up to heaven, etc. Let the wicked man or hypocrite come to never so great excellency, though he should rise so high, that nothing should be above him, yet he shall come to a shameful end, *like his own dung*. And when he is gone, folks that before have seen him, shall ask where he is, and there shall be no memory of him (vs. 6-7). He <u>enlarges</u> [*expands on*] this to the end

He shall flee away as a dream, and as a vision of the night, so shall his prosperity be (v. 8). He thinks he is rich, and a happy man, but he is but dreaming, and when he awakes, his soul shall be empty for it all, it shall be but as a vision or shadow of that which is not. Yea, he shall be chased away as a vision in the night. The people abhor him, like a thing that is not seen in the light, but they imagine they grip it and see it, but cannot let others see it or feel it.

The eye that hath seen him, shall not see him again; neither shall his place any more behold him (v. 9). He shall no more be found in the world, to set out the irrepairableness of his destruction. They that saw him shall not see him again. *Neither shall his place any more behold him*; he shall no more be found in the world.

His children shall seek to please the poor (v. 10). While he lived he made many poor folk by robbery and oppression, but when he is away, the poorest in the country shall be his children's masters, so that they shall flatter and fawn on poor folk to please them, and court their favor. And he gives the cause of it: *His hands shall restore their goods*, which were wrongfully taken from them, so he shall have nothing.

His bones are full of the sin of his youth — a comparison to hold out the wicked man's or hypocrite's destruction (v. 11). He is like a young man that has gotten a vile disease in his youth, which sticks to him all his days, and leaves him not till it lays him in the dust. So the wicked man's sin, and God's judgment therefore, shall never leave him till it destroys him (as men in youth gather marrow which nourishes the body in old age, so he treasuring up sin, it shall destroy him then).

A further comparison to set out his destruction (vs. 12-15): He is like a glutton that eats <u>meikle</u> [*much*], but he shall vomit it out again. Though he spare it and keep it in his mouth, that is, though he delight himself in pleasing his appetite, and feeds himself on his prosperity in a sensual way, yet when it is over, it shall no more be sweet, but bitter and venomous as the gall of asps in his bowels. And he makes the application (v. 15), though he has taken much pains to gather riches, God shall <u>gar</u> [*make*] him cast them up again. The meaning is, he shall have more torment in the loss of his wealth, than ever he had refreshment in the gathering and enjoyment of it.

He shall suck the poison of asps, the viper's tongue shall slay him. His destruction shall be as certain as if he were sucking most deadly poison (v. 16). *He shall not see the rivers, the floods, the brooks of honey and butter* (v. 17). He has thought much of his prosperity, that that was like these things which are evidences of a man's thriving in the world; but it shall vanish, and he shall not see the abundance of that which he had.

That which he labored for, or took much pains to obtain, *he shall not swallow it down,* an application of the former similitude (v. 18). God shall make him quit it <u>nill he, will he</u> [*willing or not*]. Yea, he shall not digest it, nor send it down to feed on it. It shall do him no good, and according to his substance shall the restitution be. He shall be as poor as ever he was rich, or, so <u>long</u> [*much*] as he has, it shall be taken from him, and he shall not rejoice therein.

The reason of this is rendered (v. 19), because he cared not how he got his <u>gear</u> [*property*], or how many were poor by his oppression, and after he had courted their favor, till he got what they had from them, [he] then cast them off. And because by violence, he had intruded himself in other folks' buildings, which he had no right to, or paid not the worth of them. And because he had swallowed down much ill gotten goods this way, he shall have no rest till he be quit of it; and that which he loved best he shall get none of it kept. He shall not save even that which he most desired to have (v. 20).

There shall none of his meat be left (v. 21). His destruction shall be so great, that there shall not be a bit of bread left in his house, and whereas every one was striving who should be his heir, that strife shall cease when he has nothing. *No man shall look for his goods.*

In the fullness of his sufficiency, when he is at the height of his prosperity, he shall be brought down, and made miserable through straits, and every wicked hand shall pluck at him as he plucked others, as ordinarily losses come with more hands than one (v. 22).

When he is about to fill his belly, and barns, like the rich man in the gospel, God shall fall upon him with some extraordinary plague and judgment (v. 23). *He shall flee from the iron weapon, and the bow of steel shall strike him through;* in flying from one judgment he shall meet with another; or, when he thinks to escape one plague, God shall cause another meet with him (v. 24). *It is drawn and cometh out of the body* (v. 25); that which is shot <u>lights</u> [*lands*] on him, and folks pull it out of him; yea, *the glistering sword cometh out of his gall;* he gets a deadly wound by the shot, or stroke which he falls under. *Terrors are upon him.* God's judgment is so terrible, that it makes him tremble, because he is as sure of destruction, as if his gall were poured out on the ground. And this may have respect to Job's words before (16:13), where he says, *He poureth out my gall upon the ground.*

All darkness, that is, every plague, *shall be hid in his secret places* — shall privily wait for him (v. 26). There is no sort of plague but it shall secretly attend him, and whatever he does to escape them, he shall not be able, and in this he alludes to Job's many crosses. *A fire not blown shall consume him.* A fire that is not blown, is a fire that kindles and none knows how. The meaning is, the fire of God's judgment, that none can tell wherefrom it came, or a fire within not wakened by human means, but by the finger of God in the conscience shall consume him. *And it shall go ill with him that is left in his tabernacle.* If anybody is left behind in his house, he shall have a poor life of it.

The heavens shall reveal his iniquity, etc. (v. 27) — i.e. when God plagues such a man, both heaven and earth shall be against him, as fire from heaven, and the weather and wind, and men on earth set themselves against him.

The increase of his house shall depart, his posterity shall take wings and fly away, *and his goods shall flow away,* like a river *in the day of God's wrath* on wicked men (v. 28).

III. The conclusion follows in the last verse. 'Whatever a wicked man or hypocrite has or may enjoy; this that I have spoken is the inheritance that he has right to, and he has not another thing for his portion. It is appointed and decreed of God to him, and there is no other that he can call his.'

OBSERVATIONS.

Zophar in all this aims to bear out the main controversy, that it went well with good men, and ill with wicked men in this life. Though an interruption might [*come*], and wicked men might prosper for a time; [yet] there is a limiting of the wicked's punishment to this life, and the godly man's trouble to a temporal outgate [*deliverance*], which Job confutes in the next chapter.

1. Observe from the preface, that oftimes that which seems to reflect on mens' persons puts them to speak, and has as much weight

on them to put them to vindicate themselves as the truth itself. Soberness at such a time should be studied.

2. He thinks himself very clear in the controversy, and that puts him to speak that which he was not clear of. Observe: (1) Folks engaged in a debate, will seem to themselves clear in the matter when it is not so; folks' willfulness and engagement, especially in men of parts, carry often too much sway, and makes that seem light which is not. (2) Folks' estimation of their own ability, brings them often in a snare, out of which they do hardly extricate themselves (v. 3).

From the sum and shot of the debate, we draw two notes. 1. Let the hypocrites flourish as they will in the world, they have a fearful and desperate condition abiding them, whatever sort of hypocrites they be, whether grossly profane, or more civil and formal (for both are put together, v. 5) or whatever their prosperity is, their triumphing is but for a moment. *Use.* Fear to trust your portion to the things of the earth, and to lose the gain that godliness has with it, else you will find that you have made an ill block [*bargain*]. It would be a good advantage, if the strokes that are come upon us, brought us more in love with godliness, and to hate hypocrisy.

2. Observe from the misapplication to Job, there is nothing so terrible and due to the hypocrite, but it may be misrepresented to a godly man as his portion. Job was no hypocrite, yet looking on this as a temptation, which the devil was furthering, it clears the doctrine. But it is one thing to have right to such a thing as is the portion of the hypocrite, and another thing to have it borne in on a man by the force of temptation, and Job in all the debate guards against this.

21

I. Job is here replying to Zophar's challenge in the preceding chapter, wherein he chops at Job as a deserted man, with whom God had a controversy, and bearing in upon him, that however God might spare the wicked for a while, yet they get not off the world without some visible token of wrath. Job prefaces his reply (vs. 1-6). II. He confutes Zophar's thesis, and the application of it (vs. 7-33). III. He closes with a reproof to him (v. 34), and the rest of his friends, for taking the way they took with him, and for making use of the grounds they went upon, telling [them] they were false in respect of God's dispensation, and their limiting of Him, and in respect of their constructing of him.

I. For the preface, *Hear diligently my speech, and let this be your consolation* (v. 2). That is, 'I have spoken much, and you have taken little heed to it; and seeing you have spoken much, and little to my comfort, let it be your way of comforting me to hear me speak. *Suffer me* patiently *to speak* my mind, and if it be not to purpose, *mock on.'* As if he said, 'If you weigh my words well, you will not have much cause to mock' (v. 3). 'And so much the more I seek a hearing of you, because it is not man, but God that I mainly aim at in speaking, and therefore you would not be so bitter in censuring me, as to construct me a hypocrite.' *And if it were so, why should not my spirit be troubled?* That is, 'though I were speaking to men, have I any encouragement or advantage from you, why my spirit should not be troubled, or that might mitigate my trouble' (v. 4).

Mark me (v. 5). 'Consider me, look upon me more narrowly, and observe my condition, carriage and affections, and you will not cast up my hypocrisy.' *And be astonied, and lay your hand upon your mouth.* 'I think not upon my case, but I am afraid and astonied at beholding God's uncouth dispensations toward me, and will you look upon me, and not be afraid at it?' (vs. 5-6).

II. Having thus prefaced, he refutes Zophar's ground or thesis more generally (vs. 7-26), and then follows the application he aimed at (vs. 27-33).

1. The refutation has three things in it, his scope being to maintain God's sovereignty to afflict whom, and how long, and after what manner he pleases. (1) He asserts that the wicked may not only live, but go to their grave in prosperity, when the godly may be afflicted (vs. 7-16). (2) He shows that as he lets some wicked go to their grave in prosperity, so he puts out the candle of many wicked men before that time (vs. 17-21). (3) He shows the reason of this to be God's sovereignty (vs. 22-26).

(1) In the first verse he lays down his conclusion just applied to Zophar's. 'If it be as you say, wherefore do the wicked live a comfortable and merry life, and become old in that life, and are not taken away so suddenly as you speak of? Yea, they are mighty in power, and die great, and they do not leave their seed beggars as you said, but they buy land and houses to them, and see their grandchildren and heirs established in their sight.' Being great themselves, they lay down a fixed way of living to their posterity (v. 8). And not only are their children well, but their dwelling-places also; and *the rod of God is not upon them*; they have the only happy life that is of it in the world (v. 9). Yea, it goes well with their beasts, the wicked man's husbandry, his corn, and cattle may thrive best, and fewer maladies come over them than on other folks (v. 10). Their children are multiplied and increase like a flock, and are married, and dance, when the godly man's children may weep for want.

'They may feast on, and dance on, and none has such a merry life in the world as they, and are not always taken away as you said' (vs. 11-12). 'Yea, they may spend their days in wealth, and die in estimation, and nobody to crave them.' As it is [in] Psa. 73:19, 4. *In a moment they go down to the grave, there is no bands in their death.* As there is no judgment seen upon them living, so there is none seen on them in their death. From all this he would reason, 'How can you say that a wicked man cannot live long without some visible judgment?'

He sets down the profanity of these men, and how they abuse their prosperity (vs. 14-15). 'It is for no blessing that they prosper and thrive so, neither make they any good use of their prosperity, but they are the more godless the better God is to them.' *They desire not the knowledge of thy ways*, nor to hear of thy directions to hem them in (v. 14). Yea, they say, *What is the Almighty, that we should serve him?* 'You speak to us of God, and his ways, and put us in fear of a reckoning, and of a judge, but what good will we get of serving God? Look to them that pray most, and see what better they are of it:' Setting out the atheism of profane folks' hearts, that think religion a fancy (v. 15).

We have Job's sense of this (v. 16): *Lo, their good is not in their hands.* That is, 'their prosperity is not in their power, although they will boast of it.' *The counsel of the wicked is far from me.* 'I am far from the way of that sort of men, my heart abhors it.'

(2) He proves this the second way, that as [God] lets many wicked men live and die in prosperity, so he has seen some others of them die ere the half of their days are gone, and their candle put out, and destruction sieze upon them <u>ere they wit</u> [*before they know it*]. And this proves their good is not in their hand; yea, the wicked's portion is sorrows, and God distributes them in his anger (v. 17).

They are as stubble. They cannot more endure God's indignation, or any judgment he brings on them, than the dry stubble or chaff can bid the stormy wind; they have no solid root or foundation in themselves (v. 18). And God's anger ends not with the wicked man's death, but *he layeth up* the punishment of *his iniquity to his children,* and *rewards,* or recompences *him* justly, *and he shall know it* (v. 19). That is, he shall see a feasible judgment pursuing them. The judgment of God shall follow their children, that walk in their steps, or though the children be gracious, they may share of their wicked fathers temporal rod as Jeroboam's child did [1 Kings 14:13].

But if hypocrites are spared for their own time till death, what care they what becomes of their children? He answers (v. 20): *His eyes shall see his destruction in his own time,* and the cup of God's wrath in a deep draught shall be put in his hand, and he made to drink it. And a reason is given (v. 21): *For what pleasure hath he in his house after him, when the number of his months is cut off in the midst?* A reason why God will not only punish the hypocrite in his children, but oftimes in his own person, because a wicked man, when the time he has set to himself is cut off, he cares not what comes after him; therefore God brings a stroke, and lets him see it in his own time.

(3) He joins both these steps, in giving the reason of this dispensation from God's sovereignty (v. 22). 'Seeing,' would he say, 'you see that God takes this different way in letting some hypocrites live and die in prosperity, and putting out the candle of others before death, would you limit God? Is it [*suitable*] that you give God, who is Judge of all the world, a lesson? Should not God, who made the

world, get leave to guide the world, to spare whom he will, and cross whom he will?'

This he enlarges in an instance or comparison (vs. 23-26). He says, 'There are two wicked men, and God lets the one of them live prosperously and at ease, and they never know a cross, but he is like a fatted beast for his temporal estate. And the other of them, [who] may be no worse, lives in bitterness, and is tortured every day with one cross upon the back of another, and never gets a meal of meat with contentment. And yet they are alike in their death. The earth becomes a bed in both, the worms become sheets and blankets to them, and cover them, and there are as many worms in the one as in the other.

2. He comes to apply what he has said to that which he aimed at (vs. 27-33). For Zophar and the other two fought to bind it on Job that he was a wicked man, and a hypocrite, because he was so sorely dealt with. *Behold, I know your thoughts.* 'I know you have not said all that you have expressed for nought, but I have a guess what you mean' (v. 27). And he repeats the argument they brought against him (v. 28). *Ye say, where is the house of the prince?* 'You think because such a stroke is come on me, my children smitten, my family scattered, my prosperity gone, and I brought in a sudden to such a low condition, that I am the wicked man, and the hypocrite that you have been speaking of. But it is not so.'

And he proves their argumentation is not valid (v. 29). *Have ye not asked them that go by, and do ye not know their tokens?* Ask the poorest that go by the gate, and their observations will be these that follow (v. 30). 'The poorest can tell you that wicked men are not [*always*] punished in this life. Wrath is abiding them I grant, but it is not always poured out here.' Or as the words may be turned, *Destruction is kept up from them, yet they are kept to the day of wrath.*

He illustrates this in a second reason (v. 31). 'Show me who there is that will __buckle__ [*grapple*] with wicked men to cross or oppose them? They are in such power and prosperity, and so proud of it, that they have always protection in their pride. Whatever folks think, who dare speak it to their face, and though they do wrong, who dare repay them, or take amends of them? Do not all rather stoop under them?'

Yet (v. 32) the wicked man *shall be brought to the grave quietly*, and have as honorable a burial, and have as much rest and ease as any other. *The clods of the valley*, or the seal or turf shall be laid on his corpse, as well as on the corpse of any other; and as he slept away like another man, so he shall get that common rest in the grave that others get, whatever becomes of his immortal spirit. There shall be nothing singular in his death more than in a godly man's (v. 33).

III. 'How then pretend you either to convince, or comfort me, seeing you do it without weight, and the grounds you go upon are unsound?' And thus he reproves them, which is the last part of the chapter (v. 34).

OBSERVATIONS.

1. Observe from the general scope, it is a part of God's sovereignty and wisdom in ordering the world, to make no difference in respect of outward things between the wicked and godly, or one wicked man and another. But the wicked will sometimes be afflicted, sometimes in prosperity, as well as godly men, to draw folks eyes off external dispensations to read God's love in some other thing. If God's love goes not [*always*] with <u>creatures</u> [*creature-comforts*], so neither goes it always with <u>rods</u> [*punishments*]. He will sometimes distribute wrath to wicked men in this life. *No man knoweth love or hatred by all that is before him; all things come alike to all*, etc. (Eccles. 9:1-2).

2. Oftimes prosperity occasions folks to vent their atheism more than adversity. It is true, adversity will hugely press it out. *This ill is of the Lord*, said that wicked king, *why should I wait any longer?* But see what the text says here (vs. 14-15), prosperity is a curse to wicked men, and it is a fearful snare to be in it, and [*lack*] the sanctified use of it. Therefore labor for the sanctified use of what you have. Better you never had house nor table, nor riches, than that they should become a snare. And yet such is the condition of many.

3. There is no more foolish thing than to take upon us to guide God in guiding the world (v. 22). It implies two things. (1) That we are given to do so, and to fret against God when his dispensations suit not our humor. (2) That there is no [more] foolish way [*than*] this. This is God's exposition of folks' fretting at wicked mens' getting up to power, and godly mens' being borne down. Shall men teach God knowledge? God knows best what is [*suitable*], and who should be up and who down. Isa. 45:9: *Shall the potsheards of the earth strive with their Maker.* (Job 40:9. Rom. 9:20; 11:34). Are you able to advise him? We exhort you in this particular not to fret at God's dispensation towards his people. When your heart says, 'Such a thing is not right,' you say God is not wise enough, and take upon youself to teach him.

4. The state that all are running to is the grave. All have gone to it, and all will follow on. Worms will cover all, and be sheets to all. Be convinced, and convince yourselves of this, that ere long you will be like worms, and lie among worms. It is often in this book, and to be thought on by us. Nebuchadnezzar, [*who*] was the greatest man on earth, and had never a cross, yet comes to the grave, and gets that for his feather-bed and sheets, and the clods and worms to cover him (Isa. 14:11). Look for, and <u>make</u> [*prepare*] youself for such a bed. It is a wonder so many die, and we are witnesses of it, and yet we forget that we ourselves will die, and come to be covered with clods, and have the worms creeping through us. Let the consideration hereof stir us up to labor to have the image of Christ stamped on the body, and that will make it shine. For it will be an ugly spectacle when the vile body shall rise at a distance with Christ, and be deformed and destitute of his image.

22

This is the beginning of the third contest that at least two of Job's friends have with him; we heard the scope and sum of their debate before. They have a mind solidly to humble Job, and fit him for the promises of mercy. They set themselves to convince him of his guilt and hypocrisy, that by forcing him to take with that, they may have the better ground to apply the promises of mercy to him: But they exceed, 1. In limiting God to guilt as the cause of afflictions. 2. In judging Job while they are not content to make him a sinful man, except he also be a hypocrite, who has nothing of the grace of God in him.

The chapter has two parts. I. Eliphaz charge to Job (vs. 1-20). II. His exhortation to Job, containing his scope, [which is] not to seclude him from mercy, but to make his acquaintance with God that he might come by it (vs. 21-30).

I. The charge has two parts. 1. He charges him for justifying himself (vs. 1-11) 2. He charges him with gross and atheistical thoughts of God, which he professes to have gathered out of Job's tenets, as so many consequences thereof (vs. 12-20).

1. For the first charge, he follows it two ways. (1) More generally, that though Job was just, what advantage can he plead God has by it. *Can a man be profitable unto God, as he that is wise may be unto himself?* 'Suppose you were righteous and sincere, and had done all that God requires of you, what does God profit by that means? A man walking so may profit himself, but God is [*outside*] the reach of man's good or ill.'

(2) A second argument is (v. 3): *Is it any pleasure to the Almighty that thou art righteous?* 'As your being righteous brings no profit to God, so it brings no new delight to him. Can there be any addition to God's perfect blessedness for you to boast and vaunt of your righteousness? Is it gain to him?' For all [*these*] interrogations supposes their

negatives. 'And what then can the end be that you have before you in that way?'

(3) A third argument is (v. 4): *Will he reprove thee for fear of thee, or will he enter with thee into judgment?* 'As your good can do God no good, so your evil cannot hurt God. Will he reprove you for fear that you by your way of living hurt him?' Or, it is a comparison from judges who put [*prevent*] a man from being hurtful, making an end of him. The scope is to tell that God [does] not chasten without a ground; as if he had said, 'it is either because you have done wrong, or for fear you do wrong, that he deals thus with you. Now, God needs not fear your doing him wrong, therefore you have done him wrong, provoking him thus to handle you.' Or, *will he enter with thee into judgment,* for you? Or, *will he enter with thee into judgment* for fear of you? is here to be repeated to tell that God is not swayed in executing judgment, either by man's ill or good. This is a doctrine that is true and sound, but ill applied; for he is not here pleading for God's sovereignty, but to prove Job [is] a wicked man, because he was so oddly handled.

(4) This he follows out (v. 5): *Is not thy wickedness great?* Is it not of a high nature? *And thy iniquity infinite* for number? 'Are not your sins great, and many? And if God had not laid his hand upon you, you [would have] sinned on still.' This general charge he follows in particulars, all tending to make out [Job's] cruelty and covetousness.

[1] *Thou hast taken a pledge from thy brother for nought.* 'There was no friend that you pitied.' And he says, 'He took the pledge for nought,' to point out these ways that Job sought advantage of his poor friends beyond the worth of anything he gave them.

[2] *And thou hast stripped the naked of their clothing.* 'If any poor body owed you, though they had nothing but a brat [*cloak*] to cover them, you took it from them, and sent them naked to beg their bread' (v. 6).

[3] *Thou hast not given water to the weary.* 'You [were so] unmerciful, that you would not give a drink of water to a weary body.' *And thou hast withholden bread from the hungry.* 'When you had bread enough in your house, you would not give a piece to them that were like to starve, as the word is, 'a height of uncharitableness' (v. 7). He aggreges [*charges*] (v. 8), 'Though you had no respect to poor men, yet you made off and fanned upon great men, who had abundance of the world, when you rode over poor folk.'

[He] goes on in this (v. 9), under *widows* and *fatherless*, comprehending all poor folks who have no protection, and alleges he <u>undid</u> [*destroyed*] them: 'The little portion they had, you soon spoiled them of it and sent them away with nothing.' The *arms* being that which upholds or supports, the breaking or destroying of them is the taking from them anything they had to maintain them, or be a life to them. The meaning is, wherever he could win over, he ran over all. Were they never so poor or indigent, they found no mercy.

Upon this (vs. 10-11), he infers the justness of God's punishing or afflicting him in four similitudes, as if he said, 'you need not think it strange that God so afflicts you, [since] you have been such a cruel man.' *Therefore snares are about you*, 'as hunters deal with beasts, or fowlers with fowls, so God deals just so with you.' And, secondly, *sudden fear*, or 'an alarm, affrights, troubles, or surprises you' (v. 10). Thirdly, *Darkness, that thou canst not see.* 'You are like a man that walks in the darkness, that knows not where to go, nor where he is.' Fourthly, *Abundance of waters cover thee.* 'Judgment is come on you like a flood,' holding out the greatness of Job's sin, and the inevitableness of wrath and judgment therefore, <u>to his conception</u> [*in his opinion*].

Now we see from chapter 31 that Job was free of [*these*] sins he was charged with here. He was so far from taking clothing from these poor friends, that he made them clothing of his own wool, and fed the hungry, etc. And when God comes in to speak, he justifies Job, and condemns his friends. Therefore this uncharitable charging him with [*these*] particular sins, flows partly from a mistake, partly from passion, and partly from the principle he maintained, that where great affliction was, there behooved to be great sins, and he instances by guess a number of particulars.

2. The second part of the charge is for his gross and atheistical thoughts of God, as if he said, 'Job you were [*always*] sinning, and thought God would not find you out, nor take notice of you; yet now he has discovered you.'

(1) The first ground for this is (v. 12): *Is not God in the height of heaven?* God is a high Majesty. He is more sovereign [*than*] the highest imaginations man can reach. *Behold the height of the stars.* The stars are the highest thing we see, and yet God is higher. Depending on none, but having all depending on him. Giving orders to all, and receiving orders from none.

This is true doctrine, which he brings in Job contradicting (v. 13): *Thou hast said in thy prosperity, how does God know?* As the wicked man is brought in, saying (Psal. 10:11): *God hath forgotten; he hideth his face, he will never see it*, 'till God found you out.' You were careless and regardless of God, as if he saw not. *And how can he judge through the dark cloud?* Implying Job's secure way of living, as if this were true of God. 'There is such atheism in your heart, that because God is above the clouds, and you see him not, you think the clouds cover God, so as he cannot see nor judge you; and you think that he walks in the circuit of heaven, as if he were regardless of men on earth' (v. 14). 'This has been the language of your heart, which may be read in your practice.' But Job was far from any such thing.

Having bound this conclusion on Job, he labors to refute him, and yet so as to bear it in upon him he was such, by showing his way had been the same with the way of wicked men before him. *Hast thou marked the old way*, etc. (vs. 15-16). 'Job, if you had taken heed to the way of wicked men, and compared it with yours, and if you had marked God's judgment on them, you would have known God's dealing with you not to be unlike [His dealing with the them], and that God takes notice of men like you.' He has respect to the old world, for they were cut down out of time because they were taken away by an extraordinary judgment before the ordinary time of death: *their foundation was overflown with a flood.*

(2) He describes these men with a special respect to Job (v. 17). 'They were atheists, and had a way of living like yours, *which said unto God, depart from us.*' We exponed thir [*explained these*] words [in] 21:14-15. They had no will of nearness with God in respect of taking direction from him, or giving obedience to him, and they give a reason of it. *What can the Almighty do for them?* They had a fair life in prosperity, and thought God could not make them better. It is like that word [in] Malachi 3:14-15. *Ye have said, it is vain to serve God: and what profit is it, that we have kept his ordinance, and that we walked mournfully before the Lord of hosts? And now we call the proud happy: yea, they that work wickedness are set up; yea, they that tempt God are even delivered.* And like Senacherib's word (Isa. 36:20) and like Pharaoh's word (Exod. 5:2), and some others.

(3) He refutes their atheism (v. 18). *Yet he filled their houses with good things.* There was nothing in their house but they had it of God: plenishing [*furnishing*], meat, drink, and all. And he rejects this horrible blasphemy of theirs: *The counsel of the wicked is far from me.* Which words Job had spoken before (21:16), and Eliphaz repeats

them with a reflection on Job, that he was far from taking it on him (as he alleges Job did) to justify wicked men.

He goes on to prove the same thing (vs. 19-20), and to overturn that which Job held, that wicked men might live and die in prosperity. *The righteous see it, and are glad.* That is, the righteous see the destruction of such wicked men, and therefore it is applied by some to Noah, but it is best to take it in the general. 'Righteous men, that pity poor folk, as you have not done, rejoice to see God give a proof of his justice on them.' *Whereas our substance is not cut down,* taking in [*referring to*] his friends, and other godly men, in opposition to Job, and other wicked men. 'God has set an hedge about us and our goods; it is not cut down. *But the remnant of them the fire consumeth.* That is, some judgment lights [*falls*] on the remnant of the wicked, and their substance, and it may be he respects the fire that came on Job's substance. He too proudly puts Job in with wicked men, and himself in with godly men.

II. The second part of the chapter contains his exhortation to Job. It is proposed (vs. 21-22), and even backed with reasons, as if he said: 'Job, if you would take a right [*way*] to happiness, take youself to another [*way*] of living [*than*] you have been upon.' *Acquaint now thyself with God.* The word is ordinary conversing, and he subjoins an argument: *Thereby good shall come unto thee.* You shall have all prosperity and happiness.

A second exhortation (v. 22) is in answer to a question, 'What way shall I make acquaintance and converse with God?' *Receive the law from his mouth.* 'Prescribe not to God, live not after your own will, but receive his *will revealed in his word,* and walk according to it; *Lay up his words in thy heart,* be careful to keep them when you have received them, that they may be a rule for your practice.'

1. And if he will take this [*way*], he proceeds to promises (v. 23). 'Job, if you take my counsel, and turn to God, *your desolations shall be built up.* God shall make up all your losses; and *if ye put away iniquity from your tabernacle,* you shall indeed be just. You shall not be oppressing, and wronging, as you have been, if you take this course.' Or it may be taken for the punishment of iniquity, 'The curse of God that is lying on you, and all you have, shall be taken off.'

2. A second promise is (v. 24): *Then shalt thou lay up gold as dust.* 'Job, you loved riches well, and if you take this way of it, you shall have enough.' They are hyperbolic expressions, to show by turning to God, he shall have abundance of that he loved best.

3. Thirdly (v. 25), 'Yea, besides that you shall have a better mercy, *the Almighty shall be thy defense.'* And this third promise is beyond all that he promised before. 'You shall not only have plenty, but you shall enjoy it.'

4. A fourth promise is [in] verse 26, and a reason [for] that which goes before, and it is a more spiritual promise, as if he said, 'you have been taken up with seeking contentment among the creatures, but by turning to God you shall have more delight in God [*than*] in all the world beside, and you shall have access to God with boldness, and lift up your face before him.'

5. Another spiritual promise is (v. 27): 'you made a fashion of prayer before, and got little hearing, but if you return to God, and make acquaintance with him, and be holy in your walking, what you seek of God, you shall get. You shall pray for delivery, and get it; and God, shall give you occasion to vow, and pay your vows.' He shall get an evidence of God's hearing him, and he shall be thankful.

6. 'Yea' (v. 28), 'whereas before you had many purposes and projects, and they were all broken, you shall thrive in what you undertake, and the light shall shine upon your ways. God's countenance, and <u>owning</u> [*accepting*] of you, shall make your proceedings and success heartsome.'

7. A seventh promise is (v. 29): 'when you shall see many cast down, you may say in your particular experience, God has lifted you up, and by this, I know there is a way of God's lifting up of them that are brought low.' And he backs this with a new insinuation as a motive, *God shall save the humble person,* and (v. 30) closes with another promise, as a second motive to take his counsel. It contains two expressions tending to the same thing. 'If you be such a humble person, you shall not only do good to yourself by your prayers, but you shall deliver others.' Or as it is on the margin, *His prayers shall have weight to prevail with God, for the island of the innocent, or, the innocent shall deliver the island.* It is spoken in the second person to confirm Job the more. 'It shall be delivered by the pureness of your hands. You shall have the same promise and privilege that the humble person has to be helpful to the saving of others besides yourself.'

OBSERVATIONS.

1. From the first part of the words, observe to how great a height mistakes may come, and grow very unjustly. Eliphaz, a wise and

gracious man, charges such horrible things on Job as is a wonder. We would beware of venting our apprehensions and mistakes of folks, and study patience when mistakes are charged on us.

2. Lay all the promises he makes to Job together. They depend on his making his acquaintance with God, and the doctrine is sound, especially in reference to the spiritual blessings. Observe there is blessing upon blessing attending folks that make their acquaintance with God, and receive the law from his mouth, who seek to be friends, and to live friendly with him. In our hard condition, and manifold straits, when no other thing can promise happiness, it is good to take this course. Grow in the right uptaking of God, and making use of him, in which true acquaintance with God consists.

23

We heard a sharp charge, and we may say a very unreasonable challenge, wherewith Job is challenged by Eliphaz in the former chapter. In these two chapters (23-24), we have Job's answer, wherein he does two things in reference to Eliphaz's charge. 1. He vindicates himself from the many great faults imputed to him by Eliphaz, and clears his innocence (chap. 23). 2. He confutes the ground which Eliphaz laid, which was the rise of his charge, that is, the alleged prosperity of godly men, and God's dealing well with them, and the severity of his dealing with wicked men (chap. 24).

He clears his innocency in this chapter two ways. I. In his expressing of his confidence, that he dare go to God with his cause, and expect a comfortable hearing (vs. 1-10). II. He shows the grounds of his confidence in the testimony of his conscience, holding forth the straightness of his way (vs. 11-17). In both which he removes some doubts and objections which might be started against him.

I. 'You think much of my words and expressions, and wonder at my impatience, but you consider little the cause I have to complain. If you knew the verity you would not charge so hardly.' *Even today is my complaint bitter, and my stroke is heavier than my groaning.* 'The weight God has laid upon me is beyond what my groaning expresses' (v. 2). Then he [*proposes*] the first way of clearing his innocence (v. 3). *O that I knew where I might find him*, etc. 'I need not fruitlessly acknowledge my complaint to you, for I get little hearing. But I dare come before God with it. And if I knew his seat, if I could get him in that capacity men are in, I would think no shame to come that near him.' And (v. 4) 'if I were admitted to speak to him, I could orderly draw up the grounds of my cause, as men use to order battles in squadrons. I would muster my reasons to defend my sincerity, and multiply arguments. My cause is so good, that I think God cannot condemn me, but he would tell me the cause of this strange dealing, that you have not yet touched.'

This may be approved in reference to his friends, in defense of his particular cause with them; yet it seems too much boldness in respect of God, and his fault is his leaving his friends, and his betaking himself to God so boldly, without considering his due distance, for which God reproves him (chap. 38).

Objection. 'Dare you contend with God, Job?' *Answer* (vs. 6-7). *If he would plead with me in his power, I durst not plead with him;* 'but he would not take that way with me, but [take] the way of grace. And if he came to ask a question at me, he would give me wherewith to answer.' He would put in a strengthening word, as it is in the original, and this agrees well with that which follows (v. 7). *There,* that is, before the throne of his grace, where God takes not an absolute way of pleading with creatures, *the righteous might dispute with him,* might in a rational way, if he have grace, plead sincerity, and for mercy — 'there I am sure of a sentence in my favor, and forever to be absolved and not called to a reckoning.'

Objection. 'But Job, how is it that you would so fain have God to reason your cause before him? He is near to all, and you in particular?' He answers (vs. 8-9), 'It is true he is near me in his absolute providence, but I have sought to get a sight of him in another way, and that which I would have is not yet come. I take much pains to get him manifesting himself to me, and setting a day to me for clearing my cause, but for as near as he is, I cannot get near to him. *He hides himself* from me, in respect of that way I would see him in.'

He gives the reason of this (v. 10): *But he knoweth the way that I take; when he hath tried me, I shall come forth as gold.* 'Though he keeps a sovereign deep-drawn way towards me, which will not do my turn, he must condescend to a more familiar way. Yet I am confident, though I cannot get to him, he knows what I am doing, and though he seems now to [*misunderstand*], he will not do so still; and though he lets me lie still for a while in this trial, I shall come out of this affliction like gold more shining. I shall get a sentence from him that shall make my innocence more clear, and the relicts of corruption in me shall also get a death stroke, and so I shall also be more clear.' And this is brought in partly to answer an objection, for it might be said, 'Job, your cause is not so good as you call it from God himself.' He answers, *When I am tried, I shall come forth as gold,* partly to encourage himself that God in due time can clear his innocency.

II. In the second part of the chapter, he shows the ground of his confidence, holding forth the straightness of his way. For it may be said, 'Job, this is far said. What ground [do] you have to be thus confident of a clearing?' He answers, *My foot hath held his steps.* 'I know well I will get a clearing, and his sentence in my favor, for I have imitated him in the way wherein he has gone before me, and carved out to me, without declining to the right or left-hand' (vs. 11). And (v. 12) he goes on in this ground, *Neither have I gone back from the commandment of his lips.* 'I made conscience to follow every direction he gave me,' or, 'I meditate upon the commandments of his lips,' because men use to give directions with their lips. He held himself by God's steps, that he went not the wrong way, and when he was in the right he sat not up in it [*he continued on in it*].

I have esteemed the words of his lips more than my necessary food. 'I would have been loath to neglect one of his commandments, for I thought more of his word [than] of my dinner or supper.' It is the same word that is [in] Prov. 30:8. His respect to the word was not like his respect to his superfluities, but that which he had to his meat which he could not be sustained without.

Objection. 'But Job, if you were so righteous and religious a man as you say, how could God so afflict you?' He answers this from God's sovereignty (vs. 13-14). *But he is in one mind, and who can turn him? and what his soul desireth, even that he doth. For he performeth the thing that is appointed for me: and many such things are with him.* That is, we must not limit God to our way. He has a way of his own [from] which none can put him off. *He is of one mind,* that is, he is of one absolute mind when he has a purpose to do a thing. Neither mens' praying, nor forbearing to pray will divert him; he has a design of his own and will take his own will. He will follow his own way, and we are not to bound him, nor can bind him by reasons; and whatever he does, he performs no new thing but what he has appointed. 'And this affliction is carved out for me as well as my daily bread;' as the one is statute, so is the other.

And he closes this answer with this: *Many such things are with him.* That is, we must not think to plumb the deep of his sovereignty in this and many other things, which we cannot reach. Then he closes the chapter with showing the ground of his complaint, and the consistence of it with his innocence, for it might be said, 'Job, [why] need you then so complain?' He answers (v. 15), 'it is not my ill conscience, but the majesty of God and his absolute way of proceeding. *I am troubled at his presence.* I dare scarcely think of God, and when I consider his greatness and absoluteness that folks cannot take up, *I am afraid,* and it is that, that makes me complain, and not these things that you cast up to me.'

This he confirms (v. 16): *For God makes my heart soft.* 'For as stout a heart as I have, he makes it melt like wax for feebleness; for it is not man that I have ado with, but the *Almighty.*' And the grounds of this trouble (v. 17): *Because I was not cut off before the darkness, neither hath he covered the darkness from my face,* etc., wherein there are two reasons of his fear and trouble.

1. Dark affliction, which is often expressed under darkness. He is afraid of that because God took him not away before that came on him; and it may include a wondering that he is not taken away under all this darkness of affliction.

2. *Neither hath he covered the darkness from my face.* That is, 'neither has he taken any way to mitigate my affliction, to hide the ugly face of it from me. He has neither taken me from my affliction, nor my affliction from me, nor mitigated the same unto me.'

OBSERVATIONS.

1. In all this chapter we may look upon Job as failing in this: in leaving off to complain of his friends, and venting his complaint overmuch on God. Observe, when men give too much way to complaints, ere they end, readily they rub on God himself. Therefore there is nothing that folks would be more cautious in than in their complaints, lest they put themselves in the lists with God [*enter into combat with God*].

2 Observe (vs. 8-9), where he holds forth God's absoluteness, that for as much pains as he took to see God, he could not get a sight of him, that when God has a mind to exercise one, he will not give distinctness of access to him, but though they seek, they will not get him. This is one of the hardest exercises that souls are put to; and yet God will put to it, partly to make their affliction an exercise, partly to let souls know that his presence is not [*always*] tied to affliction. If folks always got God's presence in affliction, they would be vain and conceited in their own eyes, and not be humbled under God's hand; therefore to learn them to stoop, he will both afflict and hide his face. Therefore for use, [*purpose*] no limits to God; no dispensation carries God alongst with it, and we would trust to none of them.

3. *But he knows the way that I take* (v. 10) — see a notable piece of Christian wisdom and courage. When he misses God, and can

ground nothing on his knowing of God, he grounds something on God, and his knowledge of him. Observe that though affliction be without, and terror and confusion be within the soul, it should not mar confidence; there is some grip to faith to hang by, even then when we look to God in himself.

4. Observe from the grounds of his confidence (vs. 11-12), that there is nothing can maintain confidence under a hard and heavy exercise, except it be backed with a good conscience. Therefore when he promises to himself to come shining out of the trial, he lays down the ground of a good conscience as the reason of his confidence; and how little soever this be thought of before [a] trial comes, yet when any hard exercise comes, it will be known what a tender conscience was, and though it be by God's free mercy that any come to heaven, yet you will have ado with a good conscience; and if it be a missing, you will find an exercise hard to <u>buckle</u> [*grapple*] with.

5. Observe from the great estimation he has of God's word, that folks that make conscience of the word of God, and have a mind to live according to it, nothing will bear such sway with them. Or, a right estimation of the word of God is one of the main things that puts folk right in their walking, and sustains them under crosses. There was nothing he thought more of than to get his lesson from God, and grace to follow his lesson in practice. It was more than his appointed food. It is a sore matter there is such ignorance amongst us, and folks care not to learn, though many lessons be given them. If many of you were on your death bed, it is to be feared few could say they thought more of God's word, [*than*] of their appointed food. Job thought it a greater happiness, [*than*] to keep his life; little estimation [*shown*] to the word in folks practice, will be ground of a sad challenge.

6. *He performs the thing that is appointed for me* (v. 14). He looks to the cross, as he did to his necessary food, to the means appointed by God, as well as the other. Observe that folks' crosses are as necessary, and as well carved out, appointed and bounded of God, as their daily bread; which should learn us to welcome crosses, to bear them well, and to look to a higher hand under crosses than we [*normally*] do.

24

We heard what is the matter that Job answers in these two chapters (23-24); having in the former chapters cleared himself of many foul faults that Eliphaz charged him with, here he overturns the principle that Eliphaz had laid down, and which lead to these absurdities. For he and the rest of his friends could not think but that Job, who was so afflicted, was a wicked man, and hence they lay another conclusion, *That wicked men go not away unplagued of God.* Job, as before (chap. 21), overthrows this ground, showing that wicked men live and die without remarkable judgments.

He passes from that which he was defending by way of transition (v. 1). *Why, seeing times are not hidden from the Almighty, do they that know him, not see his days?* 'Why [do] you dispute to maintain that question, as if God's judgments on wicked men were [*always*] remarkable?' He grants by way of concession, that there is a time set for the destruction of wicked men; but though God knows, and has a set time for their destruction, '[Do] you think,' would he say, 'that that time is always known to men?' These times are known by the Almighty, but they that know him, that is these that are nearest God, know [that] his ways and counsel are so deep, that they cannot tell before hand what shall befall wicked men; they cannot see his days, or observe God's judgment by anything that they see. And he proves through[out] the chapter, that many wicked men have lived profanely, and died without any remarkable judgment coming on them to the observation of others. This he does in three steps.

I. His first instance or proof is the oppressor and violent man (vs. 2-12). *Some take away the land mark.* Nothing was more sacred, nor more punctually looked to, [*than*] the keeping of right marches [*boundaries*], and there was no greater iniquity, [*than*] the removing of them. Yet there are some that do remove them, and yet are spared, and *some take away* other folks' *flocks*, and that *violently, and feed upon them* (v. 2). And if there be a fatherless person, who has but an ass to gain their living by, or a widow who has an ox free, they are that merciless that they will take it from them (v. 3). And they are so great oppressors, that a poor man dare not meet them in the high way (v. 4). *The poor of the earth hide themselves together.*

He goes on to describe their wickedness: *Behold*, as other men that have callings go out in the morning to follow them, so [*these*] men go out and make it their work to live in violence. And as the wild ass (which is described in chapter 29) lives in the wilderness, so [*these*] folks live rather like beasts than like men, and *the wilderness yieldeth them food.* It is a bare ground, but they will get something off it (v. 5), and their prosperity is such that none of them [*lacks*] their harvest, and their corn is neither shaken nor rotten, and they gather not only their own, but the vineyards of others (v. 6). Yea, they are that unmerciful, that they who have a few clothes, were it but a blanket left them to keep them from the cold, they will take it from them, and let them lie in the fields without clothes (v. 7). And these poor, naked folks, flying from their severe cruelty, are glad of a cleft of a rock to lie in (v. 8), for not only take they their clothes out of their houses, but when they have undone poor folks in any little thing they had, they take any <u>brats</u> [*cloaks*] they have upon them from off them. And if a poor man had but a sheaf of corn to live on, they will bereave him of it (vs. 9-10).

And a further step of their oppression is (v. 11): They will not give the poor men that work in trading their oil, meat to live upon. But [v. 12] publicly in the city the soul of the wounded by their oppression cries out. And he concludes the proof with this: *yet God layeth not folly to them.* That is, God reckons not always with them before men; they often die without God's charging folly on them, to the observation of men.

II. A second proof to the same purpose in new sins and sinners. 1 Of the murderer (vs. 13-14). 'The wicked men that I have been speaking of, and particularly the murderer, are like men that cannot abide the light. *They know not the ways thereof.* That is, they cannot abide to hear what God directs them. It is a burden to them, or take it literally, they cannot abide to be found out, for they would think shame of it. This is clear by what follows (v. 14). A man that is cruel to his neighbor, the scripture calls a *murderer, rises soon with the light,* or before it is light (whether literally to kill, or to take his neighbor's subsistence from him, all is one). *And is as a thief in the night.* When he gets opportunity he is a thief, glad to be about with it.

2. Of the adulterer (v. 15). As the murderer waits for the night, so does the adulterer, and thinks to go so quietly about it, as none shall

get wit of it, and says in his heart, *No eye shall see him,* and he sets his face in secret; and (v. 16) in the daytime they mark where to get their prey, and set on in the night to obtain it. *They know not the light.* That is, they cannot be seen in the light.

The reason of this is (v. 17): *The morning to them is as the shadow of death.* That is, the daylight is a great hindrance to them, and therefore it is to them as if death were at the back of it, lest any should say, 'Who was in that house, or took away such goods?' It is as death to them, for they look for some challenge or shame. *He is swift as the water* [v. 18]. That is, as he steals and robs in the wilderness, so he is a pirate on the seas. *He beholds not the way of the vineyards.* That is, he cannot abide the place where folk live; he had rather be in a cursed, wild place for his purpose.

Thus he describes the wicked to the full; yet to confute Eliphaz he sets down in a comparison how such men may live and die (vs. 19-20). *Drought and heat consume the snow-waters, so doth the grave those which have sinned. The womb shall forget him, the worm shall feed sweetly on him, he shall be no more remembered, and wickedness shall be broken as a tree.* Snow is not [*always*] melted by thaw, or flush of rain, but sometimes by drought or the heat of the sun insensibly. So does death come on such wicked men. They die so calmly that the world forgets them; for where folks are taken away by some terrible and remarkable judgment, there is a remembrance of it. But it is not so with them; they go to their grave like other men, and *the worms feed on them,* and are a banquet or dinner to them. They have a common lot with all men, and are not <u>an upcast</u> [*a reproach*], nor remembered as stricken with any palpable judgment; and as a tree that is worm-eaten falls over with little noise, so do many wicked men without remarkable judgment.

III. A third proof or instance to the same purpose (vs. 21-24): *He evil entreateth the barren that beareth not.* It was a sore cross in these times to be barren, but these men are so cruel and merciless, that they evil entreat such, and are so far from doing good to widows, that they do ill to them. Yea, this wicked oppressor is so high, that none <u>eschews</u> [*avoids*] him. The mighty are drawn with his power, and when he is angry there is none sure of his life. So wicked is he to invent, and so powerful to execute, that all tremble to look on him. *Though* (v. 22) is not in the original. But it is *given him to be in safety;* that is, to be quiet and secure, and he rests on that. *Yet his eyes are upon their ways;* that is, yet God's eyes are upon their ways (for Job and his friends knew when God was spoken of, though he was not named). The Lord is taking notice of him, and shall be about with him (v. 23).

They are exalted for a little time (v. 24); they get a little prosperity, but they have no cause to boast of it, for they are soon brought low, and laid among the worms. *They are taken out of the way as all other;* there is no difference between them and other men in their death. *And they are cut off at the tops of the ears of corn;* that is, they are not cut down till they are ripe. 'They die in full age, they are so far from suffering here away, as you say.'

Then he subjoins his conclusion (v. 25): *If it be not so now, who will make me a liar?* 'I defy any of you to make out the contrary, and make my speech worth nothing, for as little as you think of it, this is the truth.' It is an appealing to them that this is a sure truth that none can say [*anything*] against.

So Job here out of his experience clearly proves that as wicked men might live happy in a world to their outward condition, so they might die without a remarkable evidence of God's judgment.

OBSERVATIONS.

1. Observe that it is ill gathering [wrong to reckon] God's love to folks, either from prosperity in their lifetime, or from a meek and calm manner of dying. The greatest enemies of God on earth may live and die as those spoken of [in] Psal. 73. It is true God will by his judgments on some, make the world know sometimes that there is a God that judges in the earth. Yet he will spare others of them, because there is a day of judgment coming, at which time he will reckon with them for altogether.

2. Observe (v. 23) that wicked men desire no more if they get a present happiness, and there is no greater evidence of wicked men, [*than*] to rest satisfied with the things of the world, nor no greater snare to them. Think on it, you that may get more of the world [*than*] your neighbors, and sit down [*rest*] on it. It is one of the benefits of affliction that folks are kept from resting on the things of the world by it, especially when it is blest of God, whereas others settle in the world, never minding their decaying tabernacle, nor a tribunal of God.

3. Observe (v. 24) that the wicked man's prosperity, though he should live and die in it, is but short. Were it for an hundred or a thousand years, being compared with eternity, it is but short and not

worth naming. And it is an ill change that folks make, when for a short whiles prosperity, they miss eternity of happiness, and fall under eternal wrath. Look to the frailty of your life while you prosper; know you are but exalted for a time, and remember eternity is on the back of it. We are all wearing on, and see others wearing away. Be often thinking on that time, when at an instant you will pass from time into eternity, and how there will be no making up of losses then. And be not such fools as for the trifles in time to lose an enduring substance, but learn to make up that in God, that creatures cannot yield you.

25

This chapter contains the last onset that Job's friends have on him, and it is the third onset that Bildad the second friend has. He comes in on the answer that Job had given to Eliphaz, wherein he, 1. vindicates himself from these aspersions Eliphaz charged him with, and appealed to God as judge; and 2. disputes the common state of the question. Bildad here disputes not the last, either being overcome with Job's reasons, or because in the first he conceived there was greater occasion given him to pursue Job. Therefore he checks him for his confident appealing to God, and his check runs on this ground, that Job knew not God, [who] was greater than he could take him up. To which Job answers in chapter 26, not contradicting Bildad; and the rest that follows are Job's own thoughts, without respect to any particular charge.

In this chapter, Bildad from four grounds checks Job. 1. *Dominion*, or to rule, is with God; he has not only absolute power and force, but he has right to rule, and *fear* and terror *is with him.*

2. Ground or reason is from the effects of his government. *He maketh peace in his high places.* God guides the world so, that among the highest of his creatures there is not a mouth can be opened, neither any that dare say [*anything*] against his government (v. 2).

3. The third ground or reason is (v. 3): *Is there any number of his armies?* He has hosts and armies without number at his command.

4. And the fourth ground is, *Upon whom doth not his light arise?* Is there any creature upon whom that sun shines not? It is his light that shines on all creatures. Upon these grounds he subsumes (v. 4), *How then can man be justified with God?* Since it is so that God is so absolute, can man, that is God's creature, so far subordinate to him, be absolved before God. And this he aggreges or enlarges: Or, *How can he be clean that is born of a woman?* Can man who is such a base creature be clean before God?

He follows this in comparison (v. 5): *Behold, even to the moon, and it shineth not, yea, the stars are not pure in his sight.* Look to these glorious creatures, sun, moon, and stars; for as glorious as they are, they are not pure in God's sight. He can espy spots in them. Who then dare contest with this God, or plead purity before him?

And the comparison is applied (v. 6): *How much less man that is a worm,* or how much less silly man, or worm man. The word in the original, in the first place, is that sort of worm that breeds in flesh, and that we usually call a maik. Or a worm man, in the second place, is that long worm that breeds in the earth. So the meaning is, if these glorious creatures in the heaven cannot stand before God, how much less vile man? It <u>sets not him</u> [*does not suit him*] to contest with God.

Now in all this Bildad speaks sound; but there are two faults in his drift. 1. That he [*misunderstands*] the main ground of the debate, and takes him to cavil on some of Job's expressions. 2. That from these expressions he would bear out that Job knew nothing of the majesty of God.

OBSERVATIONS.

1. Bildad speaks well of God's majesty and absolute sovereignty, and it is a wonder to see such tender expressions of God, going along with gross mistakes of Job's way. But Job's check insinuates that he studied more words than [how] rightly to apply them. So it is <u>yet</u> [*still*]. Many from their parts and abilities may speak great words of God and his way, and yet err in application, which should make folks more wary, tender and humble, and study not so much words, as to be right in the matter itself. For Job passes by words and expressions, and examines the matter and drift of them, and so should we.

2. Observe when man is compared with God, it cannot be told of how little worth man is; therefore he is compared to the vilest of worms. It were good and profitable for us often to be laying together the greatness and majesty of God, and our vileness and baseness; and the looking upon these creatures, the worms and maiks, might give us a lesson, and <u>lay</u> [*humble*] our pride.

3. When God and man are rightly compared, or men consider God and themselves rightly, it heightens the excellency of God. If we have low thoughts of God, we have high thoughts of ourselves, and if we have low thoughts of ourselves, we have high thoughts of God. Therefore labor to have our eyes filled with the greatness and absoluteness of God, and that will bring us to right thoughts of ourselves.

26

J ob, offended at Bildad's answer, replies two things to it. I. He checks him for speaking to no purpose (vs. 1-4). II. He shows he could speak of the majesty of God (vs. 5-14), and had no more mind to wrong him than he, but had respect to him in his soul, however his infirmities [*appeared*], and therefore ought not so to be interpreted.

I. His checking of Bildad is by way of irony: *How hast thou helped him that is without power?* 'Bildad, you have done a mighty deed. You think you have done bravely to it. You came to help a poor man, and to plead for God, as if he had needed your help, and you have lifted me up well who is lying under your feet' (v. 2).

How hast thou counselled him that hath no wisdom (v. 3). 'You think me a fool who [*lacks*] counsel,' or (take it in reference to God) as the former also, 'you come in well to speak, as if he needed your counsel, and think you have abundantly declared the debate, and taken up the matter as it is. You have done much to it now.' He means 'you have done nothing to it at all.'

To whom hast thou spoken thy words? (v. 4). 'If you have spoken for God, he needs none of them, and if to me, they are not new. I know all that you have said.' *And whose spirit came from thee? i.e.* of whose spirit savors these words? Or take it in reference to Job, the meaning is, 'whose spirit is refreshed by these comforts you [*propose*]? Who [do] you think are revived in spirit by these your speeches?'

II. To let Bildad see he has no mind to wrong God more [*than*] he, he sets out God's greatness in several steps.

1. In his power (v. 5), secretly putting life and keeping life in the creatures, even in these creatures that men see not: fishes in the sea and waters, or under the waters, in the body of the earth, which is as their womb, whether they be minerals or roots of plants. God makes them conceive there, as in a womb, and sustains them by his power, and this he extends to the inhabitants both in the sea and the earth. God gives them all a being.

2. A second instance (v. 6), *Hell is open before him.* We take it literally for hell, because there is here a gradation, and afterward it is called *destruction.* 'God,' he says, 'has a dominion over hell.'

3. *He stretcheth out the north* (v. 7, that part of the heaven which was in their view, and is in ours now) *over the empty place,* and there is no contiguity between it and the earth, but a void. *And hangs the earth upon nothing.* By his power he hangs the world in the air upon nothing, having neither prop nor pillar to support it, but it is as a point or globe in the circumference of the heavens.

4. A fourth evidence or instance is (v. 8): *He bindeth up the waters in his thick clouds, and the cloud is not rent under them.* 'God is great in power, and I know it by this, that though the waters in the firmament are a heavier body [*than*] the clouds that are an airy body, yet the clouds break not till God lets a shower fall through.'

5. *He holdeth back the face of his throne, and spreadeth his cloud upon it* (v. 9). 'When I look to God's throne, I see much, yea, inaccessible majesty in it.' And this he expresses in God's covering of it, and spreading a cloud over it. He will not let his glory out and [*appear*] on the creatures, for a blink of it would consume and eat them up. Therefore as Moses put a veil on his face when he spoke with the children of Israel, so he puts these heavens between his glory and us, which is called the spreading of a cloud between him and us, that we in the state of mortality may have a being before him for a time. For if the firmament were away, his glory would consume creatures.

6. [The sixth] evidence (v. 10) is of his setting bounds to the seas. That it is a wonder how God hedges it up with a <u>pickle</u> [*little*] sand, but he does it by his decree; and this decree stands till the day and night come to an end.

7. *The pillars of heaven tremble* (v. 11). If God would speak, and give a word of *reproof* in his anger, heaven and earth would shake and tremble.

8. *He divides the sea by his power* (v. 12). God is not bounded to an ordinary way as we are. Though man cannot divide the sea, neither knows he how to be about with proud tyrants, [*God*] can smite through pride itself, as the word is. Whether this relates to the Red-sea and Pharaoh, we will not say, for the word is Rahab, but it is likely this was written before that time. However, he is speaking of God's absolute power.

9. *By his spirit* (v. 13), i.e. by the glorious third person of the Trinity, who (Gen. 1:2), *moved upon the face of the waters.* He has garnished the heavens, and he that has set the firmament with such pearls, and made it so glorious, must be much more glorious in himself. *His hand has formed the crooked serpent,* that is, the greatest and most monstrous creatures in the earth or sea, rather than that sign in the heaven, for to take it so answers his scope.

Lo these are a part of his ways (v. 14). When we have spoken all this of God and his ways, they are but parts of God's ways. Their extent tie us, and the infinite number of them cannot be taken up. *And how little a portion is heard of him?* All that [Bildad] and Job both have spoken, or that can be heard from any [about] him, is but a little portion of that which is in him. And a third word is added, *But the thunder of his power, who can understand?* Take God in his infiniteness, whereof the thunder is but a little evidence, or look to the attributes of God [*appearing*] in that one mark, who can understand his infiniteness in that and other works? 'I defy all men, angels, and saints to understand it. They are all but finite creatures that you and I have been speaking of, but his infiniteness is far above them.' So Job well and sharply checks Bildad, yet speaks tenderly and humbly of the majesty of God.

OBSERVATIONS.

1. Observe in general, that if folks would study the art of knowing God, there is nothing they look upon among the creatures in heaven or earth, but it may wonderfully set out God: not a look to the firmament, nor to the earth, and its hanging upon nothing, nor to the void between the heaven and the earth, nor to his giving and preserving life in all creatures, nor to the clouds covering the face of his throne, etc.; but it shows the majesty, power, and goodness of God. Make this use of God's creatures, not only in word, but in deed, and in effect.

2. In the last verse, [Job] quits the uptaking [*comprehending*] of God, as that which cannot be won at [*attained*]. Observe, these that study God most, will find him incomprehensible, and he is never rightly studied till he be found so to be, and these are three words well put together. *These are but a part of his ways, and how little a portion of him is heard,* when you and I, and all the world have spoken of him. *And who can understand the thunder of his power?* None in all the world can [understand] that. Think and speak reverently of the majesty of God. Set all the world together, they cannot [understand] the glory of that majesty we are called to profess and worship.

27

Job's friends are now at a stand. He had given an answer to the last onset of Bildad, and it seems there has been an interruption, Job ceasing and waiting for a time to see if any of them would reply; but none of them speaking, either because they thought Job was obstinate, or because they had not much more to say, they cede now to him (in discourse, yet not convinced in the matter), and Job goes on in his purpose, and clears himself from the aspersions they put upon him.

Moreover Job continued his parable, and said. After some interruption, he began to speak in an excellent, although dark way; and in [these] two chapters (27-28) has one continued discourse, wherein: I. he asserts his integrity with confidence (vs. 2-7). II. He removes two objections [to which] his confident asserting of his integrity was liable. The first objection he answers(vs. 7-23): 'look and see Job if in asserting your integrity, you are not a brave advocate for, and complier with wicked men.' A second objection, 'If it is so that God always punishes wicked men, why [do] you dispute against us who maintain the same thing, and say you are plagued of God for your wickedness.' To this he answers in the next chapter, and tells that though God does always punish wicked men, yet he has a secret way of doing it oftimes, that it is not obvious to the [world];[1] and therefore they were not to limit God to rules conceived by them, and draw conclusions from that, that he was wicked because under trouble.

I. The first part [on] his asserting his integrity has four things in it. 1. An asseveration, *As God lives, who hath taken away my judgment.* 'Who leaves me as a condemned man? so long as I live I will not quite my integrity.' It is an entire ground, which is asserted by way of asseveration [*emphatic declaration*], bearing these particulars. (1) As the Lord lives, ordinarily was an oath even among the Hebrews. (2) 'Will you attest God, who seems to condemn you, and takes away

---

1 In the original edition this read, "not obvious to the word," with no correction indicated in the errata. It appears it should be world.

the sentence of your absolution?' He answers (v. 3): *All the while my breath is in me,* to show the inconstancy of his life. It is but a breathing, *and the spirit of God,* that is, the spirit that is from God, *is in my nostrils, my lips shall not speak wickedness.* 'I shall not assert this untruth that you bind upon me, that I am a hypocrite, for that [would be] lying against the grace of God in me, and uttering wickedness and deceit (v. 4).

2. The second assertion is (vs. 5-6): *God forbid that I should justify you.* 'Let it not be, let my soul abhor such a thing.' What he spoke more obscurely before, he holds it forth more clearly: *My righteousness I hold fast, and will not let it go.* He does not absolve himself before God, but stands for his own uprightness and sincerity. *'My heart shall not reproach me* in this defense of my righteousness, for I do it with a good conscience.' Or, 'I will not lie against the grace of God in me, to give my heart or tongue occasion to condemn myself, for speaking against God's grace, and siding with temptation.'

II.   In the second part (vs. 7-23), he declares that he abhors as much as any, siding and complying with wicked men, though they thrive in the world for a time; and he answers the doubt two ways.

1.   Though the wicked had prosperity all their days, there is another thing [that] would not let him choose to be a wicked man: his present delight in God, and hope of heaven, that the wicked man [does] not have (vs. 7-11). 2. Though some wicked men are spared, yet others meet with judgment in this life, and some time all will meet with it (vs. 13-23).

1.   If anything is worse [*than*] another, they wish it to their enemies, and he says he is so far from esteeming of or complying with wicked men, that he could wish for no worse to his enemy than he wishes to them, and he gives some reasons of this. (1) What has the hypocrite gained when *God takes away his soul?* He has no hope of heaven, and 'I would not lose my hope of heaven for all his gain (v. 8).

(2) A second reason why he casts at the wicked for all his prosperity (v. 9) [is] because the wicked have no access to God in prayer [when] under trouble, for all their happiness.

(3) A third reason (v. 10) is though the wicked man may have many outward things, yet he has no delight in God. 'I would not lose that delight I have in God for all his prosperity.'

(4) A hypocrite in the time of prosperity may bide [it] out, and carry a profession for a time, but will he continue in all difficulties

and trials to *call upon God?* That he will not. 'But I continue yet calling upon God, and <u>do not sit up</u> [*do not neglect it*], which is an evidence that I am no hypocrite. I do not like their [*way*].'

2. He goes on unto a second answer (v. 11) whereby he grants that he disputes not absolutely that wicked men are [*always*] spared, but often they are. '*I will teach you being in the hand of God;* that which he has taught me in such a condition, and you may take it off my hand, seeing what I teach is concerning God's sovereignty, and you yourselves have seen, and might understand it in your experience. Why then are you thus idle and vain in heaping up words to no purpose?'

Then he goes on (v. 13) to what he would say, and describes the wicked. *This is the portion of a wicked man;* this is the portion the wicked have right to by virtue of the covenant of works, and their portion is the curse of God, which he goes on to describe (v. 14).

(1) *If his children be multiplied, it is to the sword.* This is the first curse they often meet with, or have to look for. There is [*ever*] a judgment abiding them and their children; or if their children live, it is to a sorer judgment.

(2) They shall be miserable in their life and in their death; and they shall be such horrible monsters of misery, that their own wives shall not weep when they are dead, thinking them well away. And this is a second part of their curse or judgment, a miserable life, and an unlamented death.

(3) A third part of their misery (vs. 16-18): they may take much pains to gather the world, and heap up riches, but they have not the promise, nor sanctified use of it, nor God's blessing with it. 'I am far from thinking that the wicked have a prosperous estate, for his house is but like the moths house in cloth, or like a lodge which a man builds in a yard for a time.'

(4) A fourth part of their misery (v. 19): *The rich men* may think themselves happy, but *they shall not be gathered* to the burial of their fathers. He may think much of it when he goes to bed, and have much <u>pelf</u> [*goods*], but he shall not be buried with respect. *He opens his eyes, and he is not;* or, it is not. A wind comes and blows all his wealth away, and he cannot fasten his fingers on his riches.

(5) A fifth part of his judgment (v. 20) is, as a tempest comes on men by night on the waters, and strikes them with terror, so shall judgment come on them. This is set out by another similitude of a

tempest by land (v. 21). The east wind sunders him from his happiness, and he is taken from it as stubble or straw is carried away by a flood. Both similitudes show the sudden judgment that oftimes comes on the wicked in their prime and flower.

And he gives a reason why he must be miserable, live as he like; for when God reckons with him, he keeps no measure (v. 22). *He casts upon him, and does not spare,* and when he *would fain flee,* or <u>wind</u> [*loose*] himself out of God's hand, God's judgment grips them sorer than they can escape. This is summed up (v. 23), *Men shall clap their hands at him,* and shall *hiss him out of his place;* a word that not only holds out his loss, but the shamefulness of it. All shall rejoice at it, and think, and say, it is <u>well wared</u> [*well earned*]. Thus Job shows he was far from playing the patron for wicked men, knowing the ill both of their prosperity, and of the judgment of God on some, and abiding [on] others of them.

OBSERVATIONS.

1. Observe on his two assertions and oaths, that he is an upright man, and that he will maintain it, that it is a thing attainable, and we should not rest without it, to be clear and confident of interest in God. Try well the grounds of your interest. Many think they have interest that dare not swear it, nor confidently assert it, as Job does, but it is a notable length in religion to be clear in it, and able to swear it.

2. He counts it a horrible crime to deny his integrity and interest in God. Observe that true tenderness will be as wary and loath to deny the grace of God, and lie against it, as it will be to presume and play the hypocrite in saying he has grace when he has none. Many think they guard well against hypocrisy by denying their interest in God. But you would learn to walk tenderly on both hands; when too much liberty is taken on this hand, it may provoke God, as well as when you presume upon the other hand.

3. Observe where there is integrity and an interest in God, and it is set upon and assaulted, folks would the more willfully stick to it and assert it, and steadfastly debate for it, as Job being put to it, swears he will not quite it, and yet with tenderness to God, and loathness to take on new guilt. And his doing this when God <u>keeps up himself</u> [*hides himself*], commends his practice the more; when God has *taken away his judgment,* to maintain an interest, is a singular practice.

4. As long as the hypocrite [*lacks*] access to God (vs. 8-10), calls not on God, has no delight in God, Job will not exchange estates with him. Observe: 1. To have access to God in prayer is a happier condition [*than*] all prosperity, and sincerity does much contribute to this; and therefore to be sincere is better than all prosperity. 2. It is a mark and privilege of a sincere person when he has no delight in the world, to delight himself in God. It is a discriminating mark when all things in the world go cross like, to make it up by delighting in God; thus David *encouraged himself in the Lord his God* (1 Sam. 30:6).

5. He insinuates the hypocrite may make a fair break or be afraid at religion, but he sits up. Observe: It is a good token of sincerity, when difficulties, thorter [*opposition*], and cross dispensations, do not mar folks in their communion with God, and in the exercise of piety, and discharge of religious duties, but rather further them.

28

When we spoke of the former chapter, we showed that Job is here clearing himself from an aspersion that might be laid upon him, because he alleged that they were not always wicked men whom God punished, and many wicked might win away without punishment in this life. Some might think he patronized and complied with wicked men; therefore in the former chapter he clears that his doctrine did not loose reins to them, for though God spares them long, yet he always punishes them, some in this life, and others in the life to come. Never one of them escaped God's judgment that continued so.

In this chapter, he answers a second objection. 'Job, does not this stand well with what we say of you, and prove that you are plagued of God for your wickedness?' He answers and removes this objection, telling them that though God did never suffer wicked men to escape his judgment, yet it will not follow that it was so with him, or that he was plagued as such. God's way was so deep that none were to draw conclusions from outward dispensations to conclude men wicked, nor to limit God to rules conceived by them. For clearing of this, he sets out the deepness of God's wisdom, understanding, and holiness, and shows their mistake flowed from their ignorance or mistaking of this. I. And shows what length a man's wisdom will come in natural things (vs. 1-11). II. That for as far as men by their natural wisdom come, yet they never win to search out the infinite wisdom of God in his dispensations and providence (vs. 12-22). III. And he lays down two solid reasons of the former grounds, as conclusions to sum up the debate (vs. 23-28).

I. In natural things, man's wisdom may go far, and that in four things not obvious to sight (vs. 1-2).

1. *Surely there is a vein for silver*, etc. In searching out silver and gold, surely there is a coming forth of silver and gold. By man's art it is brought forth of the mineral. 2. There is also a place where *they fine it*, when it is mixed with dross. 3. Iron that is profitable for men,

is by man's art taken out of the earth. 4. And brass that is fastened among stones, is molten out of them. Whether this be ore of it or not we shall not stand, but by art it is sundered from it.

He goes on (v. 3) to show man's skill in seeking out these things. *He*, that is man (as this verse compared with verse 12-13, and the wisdom of God that is opposed to this, clears) *setteth an end to darkness*, etc. Albeit man cannot find out God's wisdom, yet there are four or five difficulties that he overcomes by his diligence.

1. He sets an end to darkness, or cuts off darkness, whether of making of eyes in the earth, as in coal-hews [*coal pits*], or by carrying in light, by which means there is nothing in the bowels of the earth, which lie buried as in a grave, but man's skill finds it out.

2. Ordinarily waters trouble men in such works, even waters that were not before seen, when men dig deep, do spring up, and are discovered, which were not before trod upon like other rivers (v. 4). Men by their skill dry them up, and take them out of their way.

3. A third difficulty removed by man's skill is (vs. 5-7): the earth is profitable to men, not only for the outside in bearing corn and all manner of grain, but under the earth are brimstone and coals, precious stones, and ore of silver and gold. But the difficulty is (v. 7) how to attain to all [*these*] things, for the way how [*these*] things are gotten is not a high-way, but such an unknown way that the most sharp-sighted bird, or wild beast, never found it out, and yet men by their wisdom, diligence, and art, find it out.

4. The way is set down (v. 9): *He putteth forth his hand upon the rock; he overturneth the mountains by the roots.* These things may be under great crags, and highest mountains and hills, yet man puts forth his hand upon the rock or hill, and by work obtains his end.

5. And (v. 10) there is a new difficulty his heart[1] overcomes. *He cuts out rivers among the rocks*, whether by making way to waters that trouble him, or by bringing out waters by mills, or such engines to further him. *And his eye seeth every precious thing*; he comes by his diligence to see these things that were dark and hid from him before.

Further (v. 11), *He bindeth the floods from overflowing.* Another part of man's skill: he dams up the waters that were like to overflow. He

---

1   The original text had 'heatt,' with no notice in the errata.

makes a dam or fence that (as it is in the original) not a tear or drop drops through.

II. By setting out how far man's wisdom goes, in opposition to it, he argues and sets out the wisdom of God (vs. 12-13). *But where shall wisdom be found? and where shall the understanding* of the holy mysterious and sublime ways of God's dispensations and providence be found? He denies that man can [*understand*] that; *Man knows not the price or place thereof,* as the word may be rendered. 'All my wisdom cannot find out the reasons of God's providence.' And hereby he would check his friends that were so peremptory in giving reasons of it, and thereupon condemning him.

Then (vs. 14-22), he gives particular instances to prove this. Would men dig into the sea, it shall not be found in it. And not only the place where it is, but the worth of it is unknown (vs. 15-19): *It cannot be gotten for gold, neither shall silver be weighed for the price thereof. It cannot be valued with the gold of Ophir, with the precious onyx, or the sapphire. The gold and the crystal cannot equal it: and the exchange of it shall not be for jewels of fine gold. No mention shall be made of coral, or of pearls: for the price of wisdom is above rubies. The Topaz of Ethiopia shall not equal it, neither shall it be valued with pure gold.* Take all the silver, and gold, and precious stones, they cannot be compared to this; for as much worth as the gold of Ophir, which was the most precious gold, and for as precious as [*these*] stones are, they are not to be mentioned, far less equaled when this is spoken of. The most excellent things among men, and these precious stones in most estimation among men, and brought from far, are noways comparable to it.

He renews the question (v. 20). *Whence then cometh wisdom,* where shall it be gotten? *Seeing it is hid from all living* (v. 21); neither can it be found out by men, nor the sharpest sighted among other creatures. And this is enlarged (v. 22): *Destruction and death, say we have heard the same thereof with our ears.* Go to hell itself (for the word is so expounded, 26:6) and to the place of the destruction of all, they will say they heard of it, and its fame. If they could speak out, folks will admire it; but they cannot sound the bottom of it.

III. 1. Having answered negatively where it is not to be found, he answers positively (v. 23), *God understandeth the way thereof, and he knoweth the place thereof,* which is the first reason why it cannot be gotten among the creatures. God has kept it up as his own prerogative. No creature is capable of it. And having before secluded all creatures, it is here to be understood exclusively of them, and that God only knows it. This is enlarged (v. 24): *For he looketh to the ends of the earth, and seeth under the whole heaven.* He, whose understanding is infinite, with one glance of his eye, takes up and sees thorough all things in heaven and earth.

(2) And a second reason why he cannot but understand his dispensations of providence is (v. 25) because the winds and weather that are reasonless creatures, and seem to have their motions at random, he has weighed them as in a balance, how much wind shall blow, and rain shall fall, that not a blast of wind blows, nor a drop of rain falls, but by his knowledge.

(3) A third reason (v. 26): [*these*] are no new things to God. *He made a decree for the rain, and a way for the lightning of the thunder.* Whether for the coming of showers, or the quantity of the rains, or the coming of the thunder where it shall light, and the quantity of it, he has decreed and carved out both, that [there is] not a spark of rain or crack of thunder but by his decree, as if he had hedged it up on every side. He has made a way to it.

He confirms all he has said before (v. 27), *Then did he,* that is, God, *see it,* that is, not only in his wisdom he foresaw it, but as in the words following, he *prepared* and appointed it in his decree; partly to let us see that none can claim this propriety but God, partly to teach us that things most difficult to man, are plain and easy to him.

2. A second reason of the conclusion is (v. 28): *And unto man he said, Behold the fear of the Lord, that is wisdom, and to depart from evil is understanding.* Because God has given man another task, he has given man a practical wisdom how to know and obey him, and not to search out his counsels; to walk according to his revealed will, and not to meddle with his secret will.

And this is comprehended under two words, *The fear of the Lord, that is wisdom, and to depart from evil is understanding.* To fear God and eschew evil, two words under which Job's integrity is held forth (1:1). To be careful to know his will and practice it, and to eschew sin, and the occasions of sin. It is to that purpose (Deut. 29:29); secret things belong to the Lord our God, but things revealed to us, and our children, that we may do all the words of the law. And from all this Job would say, 'had you who are my friends been more taken up with your duty how to fear God and eschew ill, you had not been so ready to mistake me, and to conclude from God's dispensations (which are a mystery to man) that I an hypocrite.'

OBSERVATIONS.

1. He points at this as the cause of their mistake in all this debate between him and them, that they mistook plain practical things, and did pry into God's deeps. Observe: (1) It is one of the great grounds of our mistakes, and the fountain from whence they rise, when we mistake plain practical things, and go to search out God's mind in things not so needful to be known, and not so easily won to. (2) And the remedy of this is on the other side, to be more studious to fear God, and eschew evil.

2. He said to man, *Behold to fear the Lord,* etc. Observe, there is no part of knowledge and understanding so profitable as that which is practical, and consists in the duties of holiness. All other knowledge is worth nought in comparison (Deut. 4:5-6): *I have taught you statutes and judgments, keep therefore and do them, for this is your wisdom and understanding in the sight of the nations which shall hear all these statutes, and say, Surely this great nation is a wise and understanding people.* Wisdom is a precious gift of God. Take it for a truth; they have most wisdom that practice most (Psal. 3:8): *The fear of the Lord is the beginning,* chief part or head *of wisdom, a good understanding have all they that do his commandments.* There never was a wise man in all the world, but in so far as he aimed at this. And it is good to take this rule to try wisdom by, not which folks can talk most or dispute a question about religion, but who are these that fear God, and eschew evil; and look upon that as wisdom, and these as the wise men.

3. Mark the exposition between [*these*] two: the task that God has to guide the world, and the task that man has to fear God and eschew evil. Observe, there are even some things in the way of God's providence and dispensations, that folks are not called to study, or to be anxious about, though they cannot find it out. God has reserved that as his prerogative to know the secrets of providence, and the reasons of deep dispensations; that is not properly darkness, but secrets, the reasons whereof God has thought good to keep to himself. And, on the other hand, when God keeps up some things, it is surest to be practicing the plain things we know, and not to be curious nor anxious in seeking to find out secret and hid things; though there is a difference among us about some things, yet there are many things about which there is no difference, as about prayer, making use of the scripture, holy walking, etc. And when God takes a mysterious and indiscernible way of doing things in his sovereignty, it is surest and safest for us to be taken up about the practice of holy duties, rather than to pry into his depths.

God has taken a sovereign way of proceeding with us, and though we will be loath to cast at anything that is allowed us for duty, in respect of, or in reference to the finding out of God's mind, yet there may be an exceeding on that side in searching out what he has kept secret. We will not condemn the work, but the fruits show there has been too great inclining to that hand. And it were better for us if we were more in the practice of things plain and obvious to all, than so exercised.

29

In the two former chapters we heard that Job continued to vindicate himself from the unjust imputation of his friends. Having done with that, there seems to be some intermission. Job waits to see if any of them will speak, and none of them offering to speak, he takes up his discourse, and clears himself in this, and the next two chapters, setting out his prosperity that once he enjoyed (chp. 29), his adversity in opposition to his prosperity (chp 30), and his integrity (chp. 31). His scope is partly to draw his friends to look upon some other causes of his affliction than his guilt, at least that gross guilt which they imputed to him; partly to show the great change that was befallen him, and therefore no wonder he had some harsh and ill [*chosen*] expressions under it.

In this chapter, besides his wish (v. 2), we have his prosperity in times past set down in four parts. I. In his happy estate between God and himself, as the fountain of all the rest (vs. 3-5a). II. In God's blessing of him with children (v. 5b). III. In external blessings which he enjoyed (v. 6). IV. In his outward grandeur in reference to his public employment (vs. 7-25). There is first his wish, as an introduction to what follows (v. 2). *Oh, that I were as in months past*, setting out the great change that was come, that he was not as he [once was]. In the wish he meets with an objection that he had abused prosperity when he had it. In answer to which, he wishes it again, to tell that he was not ashamed of his carriage under it.

I. 1. The first part of his prosperity is in the happy condition that he enjoyed between God and himself, *as in the days when God preserved me*. [He says] that the great cause of his prosperity was God's watchfulness over him, and preservation of him, and not his own wisdom.

2. The second step hereof is (v. 3): *When his candle shined upon mine head*, i.e. 'When I had God's special direction as a candle; when I was guided by him in the greatest strait I met with; *when by his light I* was helped *to walk through darkness.*' Whether difficulties in respect of

sinful courses, or afflictions, and temptations, by God's light he was guided right between straits.

3. A third step is (v. 4): *As I was in the days of my youth.* 'I would love that condition well which I had when I was a young man.' And what was that condition? *When the secret of God was upon my tabernacle;* that is, 'his secret way of providence hedging me and mine round about among the midst of wicked men.' Or it is God's revealing himself to him, which is ordinarily called a secret or a mystery, as Psal. 25:14, *The secret of the Lord is with them that fear him,* and so the meaning will be this, 'when there was a more intimate fellowship between God and me.'

4. The fourth step or instance which seems to confirm the last exposition is (v. 5): *When the Almighty was yet with me.* 'When God by his care and providence to my outward condition, and by his revealing himself to my soul, was yet with me;' which imports he had now withdrawn himself in respect of his [*Job's*] inward and outward condition.

II. The second part of his prosperity is (v. 5b): *When my children were about me;* 'at that time when my sons and daughters were alive, and not destroyed (which [in] Psal. 144 are set down as a part of man's happiness).

III. The third part is in external blessings of this life (v. 6): *When I washed my steps with butter,* an ordinary expression wherein folks' wealth was expressed. The meaning is, when [he] had abundance of wealth, as if [he] had butter (a commodity that abounded in that land, and in these times) to make any use of he pleased, and such abundance of oil, as if the rock had poured it out in rivers to him. Therefore (Gen. 49:11) it said of Judah he should *wash his garments in wine,* meaning the abundance he should have, that he should make any use of it he liked.

IV. The last part of his prosperity begins [at] verse 7, and in this he insists in four steps, because it was public to the view of others.

1. He sets out how he was looked on when he came to and sat in the place of judgment (vs. 7-12); the gate being the place where the judges sat, and judgment was administrated. The honor and reverence he had there was from all sorts of men.

(1) From the *young men* and children (who afterward in his adversity mocked him, 30:1). *When I went through the street* to the seat of judgment, *the young men saw me, and hid themselves,* 'because I used

to take order with them, and curb their insolencies, and *the aged arose, and stood up,* and gave me reverence (vs. 7-8).

(2) In reference to all degrees and ranks of men. [1] The princes and prime men stood in awe when I came out and began to speak, and were loath to vent their discourse before me (v. 9). [2] The same is expressed of the nobles, a degree or rank inferior to the former, none of these opened their mouth when he spake (v. 10).

(3) It is set out in reference to all sorts of people. *When the ear heard me, then it blessed me* (v. 11); 'there was never any person, who with their ears heard me speak in judgment, but they were so convinced of the equity of my sentence, as they blessed me, and when they saw me afar off, they gave me a testimony of an upright and straight man.'

2. In the next place or step he meets with an objection. 'There are many folks [who] get respect that are not worth much.' To this he answers (vs. 12-17) by way of reason, *Because I delivered the poor that cried,* etc. 'The poor and fatherless that none would help, and have few to befriend them, I helped them. And many a poor body that was *ready to perish,* and the poor widows for many a good turn I did them, gave me their blessing, because I made *the* poor *widow's* heart glad, and *to sing* within her *for joy* (v. 13).

Yea (v. 14), *I put on righteousness, and it clothed me.* 'Great folks use to [*commonly*] seek respect by their outward robes, which they did wear suitable to their place and grandeur, but the best mantle or robe that I thought to be clothed with, was the doing of justice, that none might see a hole in my coat in that respect.' *I put on righteousness, and it clothed me;* or, as it is in the original, *it put on me.* 'I esteemed righteousness above my robe; and righteousness made me have estimation; I counted it the greatest honor that I could think of, and it gained me true honor and respect, and not vain applause.'

I was eyes to the blind, and feet to the lame; 'I gave counsel and direction to poor folks who had a good cause, and [*lacked*] means and moyen [*agency*] to back it, how to carry their cause, and these that had no means I furnished them (v. 15).

I was a father to the poor; 'when they were miskent [*ignored*] in their straits, I took upon me their protection, and suffered them not to [*lack*].' *And the cause which I knew not, I searched out;* 'I spared no pains to seek out the truth of matters that came before me, and whether there was any secret oppression in causes, or any other wrong under-hand dealing, I had my own secret ways of finding it out (v. 16).

Then he tells (v. 17), he was far from respecting persons, or seeking applause of wicked men; *I brake the jaws of the wicked.* 'Though they had been never so proud, I spared them not, but brake them; and though they were like wild beasts, that live on prey and rapine, *I plucked the prey out of their teeth.'*

3. He expresses his happiness in his security (vs. 18-20); not carnal security, but his security in respect of God's favor, and the favor of his people, for he thought he was in a good condition, having ease and peace, not only without but within. *Then I said, I shall die in my nest,* i.e. 'I thought I should get liberty to live quietly, and die so, and all my children about me,' and then expresses the cause of this his confidence (v. 19) in a similitude. 'I was as a tree that has water at the roots, and dew upon the branches.' And another similitude to the same purpose is (v. 20): *My glory,* that is the respect which he had, *was fresh in me;* that is, it was always growing, by some new evidence or fruit in him that procured it, and it was not like that respect that wears piece and piece away. He was like a man that after one bow is broken gets another put in his hand; or his strength, power, and greatness did still increase (v. 20).

4. He returns and sets out the great weight his word had in public matters (vs. 21-25), and what success. *Unto me men gave ear, and waited* to hear speak; *and they keeped silence at my counsel.* 'They desired to hear me speak, and waited till I spake; and when I gave advice, God helped me to be so plain and convincing, that there was none that contradicted it. As v. 22, *After my words they spake not again;* 'they acquiesced in my advice, as if it had been an oracle.' *And my speech dropped upon them;* 'they seemed to be refreshed with my words' (Deut. 32:2). And (v. 23) 'they waited for me as for the rain; the shower was never more longed for, nor refreshing to the earth, when the seed is sown, [*than*] my counsel was to them.'

If I laughed on them they believed it not (v. 24). 'I was so composed and grave, that if I had at any time smiled on them, they thought that in the midst of my laughter I was in earnest, they could not think or believe it that I could sport any at all.' *And the light of my countenance they cast not down;* 'never one thwarted me in anything. *I chose out their way* (v. 25) when any difficulty came; I gave out the orders, and directed what should be done in everything, and they did as I directed them.' *I sat as chief, and dwelt as king in the army.* 'I was head, and there was none to top with me, and I was had in as great reverence as if I had been a king with an army at my back.' A*s one that comforteth the mourners;* 'and I was not only in estimation and respect for fear, but as being able to speak a word to poor folks in affliction. I was of a sympathizing spirit with them, and was refreshing to them, and so esteemed.'

OBSERVATIONS.

1. Job in going to reckon his prosperity, acknowledged God in it as he did in his adversity (26:11) and he begins at this. Observe, they will never bear affliction well who have not learned to bear prosperity well, and acknowledged God in the one as well as the other. The one of them will never be rightly borne, when God has not been sought and served in the other.

2. In verse 5 he looks to God's presence with him aforetime, and to his absence now, and constructs of it according to outward evidences that were sensible to him. Observe, it is a rife [*common*] thing for God's people to count and construct of God's presence and absence by outward evidences and dispensations.

3. The sum of the rest of the chapter following shows (1) what reverence is due to men in place, especially good men. (2) And what is the way to get reverence and respect; there is no such sure and good ground for respect, honor and reverence, as to walk straightly, to be religious and godly in our callings and stations, and righteous towards all men. It has God's approbation, and has true respect among men (1 Sam. 2:30). *They that honor me, I will honor; and they that despise me, shall be lightly esteemed.* Folks may by sinistrous and sinful ways take respect to themselves, and climb to places of preferment, but God will spit on that respect, and tread that honor in the dust that is not founded on piety. To give God his due, is the best way to attain the honor and respect we would acquire.

30

Y ou heard how Job laid out his prosperity in the former chapter; here he lays out his adversity, that by laying the one against the other, his prosperity against his adversity, his adversity may take the deeper impression on these who hear of it.

He speaks last of his respect and reverence which he had in his prosperity, and he lays opposite to that his adversity in six or seven steps, drawing his adversity to so many heads as it were (vs. 1-24); and (vs. 25-31), <u>aggreges his affliction</u> [*shows how much more grave his affliction is*] from the unanswerable meeting he got from others, common to all the steps of it, and from the effects it had on himself.

I. 1. He sets down the reproach he met with, that whereas he was in great respect, now he was in as great reproach and contempt. (1) This he sets forth in respect of the persons [*despising*] him (vs. 1-8), [(2) how they dealt with him, vs. 9-10], and (3) v. 11 is the cause. This is the first step of his adversity.

(1) The persons that [*despised*] him were *young ones*, or young men; these *had him in derision*. He tells [that *these*] young men were not of the best sort, but of the basest sort of the people, such as he describes thus: *Whose fathers I would have disdained to set with the dogs of my flock.* That is, 'who were a kind of beggarly folks, that I would not have <u>concredited</u> [*entrusted*] to keep my flocks with the dogs; not to have given them a dish of meat with the dogs.' This he speaks not in his pride and passion, to cry them down and himself up, but to set out how unworthy wretches they were that mocked him now.

He describes them further (v. 2) as unfit for any use or labor, that if he had never so much ado with folks, he would not employ them; partly because they were so idle, habituated to idleness and <u>beggary</u> [*were beggars*], partly because they were so unqualified that though they were willing they could do him no good. Neither in their youth nor old age, could they ever have done him a good turn, and yet now they run him down.

He sets them out by their misery (v. 3). *For want and famine they were solitary, fleeing into the wilderness.* They were ashamed to live among men, and fled to desolate places, being unable to pay what they were owing.

They cut up mallows by the bushes (v. 4). They were so miserable, that they had no bread to live on, but were put to live on roots, and these not of the best sort, but such as served poor people for food.

A fifth step [dealing with] their misery is (v. 5): *They were driven forth from among men.* These men were so base, that though they would have abided, they were not suffered to reside among men; but they were so [*despised*] by all, that men drove them out and raised the hue and cry after them as after a thief.

And (v. 6) the lodging that was allowed them, was the clefts of the rock and caves of the earth. And (v. 7) when they were driven out, *They brayed among the bushes,* that is, they cried for meat and could get none (as Job 6:5, the wild ox or ass is said to bray when he wants fodder), and all their lodging was a bush of nettles. *They were children of fools,* and *base men;* for their kindred base, and for their qualifications base; *more vile than the earth* — expressions to set out their unworthiness and vileness, and little estimation (v. 8).

(2) He sets out how all [*these*] men dealt with him, which is the scope of all vs. 9-10. *And now I am their song and byward* (as the phrase is used, Psal. 35:15 and 69:12, and Lament. 2:16). He says they made their song of him, as profane, graceless men did of David, and he was their byword. Scarce had they another discourse [*than*] of Job, and they that dared not look him in the face before, *abhorred him,* and could not abide to see him, such a filthy man was he to them. Or, if they came near him, they *spit in his face;* it may hold literally, or it is an expression used to hold out their utmost contempt.

(3) There is the cause of all this (v. 11). *Because He,* that is God, *has loosed my cord,* that is, 'my authority,' and *laid my honor in the dust.* 'While I was in honor and respect, God bridled them, and now in my affliction he has let them loose. But I look to God, who gave me authority, loosing the cord of it again,' as it is said before [in] 12:13, *He looses the bonds of kings,* etc., To tell that authority comes not from folks' place and parts, but from God.

2. The second step of his adversity is the violence he met with (vs. 12-14). *They rise upon my right-hand,* etc. 'They are not satisfied with scorning of me, but they rise up against me. *They push away my feet;* they use means to make me fall; *They raise up against me the ways of*

their destruction; as enemies besieging a town, mount up works against it, that they may get entry.' So they not only cast blocks in his way to make him fall, but used all means to add to his affliction. Therefore he says, *They marred his path, and set forward his calamity. They have no helper.* That is, they are not respected by any, yet they are enough for me, or they need none to help them in this ill turn; a very little thing will do it, and this is set out further (v. 14): *They came in upon me as a wide breaking in of waters.* As waters break in when a vent is made, so do they break in on [him]. *In the desolation they rolled themselves upon me,* or 'they tumbled over on me.' They were ready so soon as ever God took down the hedge to take advantage of [him].

3. The third step of his adversity is in the afflictions that were on his spirit (vs. 15-16). *Terrors are turned upon me.* 'As I have straits without, so I have terrors within; terrible apprehensions of God's anger.' And these terrors pursued his soul as the wind does a light thing, and *my welfare,* that is, 'all my temporal happiness *passes away as a cloud,* that soon vanishes.' A second expression of his inward trouble is (vs. 16): *My soul is poured out upon me.* 'When my soul was in good condition, it was whole; but now it is poured out or melted, or melts upon my hand.'[1] *The days of affliction have taken hold of me,* 'seized upon me, [so] that it has captivated me.'

4. The fourth step or part of his adversity and grief, is the strait that his body was in (vs. 17-18). *My bones are pierced in me in the night season; and my sinews take no rest.* The health of the body consists mainly in two things, that is, in the soundness of the bones and sinews, and neither of these were sound in him. When others were sleeping, he was kept waking through the yerking [*twitching*] of his bones that suffered him not to get rest, and the drawing in of the sinews was a continual pain to him. And an effect of this is (v. 18): *By the great force of my disease is my garment changed.* 'I am grown so loathsome in my body, that that which runs out of my sores makes them change their color, and [causes] folks to think they are another thing [than] clothes' (as the following words clear). *It bindeth me about as the collar of my coat.* 'My garment, or clothes, that should ease or refresh me, are grown so stiff, and barkened [*crusted*] with the matter that runs from my boils and sores, that they are as a band binding me about.'

5. The fifth step is an aggravation of his misery from the apprehension at least of God's dealing with him (v. 19). *He hath cast*

---

1   Durham: As Psal. 42:4, *I pour out my soul in me* — an expression that is used when affliction melts the heart, and faints, and pulls away all inward courage.

me into the mire, and I am become like dust and ashes. As if he said, 'How can it be otherwise with me; God has laid me in a gutter, as it were, and tramped upon me, and made me contemptible, as a man would do with another that he is angry at.' And he sets out God's dealing in several particulars in the words following.

(1) That he speaks and cries to God, and gets no answer, and *though he stand up* (that is, persevere), and be earnest in prayer, *yet he is not regarded,* [any] more than if he were [not] praying at all. [He is] speaking from sense, and somewhat out of passion, for he said before [that] God had heard him.

(2) A second instance is (v. 21): *Thou art become cruel unto me.* To all his outward affliction [God] added this great aggravation, as to seem unmerciful and cruel, an ordinary exercise to the saints when they are under outward affliction, to be also under inward desertion; and as ordinary in such cases to construct hardly of God, so weak are we to bear many troubles together. *With thy strong band thou opposest thyself against me.* 'Thou guides me as a man does his adversary against whom he puts forth all his power.'

(3) Yea, *Thou liftest me up to the wind,* etc. (v. 22). 'Thou handles me as folks use to do things that they would have blown up and down with the wind, and made [me] an object to all beholders, as corn is winnowed.' *Thou causest me to ride upon it* — 'thou hast kept me in this trial.' *And dissolvest my substance* — 'thou hast undone that which made me respected before others.'

4. He aggreges this from the desperation of his condition,[2] *I know that thou wilt bring me to death* (v. 23). 'I know thou wilt not leave off till thou bring me to the grave, the house appointed for all living, for all <u>tryst there</u> [*meet there*].' And he adds a consolation against this (v. 24): *Howbeit he will not stretch out his band to the grave.* That is, 'though God pursue me with trouble to the grave, yet he will not pursue me when I am there.' 'When I am dead, his anger towards me will cease, and I will find no more pain.' *And though they cry in his destruction,* that is, 'though these that [*despise*] me now cry loud when I am destroyed, and it likes them well to see me thus handled, yet it comforts me that then he will cease pursuing me any further.'

II. In the second part of the chapter (vs. 25-31), he aggreges his affliction.

---

2 i.e. He *shows how much more serious* his situation is from the desperation of his condition.

1. From the unanswerable meeting he got from others: *Did not I weep with them who are in trouble?* 'When they were in trouble I sympathized with them; my soul was grieved when any of them was made poor.' The like we have in David (Psal. 35:13), *When they were sick my fasting was sackcloth.* But he got an ill meeting, and so did Job.

2. He aggreges it from this, that it was unexpected. *When I looked for good, evil came unto me.* 'I thought in my prosperity to have died in my nest, but instead of continued prosperity, adversity is come upon me.' He sets [this] out in particulars.

(1) *My bowels boiled, and rested not.* 'My bowels for pain are like a seething pot.' (2) *The days of my affliction prevented me* (as chap. 3:26. *I was not in safety, neither had I rest, nor was quiet, yet trouble came*). 'I could not refrain from crying; I cried in the great congregation.' His trouble was so great, that it put him, a grave man, [*outside*] the bounds of modesty. (3) *I am a brother to dragons, and companion to owls* (v. 29, which explicates the former). 'My company now is such creatures that I affect more than the society of men' (as Psal. 102:6. *Like a pelican in the wilderness, like an owl in the desert*), setting out his abstractedness from society. (4) *My skin is black upon me.* 'My pain has this effect upon me, that it has changed the color of my skin, and no marvel, *for my bones are burnt up with heat.*' (5) *My harp is turned to mourning, and my organ*, etc. '[One]time I had the lawful use of mirth, but now I have nothing but weeping and mourning; I have no other music now.' Thus we see the sad case Job is now in, especially compared with the case he was in.

OBSERVATIONS.

1. Observe from the sum of the chapter, comparing his prosperity in the former, with the change in this chapter, how little outward prosperity is to be trusted in, when it may be in a moment turned to adversity, and a man so respected before is now [*despised*] of all, and mocked by the vilest of men.

2. When we look on Job's cross, we should think little of any cross that can come on us; therefore beware of complaining while we have no cause. Cry not out, 'Was there ever a body handled as I am?' Is there anything you are under to be compared to this? And yet this is a man approved and beloved of God.

3. Let us learn to give God much liberty in his sovereignty, not being anxious nor solicitous in seeking out the reasons of it, but reverence and adore him, giving him his will, in lifting up and casting

down. God aims at this in great part in the dispensations in hand, to learn all flesh to him.

4. Know that folks have much ado to keep good thoughts of God in times of straits. Sense and suggestion will then readily present God as an enemy, and cruel; and when patient Job is thus to express himself, we had need to guard well against such a temptation.

5. Seeing God took this way with Job, and he takes much scouth [*opportunity*] to take temptations part against himself, when his friends held their tongue, whereas before he spoke for God against his friends when they opposed him: Mark when folks fall off from taking God's part against temptation, readily they will take temptation's part against both God and themselves. It is good [for] folks [to] be balanced on both hands to keep them even, and you would guard against extremes.

31

Whenen Job is done with laying down his prosperity and adversity, he goes on to answer his friends challenge (chapter 22), to wit, that it was all <u>well warred</u> [*well-deserved*] that was come on him, for he was a heinous offender. This chapter is a continued vindication of himself from this challenge, and an asserting of his integrity, mixed with vehement asseverations, implying a curse on these that are guilty of these heinous transgressions he purges himself of.

There are ten or twelve sins that he purges himself of in this chapter.

1. From the most secret and unknown degrees of fornication (v. 1), as if he said, 'I was so far from being taken away with that vileness, that neither by the outward eye, nor by the inward affection of the heart that vents itself by the eye, was I carried after it. Yea, I was so abstracted from it, as if *I* had *made a* bargain or *covenant with mine eyes*, not to look a wrong look that way;' a thing that folks think not much of (Matt. 5:28). Christ makes it a degree of adultery.

He gives these three reasons of his abstinence from, and abhorrence of this sin. The first is (v. 2): *For what portion of God is there from above?* etc. He would not lose the portion he expects from God, for any pleasure that sin could promise him, for if folks live in that sin, they can expect no portion from heaven. A second reason is (v. 3): *Is not destruction to the wicked?* These that follow that sin can expect nothing but strange punishment and wrath. A third reason is (v. 4): *Doth he not see my ways, and count all my steps?* 'I know it was not men I had to deal with, but with God, who counts all my steps; and I looked on God as having an all-seeing eye on my secret thoughts and looks;' a notable precedent to follow, and a rule to try ourselves by, when others can espy nothing reproof worthy in us.

2. The second sin he purges himself of is defrauding or deceit, in two particulars or steps.

(1) The first is (v. 6): *If I have walked with vanity, or if my foot hath hasted to deceit; let me be weighed in an even balance, that God may know mine integrity.* 'If I have taken any vain or unapproved way to get gain, that will not bide the trial; or any deceitful way to make up myself, I am content to abide God's trial of the sincerity of my proceeding, and that I have approved myself of no degree of this sin' (as David, Psal. 129: *Search me*, etc.).

(2) A second step is (vs. 7-8): *If my step hath turned out of the way, and mine heart walked after mine eyes, and if any blot hath cleaved to my hands: Then let me sow, and let another eat; yea, let my offspring be rooted out.* 'If I have stepped out of the right way to compass anything, and if looking on anything that was not mine own' (as Achan did) 'I have coveted it, and if aught has stuck to my fingers of that which did not belong to me, and so I have left a blot on my conscience that way, I wish it may never do me good, that both my estate and children may be blasted of God in his anger.' Folks' fingering of things, in an unlawful way, oftimes makes their estate vanish, and they know not how.

3. The third sin he purges himself of is adultery with a married woman, in opposition to a maid (that he mentioned [in] v. 1). And to show his freedom from this sin, he uses an imprecation that he may be so met with himself (vs. 9-10). *If mine heart have been deceived by a woman, or if I have laid wait at my neighbor's door: Then let my wife grind to another, and let others bow down upon her.* He gives two reasons of this.

(1) It is a heinous crime worthy to be punished by the judge. The laws of man should take order with such a sin, and the moral law of God taught that such a sin deserved death (Deut. 22:22), not only in the woman, as some would have it only, but also in the man.

(2) A second reason is (v. 12): *For it is a fire that consumeth to destruction, and would root out all mine increase.* Though this sin should escape the punishment of men, yet it is a destruction to a man's estate, and to his soul, as a fire kindled that consumes both; and who knows but this sin may be destroying men's souls and estates, and they not know of it?

4. The fourth sin is austerity and rigorousness in his family (v. 13). 'I am not an oppressor of others, as you call me; yea, I am so far from being accessory to that sin, that I despised not the contest of my servant, whether it was justly or unjustly wakened.'

He gives two reasons of this. (1) The first is (v. 14) because he knew he was not so great or highly lifted up above his servant as God was above him. Therefore the awe of God swayed him in that. (2) A second reason is (v. 15) from the sibness [*similarity*] and likeness that was between him and his servant. They were both alike fashioned in the womb of one matter, and one workmanship, made by one workman, as it were, that is God, who made them both.

5. The fifth sin he purges himself of is oppression, and [*lack*] of charity, which he instances in several particulars.

(1) That he was far from having and letting the poor [*lack*], that the poor widow never looked for charity from him in vain (v. 16). (2) That he never sat down to his dinner, but he was ready to give the fatherless a share of it (v. 17). He enlarges this (v. 18) and tells that since ever he had a house, the poor were brought up with him, and that he gave the widow direction and counsel since he was capable to do it. (3) He instances in the matter of clothing (v. 19). 'I not only bestowed meat upon the poor, but spared no cost to clothe them, and by putting clothes on them, and warming of their loins, I provoked them to bless me. Yea, the wool of my sheep can bear witness for me; this is true which I assert' (v. 20). And by comparing this with the beginning of the former chapter, he says there were some that he would not set with the dogs of his flock, it was clear that he was a wise man in the distribution of his charity; that it was not to idle vagabonds, but to fit objects of charity that he was liberal.

6. The sixth sin is his taking advantage of weak ones (v. 21). *If I have lift up my hand against the fatherless.* 'When I saw an advantage to be had of weak or fatherless, and saw none to control me among men, but upon the contrary might have gotten a scug [*cloak; cover*] of law for my practice, though I had taken advantage; if I have done so then (v. 22) *Let mine arm fall from my shoulder-blade.* I wish that neither my hands nor arms may do myself any good.'

He gives a reason of this (v. 23), because though he might have been borne through before men by a scug [*pretense; cover*] of law, yet he could not bear out before God; and he adds two words that scared him. (1) *Destruction from God was a terror to me* — was more terrible to him than an army of men. (2) And God's highness calling him to a reckoning had influence on him. He adds [*these*] reasons to show, that it was neither his natural temper so inclining him, nor applause of men, nor baseness of spirit, that made him forbear such things, but the awe of God, which was the principle of his acting and forbearing.

7. A seventh sin is excessive covetousness in laying too much weight on wealth. There are two sorts of covetousness. (1) In gaining wealth which he spoke of before (vs. 5-7). (2) A second sort is a resting on wealth, which here he purges himself of. As he was not covetous to get it, so he tells he never thought his state the surer of it, more than if there had not been a penny in his purse (v. 24). And a second degree of this (v. 25) is he did not rejoice, nor delight in wealth. It never got his heart.

8. An eighth sin he purges himself of is (v. 26) giving religious worship (and it is false worship and idolatry), or signs of religious worship, to the sun and moon, which is thought to be the first idolatry that folks were carried away with. *If I have looked to the sun, or moon, when they shined,* and given them any respect or reverence due to God, *and my heart hath been secretly enticed* — that is, 'if by their brightness I have been stolen off my feet to give them God's room in my heart.' Or *my mouth hath kissed my hand* — 'if I have given them any sign of divine honor, or outward reverence, more than was due to creatures.'

He gives two reasons why he would not do this. (1) Because it is a heinous sin; for as little as folks think of false worship or idolatry; yea, *an iniquity to be punished by the judge.* Job was not of their religion that plead for toleration. He knew that God's law gave warrant to them then (and it gives also warrant to us now) to punish idolaters, and the judge ought to do it. (2) A second reason is, because he should then *have denied the God that was above.* If he had put a creature in God's room and God out of his room and place, he should have denied God (v. 28).

9. A ninth sin he purges himself of, is bitterness and revenge. *If I rejoiced at the destruction of him that hated me,* etc. As if he said, 'I never did it. Not only did I not revenge myself, but I never rejoiced when the Lord took vengeance on him another way.' And *when his evil,* that is, his iniquity; *found him out,* 'I said not in my heart, such a man did me wrong, and it is well warred [earned] that is come on him, that he has met with a miresnipe[1] (v. 29). Neither dared I suffer my mouth (v. 30) to utter an imprecation upon him' (and, O! that such considered this, who upon any petty injury will belch out curses upon their neighbors). He sets out his not being given over to revenge by a provocation to which he had at home (v. 31) when *the men of his tabernacle* provoked him to revenge, he was restrained. The

---

1   *Miresnipt* — To fall in the mire; an accident or mishap.

like we have in David, when Shimei railed upon him, and reviled him.

10. The tenth sin he purges himself of is want of hospitality (v. 32). *The stranger did not lodge in the street; but I opened my doors to the traveler.* As he gave folks meat and clothing that needed, so he gave lodging to them that wanted it; for they had not common inns at that time for lodging as we now have.

11. The eleventh sin he clears himself of is (v. 33): *If I covered my transgressions as Adam; by hiding mine iniquity in my bosom.* He covered not his sin as Adam; he never took the course that Adam took, and all men ordinarily take, to cover or extenuate their sin. But he ran away to God, and confessed it; whereby it is evident Job took with sin,[2] though he maintained his sincerity against his friends, who would have him granting he was a hypocrite.

12. The twelfth sin he purges himself of is faintness and cowardliness in his duty (v. 34). *Did I fear a great multitude* — when he was called to suppress and bear down evil doers, to break the jaws of the wicked (as chapter 29:17), he went on in his duty, and stood in awe of no hazard.

He adds an attestation to confirm all that he has said (v. 35). 'I am so clear of these things, that I am content to appear before God's throne, and if my adversary or pursuer, would write a book of the legend of my life, heinous transgressions; yea' (v. 36), '*I would take such a book on my shoulder, and bind it to me as my crown* and glory. And' (v. 37) 'if any would call me to a reckoning, I would not decline him, but I would be content not only to lay out my way in the general to him, but tell over all the particular steps of it. Yea, *as a prince,* with a deal of confidence, *would I* go near unto him.' Job here has much sincerity within, and much provocation without; yet he speaks with too much confidence and grossness of his sincerity, and therefore is found fault with hereafter by Elihu and God.

13. The last vindication (vs. 38-39) is that neither his land, nor the masters or tenants upon it, cried against him. He used no sinful shift to get, and he never put men out of their possessions, nor made men labor for nought. And [he] closes with an imprecation that, if it was so, or otherwise than he asserts, *Instead of good grain, let cockle grow upon it,* and such other noisome weeds (v. 40).

---

2 *Job took with sin* — i.e. Job didn't think lightly of his sin; acknowledged or knew his sin.

The words between Job and his friends are ended, in respect of any more dispute or debate.

USES.

1. Behold a live pattern of a holy man who gets God's approbation, and it was not for nought that God gave it him. Labor to imitate him.

2. Search and see if you are so free of these and the like sins as he was; if as a prince you could go before God, having the testimony of sincerity as he had. It is the most princely thing to go before God with a good conscience.

3. Be painful in the exercise of holiness. Job was under a covenant of grace, and so are you, and yet how exact is he in his walking. Censure yourselves for being so far behind so holy a pattern; think shame when you read, or hear these things read or spoken of such a holy man that has been so watchful in prosperity, and we take such liberty.

4. Folks that would be holy without, must be also holy within; yea, holiness must begin there, and these that pretend to heart holiness must also prove it by their outward fruits of holiness, and in all things be watchful and circumspect. And the reason why Job got to such a measure of holiness, [is] he watched over little things, even his very thoughts, and suffered not the least temptation to have access. For let in one temptation, more will follow it. Think on [*these*] things and the asseverations Job puts to them, and if God should call you to a reckoning (and he will call to a reckoning), what you would have to answer for yourselves. And if the sins of thoughts, looks and words, bring on destruction, what will deeds do? Fear and tremble to look upon it. It is no easy thing to fall in the hands of an angry God. If wrath, and the curse come (as it will come, if use be not made of Christ for holiness and pardon of sin), fearful will be your portion who shall be found out of him in that day.

32

You heard long debated through many chapters this controversy between Job and his friends. Now from this chapter to the last, the controversy draws to a decision. First by Elihu's stepping in (chapter 32-38). And secondly, by the Lord's taking it off his hand in the rest (chapter 39-42).

This chapter contains a preface which Elihu has to the following discourse. When he has waited on long, he comes on as one hearing both parties' reasons, and displeased with both, tells his judgment of both.

He sets down first that which gave him occasion to speak (vs. 1-5), and second (vs. 6-22) his preface, aiming at three things. 1. He removes an objection or impediment that hindered him to speak. 2. Sets down the motives that made him overcome that objection. 3. He [*proposes*] the way he will proceed.

I. That which gave him occasion to speak (v. 1): *These three men. Job's friends ceased to speak.* There was no answer among them; they held their peace. And the reason is, *Because Job was righteous in his own eyes.* They thought Job rooted in the conceit of his own righteousness, that they were desperate, and had lost hope to convince him, and therefore they quate [*quit*] him. It is often a fault in men, when they cannot prevail in a matter they undertake at first, to give it over, as if the fault were in these they have to do with, when it is in themselves.

2. *Elihu his anger is kindled* (v. 2). Anger is like a fire within him, and kindles or wakens up. It is not carnal passion, but holy zeal, like that commanded [in] Ephes. 4:28. *Be angry, but sin not.* The objects of his anger are Job and his friends, and the reason why he is angry at both are set down.

(1) The reason why he is angry at Job is *because he justified himself more than God.* That is, because he was more careful to justify himself, than he was careful to keep himself from reflecting on God in his

discourse and dispute. It is likely Job being so sorely assaulted to grant that he was an hypocrite, he had set so to guard against the taking with that, that he guarded not equally against the other extreme of reflecting on God; and for this God charges him in the end of chapter 38 and beginning of chapter 40.

(2) The reason why he is angry at his friends (v. 3) is because they had condemned Job for a hypocrite, and had not made that out by sufficient answers and reasons, and yet they stood by their point, and alleged that Job was obstinate, and they in the right, when they had no reason for it (a fault that is incident to men in debates).

(3) A third occasion is (vs. 4-5): Elihu having waited long because Job and his friends are elder [*than*] he, to see if they would quit the end of the string that they held, or take another [*way*] to convince Job, and none of them speaking a word, after long waiting on he steps in and speaks.

II. His discourse begins in v. 6. And because it may be objected, 'Elihu, will you who are a young man, undertake that which grave and godly men cannot do?' he answers, and yields to that, that *he was young and they aged*, and that this swayed him for a long time to be silent (vs. 6-7). For *I said, days should speak, and multitude of years should teach wisdom.* 'I thought, and I know it is a common maxim, that it is incumbent to aged men to speak before young men, and it is supposed they should be wise and able to clear doubtsome cases.' This by way of concession; but (vs. 8-9) he says, wisdom is God's gift, and old men may have lived many years and know little, and young men gifted of God may know much. It is not years, but God's spirit that makes either old or young wise in his matters. Therefore he concludes, *Great men are not always wise, neither do the aged understand judgment.* Though they are great men and wise men, if they are left of God in a particular, they may miscarry, and not get to the uptaking of God's mind. And on this ground he proceeds to speak.

He gives two reasons of his undertaking. The first reason (vs. 10-11) is: *Therefore*, that is, because it is God's spirit that teaches men wisdom; *I said, hearken to me*, and hear me, and the same is repeated (v. 11). 'I have been long a stander by, and have waited on, and heard what both you and Job have said.' The doubling of the words import that he had weighed and considered what both had said, and understood it. Oftimes bystanders understand the play better than the gamesters do.

And a second reason is (v. 12): *There was none of you that convincingly* or pertinently *answered Job.* 'Therefore I will essay to do it; for though you have spoken much, it is not to purpose.

And (v. 13) he gives a reason why they had spoken so long, and had not convinced Job. God would befool them, and put them from the conceit of their wisdom, and let them see that it was he that put down Job, and not they. So to humble them, God would not have them to convince him. As if he said, 'you think you have convinced Job, and you have done nothing. Any other man may do more than you have done to purpose.' And this is a third reason why he will speak.

A fourth reason (v. 14) is: why? He was in a greater capacity to deal with Job than they were. Job and he were not engaged, [neither] of them had reflected on [one] another; therefore he will take on him to answer. And he will not take their thesis, nor their manner of speaking, to reflect bitterly on them as they did, for that was not the way to gain him.

A fifth reason (v. 15) is: *They,* that is Job's friends, *were amazed,* confounded in themselves, and had no more to say; therefore 'wonder not that I speak.' A proof of this reason (v. 16) is: 'I waited long, and they spoke nothing to purpose.' Therefore (v. 17): *I said, I will answer also my part, I will shew my opinion.*

And he adds the last reason (v. 18) of his undertaking, partly zeal for God, seeing a good cause ill handled, and partly indignation at Job's friends, seeing them do nothing to it; partly love to reclaim Job, and partly finding the impulse of the Spirit within him helping him. This made him hopeful to do more good than they had done. Therefore he says (v. 19): *Behold, my belly is as wine which hath no vent, it is ready to burst as new bottles.* He is like a vessel filled with wine, that will burst if it [is not vented]. For which cause (v. 20) he will speak, because he has no other way to be eased, but to pour out his mind, and tell what is right and what is wrong in this matter that they have been debating.

In the last two verses, he tells in what manner he will proceed. He will shun two faults. 1. He will not be swayed to judge of the cause by any person concerned in it; a fault wherewith Job charged his friends (13:8). 2. He will not give flattering titles to men; he will be loath to hide what he finds wrong either in Job or his friends. And he gives two reasons of this (v. 22). (1) *I know not to give flattering titles;* 'as I love, so I will use plain dealing.' (2) 'If I *should do* otherwise, I should not be approved of God. Therefore lest *God's judgment take me away,* I must do it.'

This being our entry upon the third part of the book, it is necessary we consider: 1. What Elihu was — an eloquent and gracious man though young. 2. That for the matter of his discourse, it is to be approved beyond Job's and his friends. He was in the right way, which we clear by three reasons. (1) Because when God quarrels Job and his friends he is not spoken to. (2) Because God begins on the same score that Elihu left off at. (3) Because Job never missed an answer to his friends, but he is stricken silent with what Elihu says, and acquiesces.

Wherein differs he from Job's friends and from Job? 1. He differs from Job's friends in these: (1) Though he debates against Job, yet not on the same ground. For he does not say, 'You are afflicted, therefore you are wicked.' (2) Though he censures Job as going wrong sometimes, yet from these faults he never condemns Job for a hypocrite. (3) He differs from them in the manner of his proceeding. They proceed more passionately and carnally, he more meekly and spiritually, mixing in friendly words to mitigate what he spoke to Job.

2. He charges Job with three faults. (1) That he was not in his practice suitable to what he said of God's sovereignty in words, but did exceed in retrenching and limiting God. (2) That though he allowed him to justify himself as being no hypocrite, yet that he went too far on in justifying himself, reflecting on God, for he had said, 'Wherefore contends thou with me?' He kept not the right bounds, as if God had no ground of controversy, or might not have had a controversy with him. (3) That he had unsuitable and passionate expressions in his dispute, even when he was defending that which was right for the matter.

3. Yet in all this Elihu fails, and had his own faults, especially these two. (1) In drawing consequences from Job's words separate from his meaning. (2) That though he is more kindly to Job, and strikes not at the root of his interest in God, yet he was exceeding sharp, although he was straight in respect of the matter, [and] he gains more ground on Job, and is more countenanced of God, than the rest of Job's friends.

OBSERVATIONS.

1. Observe a fault insinuated to be in gracious folks (v. 2). That they are too soon ready to conclude harshly of men, and to count them desperate that come not up their length in a dispute, when the fault may be laid elsewhere on themselves, rather than on these they so judge of.

2. Another fault in debate that folks would beware of, and that is to condemn folks that are not of our mind, beyond any reason or solid ground we have brought or can bring.

3. A third fault in dispute, which Elihu professes he will shun, and that is the accepting of persons. Observe that oftimes folks judge of causes and cases by persons engaged in them, and this is a thing [that] may stumble and wrong many.

4. The right way of proceeding, when we would have folks bettered by what we are to speak, is not to follow a carnal reflecting manner of speaking, but an edifying and calm way. And if folks would follow this way, they would through God's blessing come more speed, and gain more ground of any they would convince, than ordinarily they do.

5. Oftimes when folks are sore engaged in a debate, they are not so impartial as they should [be]. Therefore Elihu lays down his not being engaged[1] as a great furtherance to him in what he was to say.

6. On the general ground he goes on, and occasions of his speaking, lest they should think themselves wise in their own eyes, observe that God will sometimes darken men that probably should know more than others, that it may be seen that neither age, nor parts, nor grace will do the turn for bringing out his mind; and that all may be convinced there is need of a humble dependence on God for the revelation of his will. Neither parts, nor greatness of parts and gifts will do the turn; therefore God will have men of gifts and parts humble, and whatever measure of understanding they come to, not leaning to it, but to him.

---

1 i.e. He was not caught up in the debate; he had not 'joined the fray' on either side.

33

We heard of Elihu's large preface in the former chapter. In this he comes more particularly to the faults he did find in Job's discourse, and he has: I. A preface (vs. 1-7), wherein he makes way to have what he was to say well taken off his hand by Job. II. He tells what he found fault with (vs. 8-11). [III.] And draws his conclusion (v. 12), [and gives] the grounds of his confutation (vs. 13-30), [and] closes his first speech (vs. 31-33).

I. He turns from Job's friends to speak to Job himself, intending to speak what he conceived Job had need of, and knowing there might be prejudice taken at him, he being a young man, he gives two or three reasons of his freedom.

1. His sincerity, that it was not passion, nor any by-end that moved him to speak, but that what he was to say should be out of the uprightness of his heart; that he minded to be both free and tender.

2. A second reason: 'that which I am to speak shall be so clear, that it shall not abide much dispute, and when you have heard it, you will not think your attention ill bestowed (vs. 1-3).

3. A third reason is (v. 4): 'Hearken to what I am going to say; for I am a man, and but a man as one of yourselves.' The first half of the verse shows how his body was formed by the power of God, and the next half shows how his soul was, and how the souls of all men are formed, by God's breathing in their nostrils the breath of life.

He amplifies this reason from two grounds. (1) That seeing he was but a man, he would draw up his words in order, and come to the field like a soldier if he had aught to say. The word is borrowed from a ranking of men (v. 5). (2) The second ground is (vs. 6-7), as if he said, 'Job you wished (9:33; 23:3) to have God to plead with, that he might lay aside his terror, and you would reason your cause with him. Now these two conditions you sought of God are here. I am a man as you are, and my terror will not make you afraid. I cannot break you with judgment, as you complain God has done; therefore come forth and debate the matter if you can.'

II. He lays down that which he minded mainly to refute in general (v. 8). 'I am not to tell you what others have told me of you, not to tell over the passages of your life; but what you have spoken in my hearing.'

2. He sets down what he observed Job [to] speak, and three particulars he pitches on. (1) 'You said (v. 9), *I am clean without transgression.* You have spoken as if there had been no guilt in you, and as if God had afflicted you without cause;' which he gathered from Job's words, (23:11-12; 9:22; 16:17), wherein Job asserted his integrity against his friends; but Elihu thinks he kept no measure.

(2) A second fault is (v. 10): *behold he finds occasions against me, he counts me for his enemy.* 'Job you quarrel with God, as if God had been picking a quarrel against you, when there was no just reason or cause.' And this he gathered from his words (9:23, 32, 34; 16:12-14; 14:17-18), when he seemed to say God had gone back far to seek a quarrel against him.

(3) A third fault is (v. 11) that he had complained God had used him roughly, and taken an uncouth way with him, and they are Job's words (13:27; 14:16).

III. He confutes Job as wrong two ways (vs. 12-30). 1. In justifying himself so far. 2. In quarreling with God. First he passes sentence in the general (v. 12): *Behold in this thou are not just!* 'I will not pass sentence upon you in respect of your state or interest in God; but in this you have failed.' And he gives a reason of it: *God is greater than man.* 'You think to limit God within your narrow conception; but God is greater than man' (that is, God is boundless and incomprehensible, both in himself, and in respect of our uptaking the grounds of his proceeding), 'and therefore you must not condemn him, though you cannot take them up.' Or it has this force: 'Though you, nor any man can see the reasons of God's dealing with you, yet God sees further, and knows well why he has dealt so with you.' 1 John 3:20. *If our heart condemns us, God is greater than our heart.* 2 Cor. 4:4. *I know nothing by myself, yet am I not hereby justified.* 'I cannot say that I am righteous for all that before God.'

2. A second reason (v. 13) is set down by way of expostulation, 'What a folly is it for you to enter in <u>the lists</u> [*combat*] with God? *Does he give an account of any of his matters?* And is it, in a word, befitting you to come in and call God to a reckoning?'

3. A third ground or reason (v. 14) is: 'Though you know not the reasons of God's proceeding, do not blame him for that; for there are many things to teach God's mind to man, but the fault is in man that takes him not up, and not in God.' For *God speaks once; yea twice, yet man perceiveth it not*; through his ignorance and dullness he takes not up God's mind. This ground he follows out largely to v. 29, where it is summed up, and which is the conclusion of all between this and that, as if he said, 'Though you know not what God is doing in afflicting man, yet he knows, and his end is to do men much good, to keep them from sin and their own ruin.' To make out this he lays down several grounds.

(1) The first is taken from God's secret way of revealing himself to men in dreams and night visions (v. 15), as if he said, 'Whether God speaks by dreams or visions, by rods or mediate messengers, God is teaching men the use and end of his dealing, and he is often teaching men when they are sleeping.' It is likely he has respect to the time before the law was written, when God spoke to men by visions and dreams, as he did to Abimelech and others. *He opens their ear, and sealeth their instruction* (v. 16). They, who when they were waking would not take this lesson, he tells them in the ear in their sleep, and he seals it up, or puts a mark upon it, that when they waken they know it is he that has appeared to them, and has been teaching them. Verses 17 and 18 may be read either with that which goes before, or with that which follows them, for it is the end of both, as if he said: 'God's end in this way of chastening and speaking in apparitions to men, is to *withdraw them from their purpose*.' In the original it is to keep or withdraw man from his work, for it is man's work to work wickedness according to his ability.

(2) *To hide pride from man*. To hide a thing is to make it as if it were not; so to hide pride from man is to make him humble, by removing that which he was given to be proud of. And when man is proud of riches, God takes them away, and leaves him nothing to be proud of.

(3) A third end, *He keeps back his soul from the pit*. By this means he keeps man from destruction, which he would have run to if he had [*lacked*] this bridle of affliction to restrain him

He sets out and describes sickness (vs. 19-23), as one of the ordinary afflictions whereby God humbles man, for it is not easy to hide pride from man, and keep him from the pit. Therefore when the word does not the turn (which he has spoken of before), he sends rods, and particularly the rod of sickness (v. 19) and *chastens him with pain on his bed.* Yea, sends pain in *his bones,* wherein his strength lies. And this pain torments him, that what he affected before he cannot bide to see it (v. 20). His appetite is marred, and he cannot bide *dainty meat,* and such curiosities as he was up taken with in health.

His flesh is consumed, or *melts away* (v. 21) and he is like one anatomized, and his bones are seen through his skin.

The third effect (v. 22) is he is brought so low, that he is like a man half dead ready to be carried to his grave, and to *the destroyers,* that is, to the worms, the commend[1] end and destruction of all men. They are called destroyers, as these that feed on men when they are in the grave.

He shows the use of and means by which God brings about the benefits of affliction to men (vs. 23-24). *If there be a messenger with him,* etc. As if he said, 'It is not sickness alone that benefits men, but when God blesses the word in the mouth of a sent minister (*an interpreter one of a thousand,* because every one is not meet to speak to men in that condition) in telling him the way to win to peace with God, and to be accepted through Christ's righteousness, which is *his uprightness,* which is the great scope that all God's messengers should have before them, when God thus trysts with sickness, and his sent minister together, and adds his blessing then (v. 24). God follows the quarrel no more, but is *gracious* to the afflicted person, and says, *Deliver him from going down to the pit.* Either it is a word warranting God's messenger to speak comfort and a comfortable [*outcome*], or it is God's intimating a word of his own to the soul of the afflicted man, as David says, *Say to my soul, I am thy salvation.*

And the ground upon which this is, *I have found a ransom,* 'I am satisfied.' A second benefit is (v. 25) the man that before was like to die [is] restored. It is like to temporary and bodily health as in these times, but if that missed, eternal life was made sure. A third benefit (v. 26): *He shall pray,* and God will hear him which he did before. And a fourth benefit: *He shall see his face with joy.* He shall get communion with God in prayer. Not only shall God take his prayer off his hand, but he shall intimate so much to him, and smile on him, and make him look heartsomely to God again as his father. And he gives a reason of this; for he will render unto man his righteousness. When

---

1   Meaning may be, 'the approved' or 'the appointed end.' Or it may be a typographical error and should read 'common end.'

man takes this way of seeking to God, he will keep his promise to him, and not deal hardly with him. A confirmation of this is [in] v. 27. God is the most easy to be entreated, and soonest made friends with of any, for *he looketh,* or has an eye *upon men, and if any say; I have sinned,* if any will reflect on their way, and take with their guilt, and acknowledge they have gone wrong, and would fain be home at God, God is ready to deliver, whether from temporal or eternal, but mainly from eternal death and destruction (v. 28). And in due time he makes this known unto them.

Then in verses 29-30, we have the sum of the argument: *Lo, all these things God worketh oftentimes with man, to bring back his soul from the pit.* Whether God teaches, or corrects, or shows mercy (as he takes all these ways with men, some of them with one, some with another, and all of them with some), it is to keep man from eternal destruction. This is the sum of Elihu's reasons whereby he would confute Job, and would say this much, that if he knew the good that God was doing to him by affliction, he would be silent in submission.

4. He has an exhortation to Job, to mark this well and hearken to him, and it is backed with reasons (vs. 31-33). (1) The first reason is, 'Look if this is not true that I have said to you, and so speak the contrary if you can.' (2) The second reason is from his respect to him and freedom with him: He was not set to condemn him as an unregenerate man; nay, he was set to justify him. (3) If this that he has said is clear, that he has nothing to say against it, he bids Job hear him out, for he has more to say yet.

OBSERVATIONS.

1. See what should be man's carriage in reference to God's sovereignty. It is good to walk with God as greater than man, as one that is incomprehensible in the reasons of his dispensations. This puts a bridle on man's corruptions, that are ready to fall out under an hard trial or exercise.

2. One of the great things God aims at in all his dispensations, is to do the persons of men good, *to hide pride from them,* to humble them, to keep them from sin and destruction. And we may by this know when God's dispensations are for our good, when they prevent the occasions of sin, or take away occasions of sin, or humble, and draw unto God.

3. He knits chastening and the messenger together, and counts it a great mercy when affliction and the word of the gospel are joined,

and so it is. It might have been said, affliction is common, therefore he subjoins to the rod, the messenger, and makes it a good token that the rod is to do some good when the messenger is beside to speak a word. When God afflicts, and gives a word, count it a mercy (Psal. 94:12). *Blessed is the man whom thou chastenst, and teachest out of thy law.* And know that our reckoning will be the greater, and we the more inexcusable, when both the rod and word are joined, if use be not made of it.

34

We heard how Elihu began to take the dispute off the hands of Job's friends, and [to] set himself to convince Job. It is likely there has been some intermission between this and the former discourse. Job has kept silence as being more convinced, or he has been meekened by Elihu's mild matter and manner of procedure, and is desirous to hear more.

In this chapter we have: I. A preface (vs. 1-4). II. The matter he has to refute in Job (vs. 5-6). III. His confutation (vs. 6-33). IV. The close of his discourse in the last four verses (vs. 34-37).

I. *Elihu answered and said.* The preface follows, and it is to stir up Job and his friends to attention, and grave and understanding men with them, to consider and judge of what he has to say. *Hear me ye wise men.* 'I deal with wise men, and men of understanding, and I shall deal prudently with you; therefore give ear to me.' He backs this with two reasons (v. 3). 1. 'I shall offer the matter I bring forth to be judged and tried, for it is with the ear in trying words, as with the mouth and palate in discerning meat. 2. A second reason is (v. 4): *Let us choose to us judgment.* 'We shall not be rash in passing sentence, but see who has the most solid reasons for them, and accordingly judge.' *And let us know among ourselves what is good* — 'Let us know by mutual reasoning together who has the best side.'

II. In the fifth and sixth verses, he draws the matter which he has to refute to two heads. 1. *Job hath said, I am righteous.* He has spoken too much for justifying himself (as chapters 13, 18, 19, 27:6), where Elihu thinks [*Job*] has spoken well and largely in vindicating himself, and pleading his own innocency. 2. He charges him for reflecting on God, as if Job had said, *God had taken away his judgment.* That is (as Elihu expounds), God had dealt more rigorously with him than there was reason or just cause. Job had indeed spoken these words (27:2), but his meaning is that God had not as yet vindicated him, but left him as a condemned man under his friends' censure. The charge is amplified (v. 6): Job has said, *should I lye against my right.* Job has said he cannot say he is guilty, except he sin, and that *his wound is incurable without transgression*, which Job said not in words, yet (chp. 27) when we compare the second and fourth verses, we will find his words to come near [*these*] words, though his meaning is different from that which Elihu would put upon them.

III. He goes on to confute Job in three or four steps. 1. The first step or way of his confutation (vs. 7-9) holds forth the absurdity of Job's assertion, wondering how such a man could speak so, in three steps.

(1) The first is (v. 7): *What man is like Job, who drinketh up scorning like water?* 'Was there any wise, gracious, conscientious man, ever spoke as he has spoken' (for in the next verse he speaks of wicked men, and makes Job a pleader for them), striving to make Job's assertion detestable, and proposing it as a thing to be abhorred.

(2) Comparing Job to wicked men in this (v. 8): *Which goeth in company with the workers of iniquity*; [for] maintaining a tenet which they do maintain — he pleads for them (Mal. 3:14). They say there is no profit by serving God, and Job says the same in substance, and so walks in one way with them.

(3) He shows the absurdity of Job's expression, by drawing consequences from it (v. 9). 'He has said it profits a man nothing that he should delight himself in God; for it is all one,' would he say, as if [*Job*] had said it. For if God takes no notice of man's righteousness, it will do a man no good though he be righteous.

2. Having teisseled [*tied*] up the absurdity of Job's opinion, he confutes it more particularly in a second way, speaking to Job's friends by three arguments (vs. 10-15). (1) '*Hearken to me, ye men of understanding*, and see if you will bind this on God, *that he should do wickedly*' (v. 10). So, he confutes Job's assertion (as he took it up), from the nature of God, who is of pure eyes, and cannot behold iniquity. It were abominable to think otherwise of God, and so he rejects the consequence with abhorrence.

(2) A second argument is from God's work and way of proceeding (v. 11). *The work of man shall he render unto him.* He proceeds with men according to the rule of righteousness, and therefore will not do unjustly himself.

(3) A third argument (v. 12) is taken from God's will: *Yea, surely God will not do wickedly*, though in his sovereignty he might do what might seem iniquity, being above all law, yet he will not do it. It is

inconsistent with his holy nature; he that is supreme, his will is our rule, but he will not do iniquity. This he confirms by two assertions, which might be new arguments. (1) If God would do wrong who could control him (v. 13)? *Who hath given him a charge over the earth?* Insinuating God's absoluteness and sovereignty, and this is followed forth in one expression or two (vs. 14-15). (2) If God pleased to draw in man's breath, or his power whereby he maintains man, or keeps in man's breath, *all flesh should perish together.* All should turn to nothing. It is as easy for him to destroy all mankind, as it for man to draw in his breath.

3. The third part of the confutation is spoken to Job himself, and it has a preface (v. 16). *If thou hast understanding, hear this,* 'and I will show you your error.' And he goes on to confute him two ways. (1) By showing the evil of Job's way (vs. 17-30). (2) By showing the way Job should have followed (vs. 31-33).

(1) In laying out the evil of Job's way he goes upon two grounds. [1] God's sovereignty. [2] His justice. [1] His sovereignty (v. 17) — *Shall he that even hates right govern?* 'Job, [do] you think [that] he who governs as supreme can hate right? or shall he that all must appeal to for decision of all causes, hate right? Shall he do wrong, to whom all must appeal to for righting of wrongs?' It is impossible. [2] His justice — *Wilt thou condemn him that is most just?* '[Do] you think it is a light matter to condemn him who is holy and just?'

He shows the absurdity of these two, by holding forth [1] God's absoluteness, mixed with justice. And [2], his <u>absoluteness</u> [*sovereignty*] (v. 18). *Is it fit to say to a king, thou art wicked?* 'Job, look if any great man will take it well off your hand to speak to him as you have spoken to God; and if it is not a light matter to speak so to man, to charge a king or prince with wickedness, [who] would not bear it well, is it fit to be so spoken to God, who is King of kings, and Lord of lords?' And yet this sovereignty is mixed with justice, *How much less to him that accepts not the person of princes, nor regardeth the rich more than the poor?* Who puts no difference between the rich and the poor. And the reason of it, *for they are all the work of his hands.* He made them both (v. 20). *In a moment shall they die,* etc. 'All these princes that you dare not speak to, he could in a night take them all away with a blast in his anger. If he should speak the word, they should return to dust. He could send sickness, or any rod he pleased, and remove them without hands. And [do] you think it a light matter to charge such a sovereign God with injustice. Secondly, he vindicates God's justice (v. 21). *For his eyes are upon the ways of man, and he sees all his goings.*

That is, 'Think not he does all this that I have been saying out of his sole arbitriment, for he knows all the ways and works of men. They are naked and bare before him. A wicked man cannot hide an evil turn from God' (v. 22). *There is no darkness, nor shadow of death,* wherein wicked folks can *hide themselves* from his eye (v. 23). *He will lay on no man more than his right,* 'for as sore plagues as he has laid on men, he never laid on any more than was right, that they should have occasion to *enter in judgment with him* (and so it is with you), or have any ground of complaint.'

[2] A second step or argument whereon he goes in laying out the evil of Job's way [is] by several instances of God's sovereignty. And the first (v. 24): God does not only what he pleases with one or two men only, but with numbers of men, *and mighty men,* whom he puts down or lets up as he pleases. And this is not unjust as he insinuates in the words following (v. 25), *for he knows their works.* He knows when there is just cause to be about with them, though men see it not, *and he overturns them at an instant. He strikes them as wicked men in the open sight of others* (v. 26). He takes a way to execute his justice more terribly before all the world, that all may behold and see in his dealing with them, a pattern of his justice.

And he gives two reasons why God vents his justice thus against great men. The first is (v. 27) because they fell from their obedience to God, and departed from their duty to him. And a second reason (v. 28), relating to their breach of the second table, is because they were oppressors of these under them, which *made the cry of the poor,* whom they oppressed, *come up to him,* whose cry he hears.

A third instance of God's sovereignty is (v. 29): *When he gives quietness, who can trouble?* God is so absolute and sovereign in his way, that he does what he will. If he has a mind to execute judgment on a person or nation, none can keep it off; and if he give quietness none can make trouble. And he takes sometimes this way, for this reason, *That the hypocrite reign not* (v. 30). That is, when he has a mind to take away a wicked governor that pretended to be for God's people, and intended to spoil and ensnare them (for the word hypocrite may be rendered 'wicked governor'), he sends trouble and prevents that snare.

(2) He sets down the way that Job should have followed (vs. 31-33), or what would have been more suitable to be his carriage. *Surely this were meet to be said unto God, I have borne chastisement.* 'I have gotten scourges for my guilt, and I will submit and mend wherein I have been faulty.' [2] This were meet to be said (v. 32): *That which I*

see not, teach thou me. 'It would have been better if you have seen any sin, to take with it, and pray for God's meaning of his rods, and to beware of doing any more that which may offend him.' He concludes with a pithy expostulation (v. 33). *Should it be according to thy mind?* 'Whether should God have his will, or you yours? [Don't] you think it an absurd thing to prescribe to God to guide the world?' And he presses the advice he has given Job by this argument: 'The way that you are on will do no good; *He will recompense it, whether thou choose or refuse, and not I.* 'Whether you take with your sin, and humble yourself before God or not, he will take his own way to humble you, and it is him you have to do with, and not I. Therefore seeing I expect you are convinced, take with your fault, or if you will speak on, speak what you know, and speak not of things too high for you.'

IV. The close of the chapter is in the last four verses, and as he began so he closes, calling wise men to judge whether Job has played the fool, and spoken rashly according to his narrow sense and [*understanding*] of God (vs. 34-35), and backs his arguments with this: 'If all that I have said convince not Job, I wish we may debate the matter over again which he has spoken, and may see what advantage he has given to wicked men, by his hot and passionate speeches and reflections of God' (v. 36). And he gives two or three reasons of this (v. 37), for *he adds rebellion to his sin.* He spoke rash words before, but now he is like to justify himself. 2. *He claps his hands amongst us.* 'He insults over us, as if we had no answer to give him.' (3) *He multiplies his words against God,* by taking occasion to cry down God's justice. Or this last verse may be read, *Why should he add rebellion to his sin, and clap his hands amongst us, and multiply his words against God?* That is, 'If we confute him not, we give him occasion to add rebellion to his sin, to insult over us, and to multiply words against God.'

OBSERVATIONS.

1. Observe from the general scope, that it is right hard for good folks, when they give way to fretting, to give God's justice, and sovereignty the right due. Job, who had no marrow for piety overshoots himself, and something escapes him, that he is justly to be found fault with. When folks fall upon a way of judging hard of God's way, it rubs [*reflects*] on God himself.

2. Consider the grounds that Elihu lays down. It may be asked, 'How is this that Elihu does so aggrege Job's faults?' Or 'How can he do it?' We think that he questions not Job's integrity, and that he was tender of him otherwise, but he speaks thus sharply to him: (1)

Because some of Job's expression, such as were named before, reflected on God, and he makes that a great fault. (2) Because he thinks that Job thought too little of such reflections. (3) It may be thought that Elihu stretches his consequences too far and beyond Job's meaning. Observe that there is no right walking under a cross and adverse dispensation without right thoughts of the majesty of God. Folks had need under difficulties to call to mind the God they have to do with. It is on this ground that Elihu proceeds, and it would calm and sober folks' spirits best of anything; and, O! but we had need to work our hearts to it.

3. From the words (v. 31): *Surely it is meet to be said unto God,* take your lesson. It is meet under every cross dispensation and afflicted condition, to stoop and submit to God; to search out sin, to take with what we know is wrong, and wherein we are ignorant to seek God's teaching, and watch and guard against the evils for the time to come that provoked God.

4. Observe from the words (v. 33): *Should it be according to thy mind?* Folks would [*ever*] have God guiding the world according to their mind and will. (2) There is not a more unreasonable thing to seek to take the guiding of the world out of God's hand, and yet this is the ground of our fretting and complaining, and not submitting to God, because we get not our will. Therefore when the heart rises, say to yourselves, Should dispensations come as you would, or as God would? This one word may stop our mouth, whether should God or we have the guiding of matters?

35

This is the third discourse of Elihu, wherein he is seeking, not to convince Job of the sinfulness of his state, yet of sinfulness in words, expression, and carriage under this trial.

This chapter follows on the former charge, and in it he challenges Job for being too much in reflecting on God's justice, and in justifying himself, he takes up his charge (v. 2): *Thinkest thou this to be right that thou saidst, my righteousness is more than God's?* '[Do] you think you [are] righteous in this, that in your heart, or in expressions, you should reflect on the justice of God? which you have done in maintaining your own righteousness more than his.' And because this was an odious charge, he hints at some of Job's words (v. 3) which are almost the same that he charged Job with in the ninth verse of the former chapter, as the ground of this charge. The words are not spoken by Job, and far less in the sense that Elihu would put upon them; for Job debated against his friends, that all things temporal came alike to good and bad, and hence Elihu concludes that Job said there was no profit to be had in seeking God. Or more particularly look to 10:15. Job had said, *If I be wicked, woe unto me; and if I be righteous, yet would I not lift up my head* — meaning he would boast nothing though he had the testimony of a good conscience; from which words Elihu, mistaking Job's meaning, concludes that he had rubbed on God's righteousness, and sets himself to confute this.

I. He confutes it (vs. 4-8) by showing the disparity between God and Job, and therefore that it sets him not to bound God. *I will answer thee, and thy companions with thee* — 'I will answer you, and your friends, or any that will take your part.' And the first ground he lays is (v. 5): *Look unto the heavens.* 'Job, you think the heavens high, and they are indeed higher than you; but God's sovereignty and absoluteness is above both heaven and earth, and will you bound God, or bid him handle you otherwise? Will you bind God by anything that you can do to a more favorable dealing? Is there anything in you to procure that at God's hand?'

He instances the contrary. 1. In Job's sin (v. 6). *If thou sinnest, what dost thou against him?* 'Can your wickedness reach to wrong God? You may wrong a man like yourself, and before men you may wrong God by being accessory to his dishonor, but it cannot reach him.' 2. In Job's good deeds (v. 7). *If thou be righteous, what givest thou him?* 'Or put any stamp of majesty on God, and if you cannot not add to him, you ought to lay no band upon him.' He amplifies this (v. 8). A man may help another man like himself, as he may hurt a man like himself, but it will not follow on that, that he can either hurt God by his sin, or help God by his righteousness.

II. He goes on to remove a second error in Job (v. 9), which comes in as an answer to an objection which might be moved against what he had said formerly for refutation of Job's reflection on God's justice, as he supposes Job had said (24:12). *Men groan from out of the city, and the soul of the wounded crieth out, by reason of the* oppression of wicked men, *yet God layeth not folly to them.* That is, he calls them not presently to a reckoning.

Elihu answers to this, and, 1. he concedes and grants that it is true indeed that oppression is rife [*common*], and many that are oppressed with heavy burdens, cry to God for help by reason of that oppression, and are not delivered. But it will not hence follow that God is unjust.

2. Therefore he gives a reason why though they cry, God hears them not (v. 10), because they cry not right. *None sayeth, where is God my maker, who giveth songs in the night?* That is, many will cry in adversity to God for help out of it, few whereof have prayed to God, in prosperity, or acknowledged their Maker for giving them matter of songs of praise; or few acknowledge him in their delivery out of straits, for turning their difficulties to the matter of a song, or for giving them a morning after a night, to lie down and rise in health and peace. And it is just with God to misken [*ignore*] them, who only cry to him in their adversity, and [*ignore*] him in prosperity; and in this he reflects on Job, as being more in crying now to God, [*than*] he was before when it went better with him.

3. And a second reason is (v. 11), as if he said, it may be indeed that such men cry to God in adversity, but there is not in these men a marking and observing of God's mercies to men more than to beasts and fowls, in teaching men more than the beasts of the earth, and making *them wiser than the fowls of heaven*, and hereby he proves there is no sincerity in their crying or prayers.

4. A third reason is (v. 12): *Because of the pride of evil men.* That is, though they be under affliction and oppression their proud heart is not humbled in them; therefore they cry, but get not an answer, because for all their poverty they keep still their proud <u>humor</u> [*disposition*].

5. A fourth reason is (v. 13): *Surely God will not hear vanity, neither will the Almighty regard it.* Their prayers are not only such as flow from proud men, but they are vainly put up, and let such men cry as long as they please, God will not take notice of them nor their prayers.

III. Then he removes a third objection (v. 14). Job had said (33:9-10), *That though God was on his right and left-hand working, yet he could not perceive him,* wherein he seems to <u>regret</u> [*mourn*] [that] God took no notice of him.

Elihu answers, that is not inconsistent with God's righteousness, though he sees not how, yet God is just; for *judgment is before him.* That is, 'Though you see not the particular cause of God's proceeding, yet he has a solid ground of proceeding, *which* is known to him.' Therefore (Deut. 32:4) it is said, *All his ways are judgment; he is a God of truth, and without iniquity, just and right is he.* He has a wise end before him, and a righteous rule he walks by. Therefore condemn not God, 'but though you see not the reasons of his working, trust in him, in a time wherein you are in the dark.'

He closes this part of the confutation with a sharp regret and challenge (vs. 15-16), as if he said, 'But what shall I say? This is not Job's case; he is not yet made to submit to God. Therefore though God has visited him in anger, he is not made to acknowledge God's hand in it.' And he closes with a censure. *Therefore Job opens his mouth in vain, and multiplies words without knowledge.* That is, because he takes not up God rightly in his passion, he speaks things that he knows not, and vents words to no purpose or profit.

Elihu in his censure is somewhat sharp by knitting consequences to Job's words that they will not bear, for his words will bear another sense than he put upon them, though they were passionately and unadvisedly expressed, though not intending either to rub on God, or to justify himself. Yet we will find Elihu rather free than rash in judging. He speaks not of Job's hypocrisy or blasphemy as his friends did.

OBSERVATIONS.

1. Observe, when folks enter on contests, they had need to take heed of reflections on either hand, knowing they are prone to weigh things severely, and to charge persons with more hard consequences [*than*] their words will bear; to lay too much weight on expressions, when there is no ground to bear it out.

2. On the second part observe a few things. And on v. 10 compared with the former, mark that oppression makes many folks pray and cry to God, while as there may be little sense of God or his goodness, and little or no religion in the heart, as in Jonah's companions in the ship and Psal. 18:41. *They cried, but there was none to save, even to the Lord, but he answered them not.* And Psal. 78:34. *When he slew them, then they sought him, and returned and inquired early after God.* But there was much unsoundness for all that; *They did flatter him with their tongue, for their heart was not right with him,* etc. Take not every fit of warmness under a cross for an evidence of soundness, or a work of grace. Fits of that kind may be, where there is nothing of the knowledge or acknowledgment of God.

3. Observe, it is a far better evidence of honesty and sincerity to acknowledge God, and think of him in prosperity, than to pray and cry to him in adversity. The one is more commendable than the other; they that will cry, as would seem affectionately in adversity, may as Jeshurun kick against God [Deut 32:15], when they are filled in prosperity, and have little mind of God.

4. Observe that one of the causes why our prayers are shut out in a strait and difficulty, is little watchfulness and thankfulness to God, when the stroke is kept off us, we make few errands purposely to thank him.

5. Observe (v. 11) that the common mercies that men have beside, or beyond the beasts and fowls, are great ground of thankfulness; that we are men and not beasts, that we have reason to look to heaven, and consider who made them, etc. [These] are mercies which we undervalue.

6. It is a great part of man's unthankfulness when he does not acknowledge common mercies, when they are not thought upon as they ought. We know not sometimes what may have influence on God's not hearing of our prayers, but certainly neglect of thankfulness, not blessing God that we are not beasts, has no small influence, and we had need to observe and mend [*these*] faults.

7. God would be in a special way acknowledged in every particular man's mercies; or we would not hold our mercies as common, but as particular to us, God teaches this mainly, that man should acknowledge his particular teaching of him, as if never another man were taught but he.

8. Observe (v. 14): 1. When God keeps up himself under affliction, we are given to fear that we will never get a sight of him, that he will not hear prayer any more. Though Job believed to see a Redeemer at the last day, yet he is put to think he shall never see God here away, for he thought the grave was waiting for him. 2. But we ought to compose our hearts in the faith of this, that God is doing well to us, whether we see him or not. Therefore (Isa. 30:18) he is said to be a *God of judgment.* That is, a God that knows how to trust [*time*] his manifesting and keeping up of himself, the times of his coming and going. Therefore the conclusion follows, *Blessed are they that wait for him.*

9. *Therefore trust thou in him.* He first sets himself to vindicate God, as ordering his way with judgment, and then bids trust God. Observe that good thoughts of God's way is a notable ground and motive for stirring up to trust in him, a notable ground to confirm faith in him. There is nothing that fosters misbelief more, nor mistakes and jealousies of God, and his way, and the end he has before him in working, and it is a great encouragement to faith to get right thoughts of God's way settled in the heart.

10 Observe (v. 15): *But now because it is not so,* etc., this is a great aggravation of Job's trial, that not only his three friends, but even Elihu also quarrels his faith; only it is with a difference. His three other friends questioned his state, but Elihu questions his faith only in this particular trial. He will not say Job had no faith, but [that] he trusts not God in this particular, and it is like this discourse has been a new set to Job. Observe it is not one of the best trials to a soul under affliction, when they are fighting the fight of faith, to be set on with this temptation, that their faith is no faith: And, looking on Elihu's discourse, there is something wherein this temptation comes carried along to Job in it.

11. He says, Job is *not humbled, therefore he opens his mouth in vain.* Observe that while folks profit not by the rod, are not humbled under affliction, it will vent wrong with them — they will utter words to no purpose that had better been kept in. Folks had need to improve a particular cross well, for if it further not mortification, it will bring

forth bitter outbreakings, and leave the person in a worse condition [*than*] it found him.

36

Elihu has been checking Job for his unsavory words of God, and his way, in several chapters before. He proceeds in this and the following, to reprove his passionate and impatient complaining of God. I. His speech has a preface (vs. 1-4). II. There is his confutation of Job (vs. 5-37:22). III. The conclusion of his dispute (37:23-24).

This speech differs from the former in that he [does] not cite Job's words as before, but generally insists to confute his passionate way of complaining.

I. He uses a preface to stir up Job to attention, knowing how hard a thing it is for men under the cross to take well with nipping and sharp words. *Elihu also proceeded, and said, Suffer me a little* — as if he said, 'I have not done yet; though I have said much, there is more to be said for God. It is such a cause to plead for God, that whosoever takes it in hand, they will never want matter' (vs. 1-2).

The second ground he goes on is (v. 3): *I will seek my knowledge from far.* 'I will not now insist on the particular dispensation that you have met with, but look all the providences and dispensations that has been from the beginning, and you will find them to plead the same for God that I say.' And the scope of all is, *I will ascribe righteousness to my Maker,* wherein secretly he gives Job a check, as if he had derogated from God's righteousness.

A third ground is (v. 4): *My words shall not be false.* 'I shall speak truth, and neither counterfeit with God, nor flatter you.' And a reason of it is, *He that is perfect in knowledge is with thee,* speaking of himself in the third place, to evidence his humility, or of God speaking in him, to tell his furniture was from God,[1] who was perfect in knowledge.

---

1 i.e. 'To show his gifting or equipping to so speak was from God.'

II. That which he has to confute in Job, is his passionate complaining, as if God had dealt unequally with him. The confutation has three parts. The first ground (vs. 5-22) is taken from God's righteousness and equal way of dealing with all. The second ground (vs. 22-25) is taken from God's sovereignty and absoluteness. The third ground is from God's greatness in ordinary causes, and in the works of creation (vs. 26-33, and followed forth in 37:1ff). And from these three, God's being just, absolute, and great, [*outside*] [the] reach of creatures, he confutes Job's taking on him to debate with God, and taking on him to censure him, as if he had done him wrong.

1. For the first ground, he: (1) [*Proposes*]; (2) Clears; (3) Applies it to Job's particular case. *Behold God is mighty.* 'God is mighty in strength and wisdom; and if we [would] look on God's strength, wisdom, and absolute way of proceeding, we [would] have little ground of complaining. But for as mighty as God is, he is equal, and will not despise the poorest. Therefore, Job, you have no cause to complain of sever dealing.'

(2) He proves this in two branches (vs. 6-7). [1] Never a poor man was in contest with a wicked man, were he never so mighty, but He did him justice, nay, he *takes away the life of the wicked, and gives right to the poor.* And [2], as he takes order with the wicked by his special providence, so he has a respect to the gracious. *He withdraws not his eyes from them*, that is (Psal. 34:15) *his eyes are upon them.* What is meant by this, the following words tell; *with kings are they on the throne,* and *doth establish them,* holding out a temporal grandeur in the latter, as in these times was more rife [*common*]. And taking it spiritually, the meaning is, that God has always a respect to them, and will manifest it one time or [an]other.

He goes on to clear and answer some objections that might be made against this.

Obj. 1 The first objection, and a great one — 'Oftimes good men are brought low, and far from reigning with kings?' The first answer to this (vs. 8-10) is: they may *be bound in fetters, and holden in cords of affliction,* but God does that for good ends. He gives two. The first (vs. 8-9) is it may be the righteous in prosperity forget both God and themselves, as they are ready to do, but he brings on affliction, and shows them their work, and wherein they have exceeded in the liberty he gave them. The second end (v. 10) is: He not only lets them see their evils, *but he opens their ear to discipline.* He gives them a lesson to amend, and by a forcible command makes them [understand] themselves. The meaning is, that God by a sanctified cross helps them to both examine themselves, and to [*understand*] their way to God, and God's way towards them.

The second way how he answers the objection is from the event (v. 11). Though God afflicts them, he does not put them from all hope of [*delivery*] if they obey and serve him. *They shall spend their days in prosperity* — they shall get a happy [*delivery*] [*from*] their affliction. And to this he opposes their not taking up of the mind of God in his rod (v. 12). *If they obey not, they shall perish by the sword, and die without knowledge,* importing that even good men do not always [*understand*] God's lesson that he is teaching them by affliction, and this makes them [to] be kept the longer in the stocks. So (1 Cor. 11) some of the Corinthians for abusing the sacrament, are made to sleep the sleep of death, and Asa and Josiah for their failings, are removed and taken away by temporal judgment.

Obj. 2. What difference is there then between the righteous, and the wicked man, or hypocrite? He answers to this (v. 13), opposing him to the righteous man he spoke of before. *The* dissembling professed *hypocrite,* he is always *treasuring up wrath,* neither does he turn to God, lay on what judgment God likes on him. And this is further explained (v. 14): *They die in youth* — How long soever they live, God's judgment comes on them ere they live out half their days. *And their life is among the unclean* — that is, their portion after this life is separation from God and good men. The word is, they have their lives among the Sodomites, after this life. Then (v. 15) he clears that even these righteous folks that are taken away by temporal calamity, are in a different condition from such hypocritical men, for God is [*always*] doing them good, for they are delivered at death. And sometimes before death he makes them take with their fault, and gives them an <u>outgate</u> [*deliverance; an end*].

(3) He applies this to Job in three particulars. [1] That if he had humbled himself, God would have given him an outgate (v. 16). *Even so would he have removed thee out of the strait into a broad place;* 'if you had humbled yourself before God, he should have brought you through.' *And that which should have been set on thy table should have been full of fatness* — that is, much prosperity and happiness should have come to him.

[2] The second way how he applies it is (v. 17): *But thou hast fulfilled the judgment of the wicked.* 'You have carried yourself like a wicked man, though I will not say that you are one. Therefore you have no reason to complain of God, though *justice and judgment should take hold of you.'*

[3] The third way of his application is by giving Job some directions. The first direction is (v. 18): *Because there is wrath, beware lest he take thee away with this stroke* — 'with a temporal judgment, though you get your soul for a prey.' Therefore it is far better to stoop to God, than to complain of his dealing. And he backs this with a reason: If God strikes, a great ransom cannot deliver; yea, (v. 19) neither gold, nor silver, nor anything else in esteem with men will be accepted.

A second direction or admonition is (v. 20): *Desire not the night, when people are cut off in their place.* 'Job you have often desired death, which is the end of all people, and which takes away people from the miseries of this life; but beware of limiting God, for you know not if death will be sweet as you take it.' And he confirms this (v. 21). *Regard not iniquity.* 'Continue not in your sinful complaining impatient way.' *For this hast thou chosen rather than affliction* — 'I have cause to bid you beware of complaining of your life, and to desire death, for you have taken this desperate way of desiring and wishing for death, rather than patient submitting to God under your trouble. [This] impatience of yours is sin and iniquity.'

2. The second ground of his confutation of Job (vs. 22-25) is taken from God's sovereignty and absoluteness. He begins every one of [these] grounds with a *Behold*, as v. 5, in this v. 22, and afterwards v. 26. And because we spoke of them [in] chapter 26, we may be shorter here.

Behold, God exalts by his power, who teaches like him? None can by his teaching cause to profit as he can, and both in respect of the means and manner of teaching, he can teach otherwise than any other can teach. This he follows with a reason (v. 23): *Who has enjoined him his way?* Who has given him a commission? Is not God absolute, and gives commission to all, but takes none from any? *Or, who can say, thou hast wrought iniquity?* Who can say, God has done wrong, or any injustice? And this way of interrogation does vehemently deny the thing; therefore he subjoins an exhortation (v. 24). *Remember that thou magnify his work* — 'Seeing God is so absolute and great, [understand] yourself Job, and be so far from complaining of God's dealing, as you make much of it; fall in love with it, and magnify it.' And a reason of this: 'because *men behold,* and see it to be God's work with you.' Yea (v. 25): *Every man may see it.* It is a thing palpable to be God's work. 'These who are not so much concerned in it as you, may be convinced that it is God that is dealing with you.'

3. The third ground whereby he labors to convince and confute Job (v. 26) is taken from God's greatness. *Behold, God is great, and we know him not.* 'Job, God is far greater than you are; he is incomprehensible, and far above all that we have said of him.' *Neither can the number of his years be searched out;* that is, he is eternal. And this he speaks to scare folks from diving curiously into the works of God's providence, and guiding of the world.

He clears God's greatness in common things. (1) *He makes small the drops of water; they pour down* — Is he not a great God, who can take up water above the clouds, and then let it not fall in a flush, but sifts it down in smalls, or like a still dropping drop after drop; and yet though he lets it fall in small drops, he makes it fall out abundantly.

(2) He puts two wonders together (v. 28) that neither the rain falls out in clouds at once, but in drops, and yet there is as much of it falls as does folks turn abundantly.

(3) His *spreading of the clouds,* and their watering to and fro, which [in] Psal. 18:11 are called God's pavilion or tabernacle, *or the noise of his tabernacle,* that is the thunder, which holds out God's terror. *Behold, he spreads his light upon it* (v. 30) — that is, God's making of the fire flaughts [*flashes of lightening*]. [All] of which sets out God's greatness. And covers the bottom of the sea, or the great gulfs and arms of the sea, that seem to be as so many roots of a tree.

He gives two ends God has before him in sending rain, wind and thunder. (1) *By them he judges the people.* Sometimes, as in the days of Noah, he sends storms and extraordinary rains for a punishment. (2) That which he makes a plague and punishment to some, he makes it a means to furnish others with plenty. And so folks have daily among their hands evidences of his greatness. He amplifies what he has said before (v. 32): *With clouds he covers the light.* When it is a clear day, he will cause a cloud come in and cover the sun, and it is dark by the interposition of that cloud.

And he closes all (v. 33): *The noise thereof,* that is of the thunder, *sheweth concerning it,* that is, concerning the rain. The meaning is, God by the noise of thunder gives warning ere the rain comes. *The cattle also concerning the vapor* — God has also a secret instinct in beasts, that they know ere a storm comes, and provide themselves a shelter. God makes himself so known in creatures above, that it is sensible to creatures beneath.

OBSERVATIONS.

1.   Observe [that] the solid ground of taking up God's way rightly, is solidly to conceive and apprehend God himself rightly. To know God rightly in these three, in his equal and righteous way of procedure, in his absoluteness and sovereignty, and in his greatness, is the way to take him rightly up in his dispensations. And it is the ignorance of God in one of [*these*] three, or all of them, that makes folk debate matters with God; therefore study to know God in this, and it will silence the most disputing mouth amongst us.

2.   Observe from his proving and clearing the first ground (vs. 6-7), that all God's ways carry in them a respect to the godly, and a stroke to the wicked. In all God's dispensations, there is a special regard to them that fear him, and a blow to them that fear him not. And this is an argument to put to silence Job's fretting and complaining, and it is a check to Job, who alleged that God took no notice to his honesty.

3.   Observe on the end why God brings affliction on the godly, that great end why God afflicts the righteous, it is one of more or both, either to let them know what is wrong, or to convert and amend what is wrong in them. For often in prosperity folks are partial in examining and judging themselves, and therefore God brings on affliction, strips them of worldly comforts, makes them sit alone, and examine matters over again. It [would be] good to learn in every particular strait and difficulty, to have an open ear to discipline, to seek out what is wrong, and depart from iniquity. Then affliction has the right fruit, when there is a discovery of sin and a turning from it.

4.   Observe that both these are not from the rod, but they are from God's gift. The ordinary time when God teaches is the time of affliction, but the lesson is from him; he must discover sin, and turn from sin, and we must depend on him for both.

5.   *If they obey and serve him, and if they obey not* (v. 12), observe that gracious folks may be under the rod for a long time, and not get the good of it. Asa is under the rod, and turns not till he is removed by death; and yet it is said of him, *His heart was perfect with the Lord his God all his days.* This should make us very humble, and to depend on God, and not on any bit of grace we have received.

6.   Observe when godly folks [don't] make use of the rod, they may come under sad temporal strokes, even unto death, as in Asa, and these [in] 1 Cor. 11, and Josiah, and others. Sad strokes may follow them till they are taken out of the world, and yet they are saved.

7. Observe that even then when it is so, God puts a difference between them and hypocrites in heart. He preserves them from having their life among the unclean, as hypocrites have. Therefore beware of being rash in judging of others, but learn ourselves to stand in awe, and fear before the Lord.

8. The directions speak themselves. (1) When wrath lies on, we would then especially beware of provoking God more. (2) Folks had then need to take heed what wishes and desires escape them, and particularly they would not desire the night of death, lest worse be abiding them. (3) Choose rather affliction than sin. (4) Remember his work to magnify it. Folks would not only be careful not to forget God's dealing and dispensations, but they would magnify his work. Labor to see God in it, and learn to speak good of God in it, and guard against anything that may make him or his work be ill spoken of.

37

This is the last part of the discourse that Elihu has with Job. The scope of the former was to check Job for his rash and unseemly censuring God, and desiring to debate with him, as if he had done him wrong. The last ground he laid to refute him was God's greatness in common things. He began at this (36:26) and follows it out in this chapter (to 37:22), wherein he concludes his debate (vs. 23-24).

I. He goes on in convincing Job by adding new instances of God's greatness (vs. 1-13). II. And he applies what he has said of God's greatness more particularly to Job (vs. 14-22). [III. The conclusion] (v. 23-24).

I. He continues his speech with an expression of the frame he was in when he thought of God's greatness (v. 1). *At this also my heart trembleth.* 'God does many great things, and when I think on his greatness, I am almost afraid to speak of it. My heart is fainting within me, and *moved out of his place*, when I am to speak more of it.'

It is conceived by some, that there was at this time a present thunder, which seems to be hinted at (v. 2), but it is not needful to make this the cause of the trembling. It was the consideration of the greatness of God, and of his works, that did so affect him. To let Job see he spoke not superficially of these things, and so might the more win in on Job, and make his speech affect him, he instances God's greatness in particulars, that made him tremble, in thunder, snow, frost, rains, clouds, that are mixed through [each] other.

The thunder is spoken of (v. 2). *Hear attentively the noise of his voice, and the sound that goeth out of his mouth* — that is, the thunder. He stirs himself up to hear attentively, and all that shall hear, not only to hear the word well, but to lay it to heart. The meaning is, 'Job, if you would hear well God's voice in the thunder, you dare not speak to God as you do.'

He proceeds (v. 3) to tell how he orders the thunder, and gives it a commission. *He directeth*, that terrible thing, *under the whole heaven, and his lightning to the ends of the earth*. And (v. 4) *After it*, that is after the lighting, *a voice roars;* for though the voice be as soon as the light, if not sooner, yet it comes to our hearing after the lightning, the sense of hearing being slower than that of seeing. Light things, that are instantaneous come to our sight before a sound effects the ear. *And he will not stay them when his voice is heard*. This may be applied to the drops of rain, which cannot be stayed when God pours them out in time of thunder.

God thunders marvellously (v. 5). He cannot get expressions strong enough to set it out; therefore he has expression after expression, to stir up to high thoughts of God the maker of it, and from this great work of the thunder he draws a general conclusion: *great things doth he, which we cannot comprehend*. All the philosophers on earth cannot know the causes of that, and his other great works.

The second instance is the snow (v. 6). *He saith to the snow, be thou on the earth*. God has no more ado, but say the word, and the snow obeys him as his soldier. And the third instance is, *the small rain and the great rain of his strength* — the least dew, and the greater rain, as it were a deluge. It obeys God as a servant his master. *He seals up the hand of every man* (v. 7). That is, when God sends the great rain, men are sealed up at home, as Noah was in the ark, and forced to keep within doors, and the beasts (v. 8) are put from the open fields to their dens for shelter from it.

And (end of v. 7) an use of this is cast in, *that all men may know his work*. He is such a great and terrible God, that he will have all men knowing him, whether they will or not; or because they will know him in a calm, he sends a storm and hems them in, and closes them up within doors, that they may study his words, and his greatness in them, which were a good use when men are kept at home, and cannot get abroad.

Out of the south comes the whirlwind, as in these places they had great whirlwinds; and cold out of the north, and this is another instance of God's greatness. The wind blows from no <u>airth</u> [*point*], but as he commands it, and no plague comes but by his orders.

Another instance is in the frost (v. 10). *By the breath of God frost is given*. And this sets out God's greatness, and the earth by the frost is hardened, *and the waters straitened in their breadth*. That is, they are made narrow when they are covered with ice, or they are drawn together by the ice that covereth them.

He comes again to the clouds (v. 11). *By watering he wearieth the thick cloud.* He makes the cloud <u>vague</u> [*roam*] and flit from one place to another to water the earth, and by watering the earth he wearieth them — not that the clouds are capable, but as if they were capable of wearying. He makes them spend themselves, and *scattereth the brighter clouds* with the sun-beams.

And (v. 12), It, that is the cloud, *turneth round about by his counsels.* The clouds go not by guess, but as God commands them to do what he has ado; he has [*ever*] an errand for them, and the errand which is spoken of in general in this verse, is branched out in three particulars (v. 13). *Whether for correction.* 1. In the original it is, whether for a rod to plague a people. 2. Or, *For* the use of *his land* in common. 3. Or, *For mercy,* that is, for a special and extraordinary blessing; and so are the ends of all [*these*] things seen that folks look little to.

II. He applies to Job what he spoke in general (v. 14), as if he said, 'Job, if you considered the wonderous works of God, you would not offer to dispute with him.' He speaks weightily of God's works, [*choosing*] words to set out God's greatness, the more to convince Job, that he knows not his greatness who offered to debate with him. *Dost thou know when God disposed them?* (v. 15). 'Do you know when God made and disposed these works that I have been speaking of? And far less can you know the particular dispensations of providence.' And *dost thou know how he causes the light through the cloud to shine? Dost thou know the balancing of the clouds?* How God hangs all things in the air, and keeps them in an equality? And speaking of the clouds, he adds a new motto on it — *The wonderous works of him who is perfect in knowledge.* He cannot speak of a cloud, but as of a wonderful work of God, and exalts God in it.

How thy garments are warm (v. 17). '[Do you] know' (is here to be repeated) 'why your clothes <u>gars</u> [*make*] you sweat now, that another time you will draw to yourself for cold, when the sun in the south shines upon you?' Though it is from a natural cause, yet he looks higher to God's hand in the natural cause, else the natural cause could have no influence in it. The word that is rendered garments, also signifies also treacherous dealing, because garments were a sign of man's treachery in breaking covenant with God; and this should keep folks from being proud of their garments.

Hast thou with him spread out the sky? (v. 18). 'Have you been with him in spreading out the firmament, which is firm and strong in respect of its pure nature, and very clear, though weak in itself, and how then can you contend with God? Are you equal to him?' 2. He expostulates with Job (v. 19). *Teach us what we shall say to him.* 'If you can tell us how to reason our cause with God, teach us. We shall be content to take a lesson from you; but for us, *we would not know how to order our cause* in spreading to him, *by reason of the darkness* of our understanding and ignorance of God.' For Job had said (23:4) he would *order his cause before God,* and offered to <u>enter in the lists</u> [*combat*] with him, [and] had given up his name to dispute. 'Now,' says Elihu, 'I will not take the cause off your hand, except you will tell us what we shall say.' *For I should be swallowed up* (v. 20). And in this he holds out a reproof to Job, for undertaking so fairly to do it, and gives a new argument to confirm what he has said of man's weakness to debate with God (v. 21). *Now men see not the bright cloud* — 'in the case we are in we do not look stedfastly on the sun, and how then dare we take upon us to meet with the Creator of the sun, [who] created light which we cannot behold?' Or it is, Elihu taking occasion to speak from the temper of the weather, 'that light we cannot see now by reason of the clouds, God by sending a wind to cleanse the air lets us see it;' and this agrees to what follows (v. 22). Fair weather (in opposition to the present foul weather) *comes out of the north,* and this is concluded, with an assertion, *With God is terrible Majesty,* or the words may be read, *To God be terrible Majesty.* Closing up his discourse with a doxology or thanksgiving.

III. The conclusion is in the last two verses (vs. 23-24), and it has two parts. The first, doctrinal. The second, pratical, on which he sums up the argument. 1. *Touching the Almighty, we cannot find him?* It is like that of Zophar (Job 11:7). He is so taken up with God, and his greatness, that he quits it as a thing impossible to take him up, and he instances this in three parts or particulars. (1) He is excellent in power, a powerful God. (2) *He is excellent in judgment,* in a moderate way ordering and exercising his power (as Deut. 32:4). *All his ways are judgment,* and therefore none have cause to complain. (3) *He is excellent in plenty of justice,* and will oppress none, as [*Job*] unjustly complained of him. That is, the words follow, he will not afflict, that is, *he afflicts none unjustly,* which is spoken to reprove Job for insinuating a quarrel, as if God had done him wrong.

2. The second part is practical (v. 24). *Men do therefore fear him, he respecteth not any that are wise of heart.* 'Job, if you considered what a God you have to do with, you would stoop to God, and leave off

debating with him.' In the original, it is men, or feckless man, shall, or should therefore fear him. 'And this should be your practice Job, for God respects none who are wise of heart.' In the original, *he sees none who are wise of heart*, that is, though this should be man's practice, yet he sees none who do so. Or, take the words as they are rendered here, the meaning is, if men will dispute with God, he respects them not. 'God is a wise God, and you will gain nothing by debating with him. Yea, God is a just God, and you will wrong him if you offer to dispute with him; and you are so far inferior to him, that he will not regard you.' And the scope of all is to bring Job to be humble, and to make him submit to God.

OBSERVATIONS.

1. Learn from Elihu's carriage in speaking of God, and his greatness (v. 1), that folks in their speaking of God should labor to be affected; they should labor to have a holy awe and reverence of the majesty of God upon their heart, and tremble and fear before this great God. Moses says, *I exceedingly quake and fear.* A humble, sober temper of spirit is rare, and a too palpable evidence of little conversing with God.

2. It may be looked on as an argument to move and affect Job. Observe that they are [most] fit to affect others, who are affected themselves, though it is God that must move the heart.

3. See how thriftily [*these*] holy men gather lessons of God's greatness from common things (the thunder, snow, frost, their garments, etc.), and all is done to gain the heart to some estimation of God. Were we spiritual, we would learn much of God out of the commonest things of God, and if we followed Elihu's way in seeking to [*understand*] something of God in everyone of his works, we would thrive more in the fear and knowledge of God. It is one of the causes why these men that had less of the word, did thrive better in the knowledge and fear of God [*than*] we do — they had a thrifty making-use of the commonest things of God. Every shower, every blast of wind, every fireflaught, every frosty night, or look to the clouds, gave them [*ever*] some new lesson of God. And if we would follow their way, it might [*teach*] us many good lessons, and bring us not only to know, but to acknowledge the majesty of God; and were it only to have the benefit of warmness and heat from our coat, it should [*teach*] us something of God.

4. See the kindly and excellent way of expressing God, and his attributes, and works, which is used by this holy man. *Touching the Almighty, we cannot find him out, he is excellent in power, and in judgment, and in plenty of justice* — words [*chosen*] to have weight on themselves, and on Job. We speak superficially of God, and his works, and disdain or think shame to take a mouthful of them. Affectation is not good, yet the scripture way would be studied, and our dulness has need of expressions to awaken and stir us up, and there is a sympathy between our heart and expressions.

5. *Touching the Almighty, we cannot find him out.* When he has spoken a while of God's works, and his greatness in them, he quits it as a thing he cannot reach. Observe that God and his works are never thoroughly studied, till they overcome men, and are seen to be far beyond their [*understanding*], and that not only in light and knowledge, but sensibly, so as men are affected with it. This is the close of many speeches in this book (as 11:7 and 26:33). The study of God is the only way to win to it; the ignorance of God mists and mars the judgment, that God is not seen in his works. How sweet a thing is it to see in everything the sovereignty of God commanding, his power and greatness in ordering, his goodness in sending it for a good end, his wisdom in guiding it right, his justice in sending it, whiles for correction, and his mercy in sending it for a blessing; and to see this in every shower. And when so much of God is to be seen in [*these*] common and little things, which may be called so comparatively, how much of God may be seen in greater things?

38

Y ou have heard a very long debate, and a very sad part of Job's exercise was in that debate between him and his friends. Elihu, a by-stander, comes in some way as more abstracted than the rest from prejudice, and he has spoken pertinently, though somewhat rigidly and severely, and yet it seems the turn is not done. Job's exercise is not yet at an end, nor is the effect of all produced.

Therefore the Lord having raised a whirl-wind, and the air speaking his terror, he comes in himself to speak to Job immediately; and as there is great odds between God and men, so there is a difference in the manner of expression, the Lord's speech here savoring of majesty and greatness.

There are three parts of the Lord's expostulation with Job, and everyone of them has a little challenge or preface. I. The first part is in chapters 38 and 39, and the challenge is the second verse of this chapter. II. The second part is chapter 40; the challenge is in the second verse, and Job's answer to it, vs. 3-5. The third part is from 40:6 and forward throughout chapter 41, and the challenge is 40:8.

I. It is said, *Then the Lord answered Job.* It is God not speaking mediately by men, as before, but immediately himself; and he speaks not to Elihu, nor to Job's friends, but to Job himself. And God steps in here: 1. To make known the weight and power of his own word, and to affect Job with it, for though it is spoken by man or angel, it proves ineffectual till God speaks it. 2. He has a mind to complete Job's trial, and Job having declined his friends, and appealed to God, thinking God would say nothing against him, the Lord comes in and brings the debate to a higher pitch for his humiliation. He takes him to Job, (1) because Job was the man mainly to be tried, and that he had a respect unto, and that he minded to leave a pattern of patience to after ages. (2) Because he had a mind to deal more sharply with his friends, therefore he will keep up the evidence of his greater respect to Job, and will first humble and compose him, to fit him to be an auditor when he should rebuke his friends. (3) Job seems as yet scarcely composed to bide God's sentence of and for himself. His heat and passion that were like weeds among his graces must be weeded out, and therefore he must first be humbled, and these must be allayed and mortified ere he speak comfortably to him, and give him a testimony of his respect.

The challenges are held forth, and they are three. The first is the ground of the other two (v. 2). *Who is this* (in a majestic way) *that darkens counsel by words without knowledge?* Who is this that speaks of the sovereignty, wisdom, and providence of God in guiding the world, but darkening it by ignorance, unadvisedness and rashness, and so spotting and muddying the native beauty of the wisdom of God? Who is this that by words without knowledge, so mars the beauty of God's wisdom and providence, speaking unadvisedly and precipitantly? And this is the challenge Job takes with in the close of the debate.

The following of the challenge comes next, and there is a difference between God's challenging Job, and his friends challenging him. His first three friends challenged him for a hypocrite. Elihu held off that, yet is very sharp. But God moderates his challenge more than any of them, and speaks without any rigidity and bitterness. He proceeds to debate (v. 3). *Gird up now thy loins like a man; for I will demand of thee, and answer thou me.* 'You have been speaking much of your desire to speak with me, and have said, you would answer me' (as 13:22 and 23:3-4). 'Now, demand of me, and I will answer.' A fair offer; but it may be Job had no mind that God would thus appear, when he wished before to have God to speak with; and because they had long garments in these countries, they used to gird them up when they wrestled, God bids him gird up his loins like a man, and make himself for it. As if he said, 'Job, you have been asking me to reason with you, now make yourself ready, and I will ask a question at you.' And he [*proposes*] a number of questions to him, the scope whereof is to show Job had unadvisedly spoken in desiring to debate with God. Every question has these two in it. 1. A holding forth of majesty and wisdom in God. 2. Infirmity and weakness in Job and all creatures. And [*these*] two being compared, God's majesty, wisdom, eternity, and absoluteness, with man's infirmity and weakness, the conclusion is: 'Is it [*suitable*] then, Job, that you should offer to dispute with me.'

The first question is from God's creating the world, in a similitude of the building of an house. And first he speaks of the foundation of it. *Where wast thou when I laid the foundation of the earth; declare, if thou hast understanding.* 'Job, gave you me counsel when I made the world? which is hung upon nothing, and yet stands as stable and firm as if it were founded on a foundation.' And when a foundation is laid, the line [*normally is*] stretched out on it, so a line is spoken of here (v. 5). *Who hath laid the measures thereof, if thou knowest?* Or, as it is in the original, 'Because thou knowest.' A sad check to Job, as if he had said, 'A man that takes upon himself to speak as you do, must know all these things.' *Who has laid the corner-stone thereof*, following forth the same similitude, 'Where were you Job, when I promoved [*began*] the building of the world?' *When the morning stars sang together?* (v. 7). This is to set out the excellency and glory of the work, the praise whereof belongs to the worker. Take them literally, 'The stars, and the sons of God,' that is the angels, 'acknowledged me their maker when I made the world, and where were you when that excellent harmony and music was among the creatures, and the angels, in the beginning of the creation, wondering at my wisdom and power in the making of all things, and think you nothing of that creature [creation] that the angels praised me so for?'

He proceeds (v. 8) to the sea. *Who shut up the sea with doors?* When the waters were as it were issuing out of the earth, and spreading over the earth, who locked them up as a man within doors? Who guides this tumultuous, raging creature? *When I made the cloud the garment thereof, and thick darkness a swaddling-band for it* (v. 9). Who has sweeled [*swaddled*] it up, and laid it in a cradle, as a man does a child, and who has by mist and thick clouds, covered it as with a garment, as a woman does a child when she sweels [*swaddles*] it up, and lays it down to sleep? And when he has drawn it off the earth, he makes a decreed place like a cradle for it, to keep it in (vs. 9-10), and God's decree and command, his efficacious sentence passed on it is the main bar to it (v. 11). *Hitherto shall thou come, and no further. Hast thou commanded the morning since thy days?* It is ordinary to see the morning after the night, but 'have you had a hand in it? made you ever a day? commanded you ever a day to come?' And every day that comes after a night, shows the efficacy of God's word (v. 12). *That it might take hold of the ends of the earth.*

He sets out the ends why God commands the day after the night (v. 13). 1. Generally, that it may enlighten all and miss no part of the world. 2. More particularly, that wicked men that love darkness wherein to work wickedness may flee away, as if they were *shaken out of the earth.* Then in two excellent metaphors, he sets out the coming of the day, and the effects it has on the earth. The first (v. 14): *It is turned as clay to the seal.* When the day comes, the earth takes impression of the light, as clay does the impression of the seal. And secondly, *They stand as a garment.* The flowers then put on a garment, they put on their clothes, and stand up as it were decked, that <u>loured</u> [*crouched*] in the night.

And (v. 15) he sets out another effect of the light, from the wicked. Their power and arm are brought to ruin by God's judgment on them when it comes. He proceeds and comes again to the sea (v. 16). *Hast thou entered into the springs of the sea?* 'Job, you take upon yourself to debate with me, but could you search out the depths or springs of the sea?' *Have the gates of death been opened unto thee?* (v. 17). He speaks of the depths of the sea, as of the gates of death, to show the hazard that any would be in to go down there, or to compare his absoluteness with Job. He *hath the keys of hell and of death* (as it is spoken of Christ, Rev. 1:18.) which Job had not. 'And if' (would the Lord say) 'you think the sea hard, I will come to dry land.' *Hast thou perceived the breadth of the earth? knowest thou it at all?* (v. 18). '[Do] you know the breadth of the earth' — importing men may well guess at, but cannot perfectly know it, and yet God is broader than the earth.

And he has a new question (v. 19). *Where is the way where light dwelleth, and as for darkness, where is the place thereof?* 'Where is all the light when the darkness comes? and when the morning comes where is the darkness? Can you know the place where either the light or the darkness is in keeping' — words that bind on Job, and all men, that they have enough ado at home every day, if they would give their mind to think on the works of God. *That thou shouldest take it to the bound thereof* (v. 20). 'Can you tell where the light or darkness are, that you may set a lodging to them? You cannot guide or direct one of these little common things, and how then will you, or can you take upon yourself to guide or direct me?' *Knowest thou it because thou wast then born?* 'Can you, who are but from yesterday, search out these things? Can you censure them that were so many years before you?' He speaks by the way of holy irony, to affect Job the more. For if Job had been born at the creation of the world, it had been enough for him to take upon him to speak so to God, or to propose such questions about his works, and more [*than*] he was able to do.

A new question (v. 22). *Hast thou entered into the treasures of the snow, or of the hail?* 'Know you the treasure or power of these creatures?' And (v. 23) he sets out his absoluteness from the use he makes of them — *Which I have reserved against the time of trouble and battle.* He keeps the snow and hail to execute vengeance on them that will contend with him, as we see in his plaguing of Egypt; therefore Job would beware to contend with God.

A new question (v. 23). *By what way is the light parted, which scattereth the east wind upon the earth?* 'Can you tell who, or what way is the morning light parted?' (that some think in these years had an east wind with it). *Who has divided the water course?* 'Was it you, or I, who have provided water courses for the rains when they come, that they may run in channels, and not overflow the earth? And who directs a way *to the thunder for the passing and lightning of it.*' And the last circumstance that concerns it — *To cause it to rain on the earth where no man is* — a further explication of the first part of the question, telling that where there is no man dwelling he causes the rain to come, to make the very wilderness fruitful. He has a care of his own land where no man takes pains that it be not unfruitful, but will *satisfy the waste ground* with flowers, to *make herbs spring* forth (v. 27).

And an admirable question (v. 28): *Hath the rain a father? or who hath begotten the drops of dew?* 'How is the rain and dew begotten? Have you or I been the father of it? Out of *whose womb come the ice?*' Who is the first cause of it? the maker and orderer of the ice and frost? *The waters are hard as a stone.* The waters that were liquid before, by frost are made like a stone, that man and beast may go upon it; and that is an instance and evidence of the power of God.

Another question of another kind, to set out further God's power and absoluteness, and [Job's] infirmity and weakness: *Canst thou bind the sweet influences of Pleiades?* These are the four stars, or constellations that have a special influence on the four seasons of the year. 1. *Pleiades,* a word that comes from sailing, for at the spring time (on which this constellation has influence), folks set forth to sea, and the earth springs with flowers.

2. *Orion* is the winter, and the word comes from folly or inconstancy, because of the inconstancy of the weather when this star rises, which is commonly called the tail of the bear. 'Can you,' he says, 'hinder the spring, or bring the winter?'

3. *Mazzaroth* answers to summer, and (9:9) is called the chambers of the south, because that time is most hot.

4. *Arcturus, and his sons,* is one great star, and some lesser stars waiting on it. 'You cannot guide, mend, nor alter a season of the year, and how will you direct me? know you what command I laid on the stars? Were you my counselor when I gave them orders? And can you make their influences effectual?' He reserves the fixing of their dominion and their influence to himself (v. 33) and then (v. 34): *Knowest thou the ordinances of heaven? canst thou set the dominion thereof*

on the earth? Canst thou lift up thy voice to the clouds, that abundance of waters may cover thee? 'Can you call for rain, and will the weather obey you? Or will the lightning obey or take orders from you as it will do from me?'

Who has put wisdom in the inward parts, who makes men wise? 'Is it not I? And [do] you think [it] [*suitable*] that man who has but a bit of wit should take on himself to debate with me?' *Can ye number the clouds?* 'Or can you stay one drop of rain' (v. 37) *'when the dust groweth in darkness?'* That is, when drought comes, importing Job could do nothing either to the keeping up of the rain, nor the making of it fall.

Then from v. 39. of this to the end of the next chapter, he speaks of his sovereignty over the beasts, fish or fowl. *Wilt thou hunt the prey for the lion?* 'Is the lion fed on your expense?' Neither the old nor the young lion gets any meat but as God provides it for them. *When they couch in their dens,* whether through infirmity or policy, it is God that provides for them, who provides for the ravens' food. Another instance of his providence in reference to fowls, though the ravens have a faculty of providing meat for themselves, yet God must find it out. And when the old beasts or crows are seeking meat, and the young ones cry out, God hears them, and here God acknowledges a creature-right that beasts and fowls have. It is he that feeds the crows. From all which God would convince Job of his infirmity and weakness, and that it <u>became</u> [*would suit*] him to speak more reverently of him.

OBSERVATIONS.

1. Here see and acknowledge God's condescension to a poor and passionate man.

2. See a glance of the majesty of God, from his own mouth, and how majestically and stately he speaks.

3. See how wary folks would be in passing sentence on God.

4. When folks are liberal in their discourses under dispensations, they often darken counsel by words without knowledge.

5. It should teach us to study more to reason ourselves to right thoughts of God, by retorting such questions upon ourselves, and the Lord is the larger in them for this very end, for though Job spoke of [*these*] things to his friends before, yet he had not learned to draw some good lessons out of them. God would by all this learn folks to drink in the thoughts of his greatness from his works of day and

night, rain, snow, etc., out of everything, to be getting some lesson. And the great lesson of all is to exalt God and abase the creature; a suitable frame for us to be in, [which] would keep us from many debordings [*deviations*] that we are ready to fall out in.

39

There is a great part of this debate now finished. After Job and his friends have had many contentions, God comes in to rid [*clear*] them, having a long time lain by as an hearer, and it is likely had not God stepped in, this debate might have lasted to their dying day, for any weight that one party's words had on another.

The Lord begins at Job, minding his reclaiming first, and respecting him most, and this chapter contains a part of his speech which runs upon several of the beasts and fowls. And it concludes: 1. Excellency in God. 2. Infirmity in man. 3. And consequently an unsuitableness that man should mistake and express his mistakes of God, and offer to debate with him, and so darken his words without knowledge.

He proceeds in his arguments to the same purpose that he was on in the former chapter, drawn from six or seven creatures. 1. The first (vs. 1-4) taken from *the wild goats and hinds*, sets out what care God takes of them, and how little knowledge man has of them. (1) And he speaks of their bringing forth. The reason why God mentions these creatures is because they are exceeding pained above other creatures in bring forth their young ones, and yet they are wild, whereby God would let us see how extensive his care is, that it reaches even to them, and would conclude the argument, much more must God care for man. (2) And it points out man's infirmity; for when Job cannot tell when they bring both forth their young ones, how can he help them? *Canst thou tell the months that they fulfill?* which is not to tell how long [*these*] beasts go, but to show Job's ignorance that he knew not the time of their calving, to wait upon them. *They bow themselves* (v. 3). They are far from the help of anybody, and put themselves to this posture to bring forth their young ones. *Their young ones are in good liking, they grow up with corn* (v. 4). To set out God's care towards them, they grow up, and are life-like, fatted, and made well-favored by God's providence. Though it is a barren wilderness they go in, yet God provides for them. *And they go forth, and return not to them* — that is, they return not to father and mother, but provide for themselves.

2. The second is *the wild ass*, and God's care of it, and how to tame it. It is a sort of ass that runs wild as colts on the hills, and there are great odds between it and the tame ass. The tame ass is dull and slow; this wild ass is swift and sharp, and this points out what difference God can put between creatures of the same kind, and hints at man's fall, and how in his fall he has lost dominion over the creatures. *Who has sent out the wild ass free, and who has loosed her bands?* 'Who has loosed her from the burdens that the tame ass has? Who has done this? You or I? It is not you but I that provide for it.' *Whose house I have made the wilderness.* 'And it is as well lodged in the wilderness, as if it were in your stable. I have provided a house for it there, and it is of that nature that it runs where it likes, and *scorns the multitude of the city*' (v. 7), 'though a whole city were called out to overtake it. And he regards not the cry of the driver of other beasts he is so swift; and if it were folly for you Job to contend with that beast, much more foolish is it for you to contend with me.' *The range of the mountains is his pasture* (v. 8). He comes not to fixed places, but ranges up and down the mountains, and has a natural instinct *to search for every green thing*, that he [*lacks*] not his food, though he comes not to an house.

3. He comes to the unicorn (v. 9). Whether there be such a beast as this here now, it is uncertain; yet there is such a beast as this God names, that is untamable, and depends on God's providence. *Canst thou bind the unicorn with his band, in the furrow? or will he harrow in the valley after thee?* 'Will the unicorn serve you as other beasts? or will he harrow your land?' *Wilt thou trust him because his strength is great?* That beast is strong enough; there is no defect in that. 'But will you lippen [*trust*] your labor to him? For folks are said to trust a thing when they look to get a thing done by it. *Wilt thou believe him that he will bring in thy seed* — an amplification of the same thing, and by the way, [*trusting*] to God on right grounds is faith.

4. He comes to the fowls (v. 13). *Gavest thou goodly wings to the peacock. Gavest thou* is added, and is not in the original, but it is to the same purpose. 'Whether did you or I, Job, make that bird stately. And if that bird be stately, I am the more stately that made it.' *Or wings and feathers to the ostrich.* A great bird, that (as it is, v. 14) where it lays the eggs, leaves them in the sand, and God by the heat of the sun, clecks [*hatches*] and brings out the young ones. God's purpose is to set out his absoluteness in creating some creatures defective of that instinct others have, and yet providing for them; and he that provides for them, will he not much more provide for man?

This is followed forth — *Who leaves her eggs in the earth, and warms them in the dust* — because she leaves them not to the sun to warm them — *and forgets that the foot may crush them.* She cares not for the egg, nor for the young ones more than if they were not hers, and is not afraid what becomes of them, whether for [*lack*] of fear or through senselessness, or trusting God with them (as beasts and fowls are said to glorify God in their own kind). *She is hardened against her young ones, as if they were not hers,* and a reason of this is given (v. 17). *Because God has deprived her of wisdom.* Men give many reasons, but God gives this for her senselessness, forgetfulness of her young. All creatures have a respect to their young ones, but God has deprived this bird of this instinct, to give an instance of his providence, and lest it should be thought stupidity in her, God says, He has given her that sharpness, that *when she lifts up herself, she scorns the horse and his rider* (v. 18). Though she be a great bird, yet she has that swiftness, that the swiftest horse will not overtake her.

5. He comes to the horse, and insists on him to v. 25, because he is a very serviceable creature, both in peace and war. He would have him taken notice of especially. *Hast thou given the horse strength?* 'Who has given that beast such strength? Was it you or I? And if he be strong, much more I, who has made all the horses in the world.' *Hast thou clothed his neck with thunder?* Words to set out the stately way how this beast carries his neck in time of war. God would have folks learning a lesson out of everything they see in the creatures. And *canst thou make him afraid as a grasshopper?* 'Can you fright a horse as another <u>feckless</u> [*feeble*] creature? *He paweth in the valley* (v. 21), as in time of war, and goes on to meet the armed man. The word, *he paweth,* signifies he digs being impatient to bide — that is, he pats with his feet, and would be forward to the battle, and he expresses not grief but joy. *He mocketh at fear.* He slights all fear; he regards not armed men. There is no hazard but he can set himself over it. *He turns not from the sword,* but runs upon it. *The quiver,* with arrows *rattling, the glittering spear and shield,* the terrible shaking of arms, are so far from discouraging this beast, that it excites him to more courage. *He swallows the ground with fierceness,* to set out his forwardness. He cannot bide a distance between him and the enemy; *neither believes he that it is the sound of the trumpet,* when the trumpet sounds. He scarcely believes it, he would so fain be at the fight, or it is but a sport to him, he thinks nothing of it. *And he says among the trumpets, Ha, ha.* If he would speak, his expressions are of great courage. *He smells the battle afar, the thunder of the captains, and the shouting.* When officers are expressing din, and soldiers are shouting, he is as busy as the best

of them in expressing his courage, to point out what stateliness must be in God who made that beast.

6. He comes again to the fowls, and instances the hawk (v. 26). *Does the hawk fly by thy wisdom?* 'Is it by your wisdom or mine that the hawk flies? who directs it in the flight?' *And stretch her wings towards the south?* It is likely some ordinary course of these birds towards the south, when the northern parts grew cold, as birds with us [*normally do*], which we see in the summer, but not in the winter, God teaching them that instinct to flee from colder to hotter parts.

Doth the eagle mount up at thy commands? The eagle is ordered in her flight, and in the making of her nest in high places; 'but comes the word out of your mouth or mine that makes her do so?' *She dwells on the rock, from thence she seeketh the prey, and her eyes behold it afar off.* She haunts not low places but high, and from thence she sees the prey, having a sagacity of sharp seeing, which God has given her. *Her young ones suck up blood.* Her young ones are ravenous, yet they are provided for by carcasses of slain men or beasts. And wherever there is a prey, she is always waiting on it to make use of it. Christ makes use of this to another purpose (Matt. 24:28).

OBSERVATIONS.

Why insists God so much here, [*overlooking*] himself as it were, and holding out the creatures to Job? 1. To let us see, if we could observe, there is much of God to be seen in the meanest creatures, and it is likely in this time, Job and his friends had not the written word, and therefore they had the more need to look upon the creatures. Here we may behold: (1) God's greatness, power, and might, his stateliness and majesty, ordering all the creatures himself, and having a hand of providence about them. Job might read, and did read God's dominion and sovereignty in these creatures. (2) God's absolute independence, his freeness in reference to his ordering the creatures, giving some wit, and holding it from others, to some a dwelling, and others no dwelling. (3) God's care and tenderness, providing for the wild goats and hinds, and waiting on them when they bring forth. It is brought in as an argument why he spared Nineveh (Jonah 4:11), that beside so many souls there was much cattle. But especially God's providence about the ostrich, and her eggs, evidences his care. He does mediately or immediately even as he likes, and this may be a comfort to poor orphans, when children [*are without*] parents, God can provide for them. He who cares for the ostrich, will he not much more for them (1. Cor. 9:9). Does God care for oxen? Comparatively or chiefly, no. God's wisdom shines here also in appointing a suitable habitation for beasts that are not profitable, the rocks for some, the wilderness for others.

2. Another reason why God insists so much on the creatures, is to point out to men their infirmity, weakness and ignorance. For when they know not the nature of the creatures, far less can the apprehend God. If man knows not when a hind should calve, how shall he know the deep things of God? (2) It points out the fecklessness [*feebleness*] of man, who cannot flee a horse, cannot take a wild ass or fowl. (3) It points out man's little respectiveness [*regard*] to God, or rather his ingratitude, who has never learned out of the creatures to thank God for making the creatures subject to him, when he cannot make them subject to himself.

3 A third reason why he insists on the creatures, is to learn Job a lesson out of them, to stop his fretting, complaining, and disputing with God. And the scope is to show it is not fit that infirm man should dispute with God, for it is probable [*doubtful; disputable*], that silly man who cannot [*understand*] the creatures, can [understand] the depths of God's providence in guiding heaven and earth, and shall he then dispute with him about it? (2) And when God's care reaches to these creatures, shall any suspect God's care to his more noble creatures? There is here a conviction to Job for reflecting on God's care about him, seeing he passes not by the ostrich egg. And Christ goes on the same ground, in guarding his disciples against carefulness (Matt. 6). *He that cares for the sparrows and ravens, will he not much more for you.*

4. All this he points out, that man is insensible of his due distance to God, who comes behind in any of the creatures in many things, and cannot command them, and yet walks not with God in that due reverence that becomes [*befits*]. And this was an evil in Job, and it is an evil in us, that we [*lack*] that due respect to God, and to his wisdom, power, greatness, goodness, providence, etc., that becomes us to have, and walk not with a due estimation of him, and with a stopped mouth before him, as becomes [*befits*].

Chapter Thirty-Nine

40

We have heard of the Lord's first charge to Job, wherein he challenges him for a rash and ignorant meddling with his counsels, speaking to the prejudice thereof, and of his wisdom and providence, absoluteness and sovereignty. It seems Job was damaged with the charge, and has not a word to speak, for as fain as he would have had God to speak with before. Therefore God goes a step higher, and puts Job more to it. The charge (v. 2) having two things in it, is a charge for presumption. *Shall he that contendeth with the Almighty, instruct him?* 'If any will dispute with God, he must think himself wiser than God, and take upon him to teach God to guide the world better, and shall any be so presumptuous, vain, and foolish? Yet it seems you take that on yourself, Job?' And to bear it the more in upon Job, he subjoins, *He that reproveth God, let him answer to it.* 'He that debates with God, makes himself wiser than God, and takes upon him to censure and reprove God, and let him answer for it. Yea, not only so, but if you are the man, Job, I call you to answer. You have been quarreling my dispensation, now answer to my charges.'

Job's answer follows, which is the second part of the chapter (vs. 4-5). He offers to speak a word, but is short in it, and he speaks very humbly and submissively, unlike his style before. And there are four things in Job's answer that holds out his frame.

1. His sense of his own vileness: *Behold, I am vile.* He gets an impression of his own vileness beyond what he had before, a good effect and branch of repentance.

2. *What shall I answer thee?* 'I will not take upon myself to dispute any more, but will keep silence.' And this is a fruit of the former, when the soul gets a sight of its own vileness, it keeps silence. It imports an acknowledgment, that God has gained, and a coming in his will. Therefore he says, *He will lay his hand on his mouth.*

3. He censures his own carriage. 'I have spoken over often, else I would speak no more.' He takes with it, that he opened his mouth in vain, and this follows well on the former.

4. He quits the dispute, and renounces the way he had taken for the time to come. *I will proceed no farther.* 'I will not reply to justify what I have spoken; I have spoken many daft words, and will add no more.' So he holds, and sists [*ceases*] here, and [*these*] four contain a right pattern of an humbled heart.

The third part of the chapter is the Lord's speech, wherein goes out a third challenge higher than the former. But why does the Lord go on to challenge, seeing Job is humbled?

1. Job is begun to be humbled, and while he is hot, he strikes to hold him going on in the work to put a real impression of humiliation on him.

2. To try Job the more, and to bring him clearly out of the trial, and to learn all souls in after generations not to mistake him when he doubles and triples challenges for the same evil that is taken with.

3. He would have Job more humbled, and he proceeds to bring him to the pitch of humility he would have him at. And if we compare his humiliation here with that which he is brought to [in] chapter 42, we will find it defective in these three:

(1) Though he speaks here of his own baseness and vileness, yet he speaks not to the justification and commendation of God.

(2) He speaks not here in express terms to the taking with of his guilt as he does there.

(3) He goes not so far on in the acknowledgment of his vileness here as there. For [in] chapter 42 he acknowledges his vileness with abhorrence and indignation, and God had this to bring forth by the following discourse, so that it is not for nought that God follows exercises, and in exercises from one challenge to another; and the last highest. *Then answered the Lord, and said, Gird up now thy loins like a man.* 'You have been provoking one to debate, now come to it, and I will go on with you.'

The charge is (v. 8): *Will thou also disannul my judgments.* 'You have ignorantly and rashly wronged my counsel. This I have charged you for, and now I charge you for coming in composition with me, as if you would disannul my judgments, and condemn me to justify yourself.' There are two parts of the charge.

1. 'Wilt thou disannul or make void my wisdom and judgment?' That is, God's wise and moderate way of guiding the world, holding out there is no such thing in God. His judgments cannot be disannulled.

2. *Will ye condemn me, that ye may be righteous?* 'Will you set yourself in my chair? You will not hold at justifying yourself, but ere you take with your fault you will condemn me, and say, that I am in the wrong.' And from these two, he concludes that Job <u>thortors with him</u> [*resists him; opposes him*]. He shows the evil of this, wherewith he charges him, by drawing Job to look on himself (vs. 9-15). Then he compares Job with two of his creatures, one in this chapter, and another in the following chapter.

But, how is this, that the Lord simply lays down the charge, and goes not to prove it as his friends did, supposing the truth of it?

1. Because God needs no testimony as man [does]. He has a witness within every man's bosom. People may answer men as they will, but God will make peoples' hearts bear him witness. 2. God rather deals with his distemper of spirit, than insists on any particular guilt, and what his distemper held forth is exaggerated that it may be allayed. 3. Because God in his dealing with Job, designed his amendment, therefore he labors not to rack up particulars, but to sober his spirit, and for that end speaks calmly to him far beyond Elihu, because he has a mind to gain Job rather than to shame him.

1. The Lord holds out this evil in Job of seeking to disannul his judgments, by comparing him with himself (v. 9). *Hast thou an arm like God?* 'Are you strong as God, to jostle him out of his chair?

2. 'Are you terrible as he?' *Canst thou thunder with a voice like him?*

3. *Deck thyself now with majesty*, etc. 'Job, you are now lying among the ashes. Can you deck yourself with glory and beauty as I am?' Words used to set out the infinite excellency in God. 'See Job, if you can put yourself in the like posture with me, and if not, is it suitable you should contend with me?'

4. [The fourth] argument is from God's justice and power in reference to proud men (vs. 11-12). 'Look up and down the world upon proud children, and lay them low, or bring them down, as I can, and as it becomes a judge to do. See, if you can break your pride, and if you cannot do that, you can far less party me.'[1] *Hide them in*

---

1   i.e. 'you can far less take sides with me or be a party with me.'

the dust together, and bind their faces in secret (v. 13). 'Put them to a contemptible condition, and make them like malefactors for the execution, whose faces used to be covered.'

He concludes this with an argument (v. 14): 'If you can do this that I have said, I will say you need not depend on me, but if not, then you would be more wary than to step into my room, and give me direction to guide the world when you cannot guide yourself.' People that cannot do for themselves had need to be much in dependence on God.

But why is the Lord so long in comparing Job with the creatures? And so short while in comparing him with himself, and after this he falls over again to compare him with the creatures?

1. Because God thinks meet to take the most obvious and common things to teach people, and to let them see how many arguments may be produced to convince them of their folly.

2. Because God does more set out his glory comparatively than by holding forth himself immediately. For if such a glory and excellency be in the creatures, God himself must be much more excellent.

3. Because our carnalness is such that we cannot comprehend God, but must have as it were a glass to take him up by.

He proceeds to compare Job with two creatures, with the Behemoth or Elephant. *Behold, now Behemoth.* In the original, it is beasts in the plural number, because the Elephant is so great a beast that it may stand for many. *Which I have made with thee.* 'It is a great beast, and I have made it, as I have made you. And if you considered the beauty that is in that beast, you would not set yourself in the chair with me. Yet I have taken cruelty from it, and have made it to *eat grass as an ox*, that it will not contend with you, nor on other creatures.' *His strength is in his loins, and his force in the navel of his belly*, sets out his strength that is placed in these parts.

2. *He moveth his tail like a cedar.* The tail here is by some translated his snout, that is, for his defense or offense, such agility as he, that he moves this as a cedar.

3. His strength is set out from the firmness of his bones (v. 18). *They are strong as brass and iron.* The bones of other creatures are hollow and brickle [*brittle*], but his bones are not so.

4. He is held forth from the end why God made him. *He is the chief of the ways,* or works of God, for it is written of this beast that it is the wisest of beasts, and comes nearest to a man in wisdom. Yet *he that made him can make his sword approach unto him,* for as great a beast as he is, God can slay him; and it is written of him, that a far less creature slays him.

5. Then his peaceable nature is set forth (v. 20). He seeks his meat beside the hills, and the least of the beasts play beside him without fear. It is not the largeness but the disposition that makes beasts terrible. *He lies under the shady trees, in the covert of the reeds and fens,* etc. (vs. 21-22). And this is another evidence of God's providing for him, or rather this beast leans on the trees, for it dare not lie down, lest it should not get up again. *Behold he drinketh up a river.* He is such a great beast, that when he comes to drink he oppresses a river. In the original it is, *he plunders a river,* he takes so much of it. *He trusts that he can draw up Jordon in his mouth.* He drinks so much that he thinks, or it may be thought, he would drink up Jordan. *He hastes not away,* but stays and takes his fill of it. *He takes it with his eyes,* he rushes so to it, as if he would sup it up. *His nose pierces,* or breaks *through snares.*

The sum of God's argument is, 'I have made this beast with you, and if it is so terrible, consider if it is wisdom to quarrel with God that is much more terrible.' It points at God's omnipotency in these creatures, and man's infirmity that is far beneath from them in many things.

OBSERVATIONS.

1 Lay all [*these*] comparisons together, it shows there is exceeding great sinfulness in fretting in God's providence — much ignorance and obscuring of the wisdom, beauty and power of God, that shines in providence, and much presumption, and pride fretting says it had been better this way [*than*] the way God has taken. *Shall he that contends with the Almighty, instruct him?* (2) Neither does fretting hold here, but it sets to thortor with God [*oppose God*], and to disannul his judgments, or wise manner of governing the world, which says there is much need of guarding against it. And it should teach us to adore the wise, just, and equal way of God's proceeding, when the reasons of it are not seen, rather than be rash in censuring it.

2. [Observe from] Job's answer, and God's reply, pressing him to be more vile in his own eyes, and more humble, that a self-loathing,

with a stopped mouth before God, is a condition profitable to the person, and acceptable to God. It is profitable to Job, both in reference to his frame, and in reference to his expressions.

3. People may be truly humbled, and yet God may have something to do to bring them further on in humiliation, in adding one challenge to another, as here in Job, he has two things before him. (1) To bring Job right. (2) To make him acknowledge his wrong. The former has brought him right, but he must be further humbled in the sense of his wrong, and must advance in the right way he is upon. Every contest of God's, or challenge from God, will not argue people being wrong; and when people are right, they will not rest here till they are in a competent measure right.

4. The appealing of people before God's tribunal is a good way to humble them. It would be good that we would put ourselves to it, what we can do for ourselves, and that will tell what we cannot do. And when we see we cannot do for ourselves, we will learn to depend more on God, and acquiesce in his dealing.

41

 T he Lord goes on to show a piece of his majesty in another creature, that by it, Job, and all mankind, may learn to know how great a fault and folly it is to contend with God. If we are not able to contend with one of his creatures, what can we do with the Creator? And so by an instance of his power, he would lay [*humble; lay low*] Job's rashness, who would [*teach*] God [how] to guide the world.

The creature insisted on here is the Leviathan, which we take to be the whale, the greatest beast or fish in the sea, and the greatest to be found on the earth. There are six sorts of them given by writers, and many things agreeing to some sorts of them, are to be found in this chapter; and the Lord does not insist in this chapter, as if he [*lacked*] arguments from other creatures, whereof he has such store, but to teach us when he spends so much time to hold them forth, men should not disdain to hear him speak of them, or to learn wisdom from them.

There are three parts of this discourse. I. He sets out in general, the strength of this creature, and how there could be no way found out for killing of it, men not being acquainted with the seas then as they now are (vs. 1-9). II. In the midst of v. 10, he applies it to Job and all men to draw them to take up a fit distance between God and the creature, and to allay the pride of men. III. Then he begins more particularly to unfold the parts of this beast (vs. 12-34).

I. He uses several similitudes to hold out this fish, and the strength it has. 1. [First] is that which fishers use to catch other fish by, and that is by a hook or a line. *Canst thou draw out Leviathan with a hook* (or a cord which is let down)? It implies an impossibility to do it. And this is amplified (v. 2) from a similitude taken from fishers, who after they have taken the fish, put them on a thorn or string to carry them home. The second similitude is taken from the carriage of a captive to him that has taken him captive (v. 3). *Will he make many supplications to thee, and speak soft words to thee?* 'Will he bring him to seek favor of you? That you will not. He defies you.'

He follows the similitude [in] vs. 4-5, when captives are taken, they are demitted with one or two, either by covenant as Benhadad — *will the Leviathan make a covenant with thee?* — or, by keeping them servants — *will he* condescend to *be thy servant?* This he enlarges: *Will you make sport with him, as with a sparrow*, as the word is. And the word follows: *Will thou bind them with thy maidens* — or young daughters, or children to play with him, or as the Philistines did Samson.

He returns to the first similitude of fishermen (v. 6). *Shall the companions make a banquet of him?* Will the comrades at fishing make a banquet on the price gotten for him? Or, *will they part him among the merchants?* Then to set out the impossibility of taking this fish, *Canst thou fill his skin with barbed irons, or his head with fish spears?* 'Can you with all your irons kill him?' *Lay thy hand on him, remember the battle, do no more* — a word of application to Job. The meaning is, it would be better to lay by weapons, and give over fighting with him. 'Remembering there is hazard of fighting with that creature, remember the battle with me, and give up; contend no more with me.' Or it may be read by way of question: 'Will you offer to struggle or fight with him? Do not that, for nothing will <u>do at</u> [*succeed against*] him.' *Behold, the hope of him is in vain.* That is, if any man would purpose to take him, his hope will beguile him, and it will prove a lie; for a man will rather be afraid to look upon him. *Shall not one be cast down even at the sight of him? None is so fierce that dare stir him up.* Suppose he were sleeping, none [would] dare waken him.

II.   The use of this follows. *Who then is able to stand before me?* 1. An argument from the less to the more, to reprove Job. And this is the scope aimed at, to set God infinitely beyond what we can apprehend, or [*understand*] in the creature, because the creatures lead us to apprehend many things of God by the senses. 2. It is to allay Job, not only in respect of God's power, but in respect of his independence and absoluteness. And further (v. 11): *Who hath prevented me, that I should repay him?* To let us see, though he is omnipotent, yet he moderates his omnipotence, that no man shall have reason or cause to complain of him. 'Show me who did me a good turn first? Who gave me advice to guide or make the world?' The meaning is, 'None has prevented me, but I have prevented all, *for whatsoever is under the whole heaven*, in the earth, or in the sea, *is mine*. I gave all things a being, and preserve all in their being, and have right to all things. Can any then quarrel me for my guiding of things.'

III.   Then more particularly he comes to speak of the Leviathan, and uses a preface (v. 12). *I will not conceal his parts*, his members, *nor his power*, and qualifications, *nor his comely proportion*, his suitableness to all these parts. And so he goes on to the excellent properties of this creature, and by a new similitude of a man's taking a horse out of a stable, and taking the sheet from off him, and putting a bridle in his mouth, sets out his strength. *Who can discover the face of his garment?* etc. 'Can you take him out, and draw the clothes off him as you will do off a horse? And can you bridle him as you will do a horse?'

Canst thou open the doors of his face (v. 14). As a horse's mouth is opened, when the bridle bit is put unto it, who [will] dare do that with him? *His teeth are terrible round about*, to tell that [these] beasts have teeth. *His scales are his pride, shut up together* (v. 15). This (and vs. 16-17) sets out his defensive strength, that some kind of whales have. The firmness and closeness of his scales, makes him proud, and regardless of what may offend him. Yea, scarce a blast of air will win in between them, far less a weapon. Neither force nor violence can sunder them.

He sets out his terror in his motion (v. 18). *By his neesings a light doth shine.* When he sets up his head above the water, he makes the sea move as if fire were in the sea — and *eyes are as if the morning were rising* before the light. *Out of his mouth go burning lamps, and sparks of fire leap out.* The same thing is pointed at in new expressions, particularly his spewing out of water, and also his violent heat and stove that comes from him, makes the sea like a fire. *Out of his nostrils go a smoke* (v. 20). His nostrils and breathing are like a seething pot and cauldron, and the reek that is above it. *His breath kindles coals, and a flame goeth out of his mouth.* The smoke, that is, his ordinary breath, is like a burning fire, to point out hotness of his nature, being very fat. *In his neck remaineth strength* (v. 22). Though this fish has not a neck, yet that place where the neck [*normally is*] in other creatures is so strong, that there is no mastering of it with any weight. *And sorrow is turned into joy before him.* Though it were never so great a stone, or never so many snares in his way, which is matter of sorrow to others, he but sports with them, or as some think, it is but a sport to him to pursue beasts and ships, which is sorrow to them. The former exposition is most native.

His heart is as firm as a stone, yea, as hard as a piece of the nether millstone (v. 24), to point out not only the natural hardness of his heart, but his stoutness and regardlessness of any danger. *When he raiseth up himself, the mighty are afraid* (v. 25). That is, of the breakings, that is, the ships and shipmen are afraid by reason of the broken waters. *They purify themselves* — that is, they betake them to God by prayer, and make themselves ready for dying. For purifying under the law was people sanctifying of themselves for near conversing with God, and so sets out here the shipmen's preparation for death, when this fish pursues them, and breaks the waters near unto them.

The sword of him that layeth at him (vs. 26-29) *cannot hold the spear, the dart, nor the habergeon,* etc. [This] sets out an impossibility to kill him by any weapon. They stick not on him; they hurt him not. He cares no more for iron and brass, [*than*] if it were straw. Arrows and sling stones, weapons that people are hurt with at a distance, do not fright him. They [do not] make him [flee]; they do him no more hurt [*than*] stubble. *He laughs at the shaking of spears* — as men would at the shaking of a windlestraw.[1]

Sharp stones are under him (v. 30), a new evidence of his hardness. He cares not where he makes his bed. *He makes the sea to boil like a pot.* When he moves he makes the sea to foam and boil. *He makes a path to shine after him.* People will see the path he makes after him in the water a great way off. *One would think the deep to be hoary.* The sea that was green before by the white foam seems to be hoary.

He sums up all (v. 33). *Upon earth there is not his like.* He is far beyond the elephant, or any other beast. *He is made without fear.* There is no beast but men can fear, but nothing can affright this beast. *He beholdeth all high things* (v. 34). He looks with disdain upon them; they are not regarded by him. *A king over all the children of pride.* He carries himself in the sea, his kingdom, as commander in chief. So the Lord sets out this creature for man's good, to bring people to know and [*understand*] themselves.

OBSERVATIONS.

1. See here how earnest the Lord is to have men knowing him, and to have them convinced of his greatness and power. Therefore it must be of great concernment to us, to [*understand*] God rightly in the creatures. It is a fault in us that we do not dwell more in meditation on the creatures, to find out God in them. Curiosity may put us to it, for a little, but we do not give ourselves to this meditation as we ought.

2. Observe from the scope (v. 10), that it is a right use of considering the creatures, from them to draw thoughts of God's greatness, and to heighten them to ourselves, from whatsoever

---

1 A dry and withered stalk of grass.

excellency we find in the creature, to ascend to the consideration of that supereminent excellency of God.

3. Though there is greater excellence and terribleness in God, [*than*] in creatures, yet man will be more afraid to grapple and contend with them [*than*] with God.

4. Not only should the greatness and terribleness that is in the creatures, bring us to apprehend God's greatness and terribleness, but it should bring us to submit to God, and to say (as it is, 1 Sam. 6:20): *Who can stand before this holy Lord?* And it should put us to wariness and watchfulness in our walking before God.

5. Observe that God is debtor to none (Cf. 41:10b; 41:11). He is in nobody's common [*debt*], and there are none but they are infinitely in God's [*debt*]. There is nothing, not a bit of bread, nor a house to dwell in, nor anything else, but it is his. And this should [*teach*] people to judge well of God, and receive anything well at his hand. There are infinite uses that arise from this one word. People cannot step but on God's ground; therefore they should walk with an eye to God, and labor to be some way suitable to, though they cannot equal his favors. God's sole interest in creatures should win our hearts more to him, and make us die more to creatures. God will seek account of them; therefore reckon them not for ours, but for his, and so use them.

6. Shipmen at the approach of this creature (v. 25), are said to *purify themselves*. Observe that these who have not much religion, when death seems to draw near, will seek to purify or cleanse themselves, and fall about religious duties for that end, as the heathens in Jonah. The sober consideration of death will put the stoutest to purification, and the right and sober thoughts of death are a very profitable meditation. If we were within reach of a whale, we would be more taken up with the thoughts of it, and yet it may be very sudden, and it is as certain as can be. It were good that we had as earnest thoughts in the study of holiness, as if death were within our view, and not an hour hence.

42

This chapter contains the last part of this book, wherein is especially the happy <u>outgate</u> [*deliverance*] that God gave Job, from his very sad, and (as it appears) right long trouble.

The chapter has three parts. I. We have a more full setting down of the effect of the Lord's discourse speaking extraordinarily on Job, or the repentance and frame of spirit it put him in (vs. 1-6)). II. We have the Lord's coming in and deciding the debate, condemning Job's friends, and absolving him, and his directing his friends to deal with Job to make their peace (vs. 7-9). III. We have Job recovery (vs. 10-17), the Lord's bringing back his captivity, and setting him free from the many calumnies and reproaches he lay under, and the great prosperity he bestowed on him.

I. The preface to what follows is in vs. 1. *Then Job answered the Lord and said.* This is the writer's words, showing how Job took the opportunity to speak, and his speech has few words, but very pithy, containing five or six evidences of a humble spirit, or of a right frame of spirit, under God's hand, or qualifications of true repentance.

1. The first is a sensible conviction of the greatness and majesty of God, which seems to be the main ground of that which follows. *I know thou canst do everything* — an impression of God's omnipotence. And the knowledge he speaks of here, is not that knowledge he had by hearsay, neither that common knowledge which he had from the grounds of faith, for he had that before. But it is a knowledge by sensible conviction and experience, settling on his mind and heart with a lively impression.

2. *And that no thought can be withholden from thee.* Or 'no thought of thine can be withheld or hindered; you can do whatever you think, and none can stand in your way' — holding out God's sovereignty. Or taking the words as they are rendered here, *no thought can be withholden from thee*, it points at God's omniscience, who knows and takes up the thoughts of all hearts afar off, and took up the carnal thoughts of his heart, in the heat of his debate with his friends, to

show his high uptaking of God, and a main qualification of repentance.

3. He has a particular reflecting on his guilt (v. 3), and he begins with what God charged him with (38:2): *Who is he that hideth counsel without knowledge?* 'Thou art a great God, and I have been a foolish man and a beast, to come to obscure thy sovereign counsel, who art such a wise and sovereign God, as I have done.' And that this is his meaning, appears by the words following. *Therefore have I uttered that I understood not.* 'I have been over malapert [*presumptuous*] to utter things above my reach, rash, through ignorance, to meddle with *things to wonderful for me.*' And here he confesses and takes not only with his guilt, but the particular fault that God charged him with. And this is another qualification of repentance, when God is seen in his sovereignty, and guilt is taken with and acknowledged in particulars.

4. We have Job's reverent address to God for new instruction (v. 4). *Hear, I beseech thee, and I will speak.* It is not like Job's disputing, but his desire of instruction — *I will demand of thee, and declare thou unto me.* 'I have been rash and foolish in offering to dispute with thee, now I will do so no more. But if thou wilt forget that, and hear my suit, I will demand of thee, or desire to be instructed of thee, and declare thou unto me.' or as the word in the original is, 'make it known to me.' Weaned from the conceit of his knowledge, he comes to get a lesson from God, as Elihu advises him (34:32). *That which I see not, teach thou me* — another qualification of repentance, when the soul is made docile and tractable, desirous to learn, and willing to be taught.

5. We have Job's special profiting (v. 5): *I have heard of thee by the hearing of the ear, but now mine eye seeth thee.* 'I heard many great things of God, and believed them in some measure before, but now the knowledge of God that I have gotten is far beyond any knowledge I had before in distinctness and clearness of taking up, as the seeing of a thing is beyond the hearing of it.' Not that he casts [away] anything he had learned, and was truth before, but what he has gotten now is like a man's seeing of a thing which is far beyond his hearing tell of it.

6. *Wherefore I abhor myself, and repent in dust and ashes* — a conclusion drawn from all the former. 'Not only find I fault with this, and that particular wrong, but now I see myself a vile creature. I abhor and loath myself' — as the promise is in the New Covenant (Ezek. 36). *And I repent in dust and ashes,* which is the kindly vent of

loathing, and holds out a turning from sin to duty, and to walk humbly before God. And if we will put all these together, it [*teaches*] us what a frame of spirit is suitable to our time, and to any of us in particular, especially when we fall under any cross dispensation.

II. In the second part of the chapter, the Lord being satisfied with Job, he turns to his friends.

1. We have the decision that God passes, wherein he condemns them and absolves Job (v. 7). He condemns them, as being angry with them, and he takes himself to Eliphaz, and he says, *My wrath is kindled against thee, and thy two friends*. Because they went all three upon one ground, in condemning Job for a hypocrite, and perverting God's way of providence, as if none but hypocrites had been so dealt with, as Job was, and godly men had always had a prosperous lot in the world. For *ye have not spoken of me the things that is right as my servant Job hath*. Comparing his thesis with his friends, he was right, and they were in the wrong. And we will hear no word, or mention made of Elihu, either of his absolving or condemning, and it seems God does not condemn him, being free of the sin Job's three friends were guilty of, neither yet does he absolve him, because though he was right in his aim, yet he [*lacked*] not very sharp expressions to Job.

2. When God has absolved Job, and condemned his friends in the particular they debated about, he gives them direction how to make their peace. He bids them *take seven bullocks, and seven rams*, whether this was before the law, as is likely, there being no place under the law where it was lawful to sacrifice but at Jerusalem, we shall not stand on it; but certainly it was known from the beginning that there was no peace to be had with God, but by a sacrifice, and this course was still kept for atonement and reconciliation, with an eye to Jesus Christ. And, because they had calumniated [*falsely accused*] Job for a hypocrite, he will have him to be their intercessor, partly to vindicate Job from that reproach, and partly to try their obedience, and partly also to confirm their friendship mutually again. And he adds a sharp threatening — *Least I deal with you after your folly* — because they were great, grave, and learned men, and had proud stomachs, lest they should have shunned the direction given them, he adds this as a motive to humble them, and to induce them to make use of the means prescribed them, for their reconciliation — *for him will I accept*.

3. We have their obedience (v. 9), and they are all three mentioned in their obedience. And it is said, *they did as the Lord commanded them*. They obeyed the direction in taking the greatest sacrifice that was appointed by the law, whereby it seems they were no mean [*common*]

men. And God performs his promise to Job, in accepting them; for it is not only for himself (which is in the words following), but for them that he is accepted. God heard his prayer in their behalf. It is likely Ezekiel relates to this chapter (Ezek. 14:14).

III. The third part of the chapter contains Job's restitution (vs. 10-17).

1. It is generally laid down (v. 10), *The Lord turned the captivity of Job.* It is called a turning his captivity, because he was under so many adversities, tortured with the devil, and vexed with his friends, under great pain of body, and inward exercise of mind. And when God calls back the commission he had given Satan, and looses his bands, it is called a turning of his captivity. The time when his captivity is turned is set down — it was when he was praying for his friends. God made choice of that time. Then, more particularly, it is set down wherewith he was blest. *The Lord gave Job twice as much as he had before* — not at that instant, but in due time before his death.

2. Then particularly the steps of this blessedness are pointed at and mentioned (v. 11). God's making of him honorable, and bringing him in respect among his kinsfolk, that before had cast him off. When they saw God was belike to do him good, they step to and are comfortable to him. And in sign of their love and respect, *Every one gave him a piece of money, and an ear-ring of gold,* pointing at the way how God began, and brought about his recovery; and to show what duty friends own to one another in their straits, as also to point out that the kindness of friends is at God's beckoning. So (v. 12), *The Lord blessed the latter end of Job more than his beginning.* To wit, in temporal things, so that he had more of them than ever he had; for he had but the half of these goods named here (Job 1). *He had also seven sons and three daughters* (v. 13). He had as many as [before]. And if it is asked then, how his children were doubled? *Answer.* Considering the children that Job had before, who were removed by death, yet living to God (as we have ground to think of them), though his cattle were not to the fore, yet these children were to the fore, and these that are to the fore, and living to God, are not lost to Job. Then follows the particular names of his daughters, and their beauty, for it is a mercy to get children with natural features, [*lacking*] none of their parts and comeliness; and this naming of his daughters is to leave a memorial of his delivery. *The name of the first is Jemima,* taken from a word that signifies the day or light. *The name of the second Kezia,* or *Cassia.* It is from a word that signifies ointment, to point at the refreshment wherewith God had refreshed him. *The name of the third,*

Keren-happuch, which signifies painting [the face], to show there was no painted beauty comparable to the life he had now in God.[1]

After this Job lived an hundred and forty years. Besides what he had lived before, he had a long life for a blessing, and in this time *he saw his sons and his sons' sons, even four generations,* not only to be a temporal mercy, but to be a witness to him, and his children, of God's goodness after his sore trial. *So Job died, being old, and full of days.* The word is, being satisfied with days, as it is spoken of Abraham (Gen. 25:8). He is content to die, and not desirous to live any longer.

OBSERVATIONS.

1. Compare this frame that Job is in with that which went before, and we shall see his tune changed. It is a good fruit of affliction, when the hand of God has this fruit with it, to make them sober and sound in their speech.

2. Yet Job's words are very short. It is not the multitude of words that has weight with God, but a humble frame of spirit, venting itself humbly and confidently. Whether the words are few or none, it is no matter, if the frame is right.

3. Compare Job's two speeches in chapter 41 and this, and it is hard to show wherein his humility vents most. Yet, as we observed before, we think this goes before the other in the commendation of God, in taking with his own guilt, in the acknowledgment of his vileness, and in the completeness of his submission.

4. Observe (vs. 5-6) that when people attain to a right sight of God, they will have other thoughts and apprehensions of him [*than*] they had before. Scarcely (if we may say scarcely) was there one on earth who had such high thoughts of God before this time; yet, when he gets a new sight of God, he thinks nothing of all he had before, but as hearing in comparison of seeing, and therefore he is affected and brought low. We are to regret our little knowing of God, when we are so little affected with what we know.

5. In the second part God proceeds to decide the debate in Job's favor, and to vindicate him. It holds out that [in] James 5:11. *Ye have*

---

1   Originally, 'which signifies paintry or farding, to show there was no painted beauty, nor farding comparable to the life he had now in God.' Paintry is the action of painting and farding means 'to paint the face.'

heard of the patience of Job, and have seen the end of the Lord, that the Lord is very pitiful, and of tender mercy. This [*appears*] very clearly here, however the exercise be long, there is a comfortable [*deliverance*], and a vindication of him at length. And though the servants of God should lie under reproach here, and go to their grave with it, there is a day coming when he will clear and confess them before men and angels.

6. Observe that God will take notice of, and be angry at the sins of his own, as well as others. [*These*] three men were reconciled to God, as God's accepting of Job for them tells; yet he is angry at them for their not speaking of him that which was right. It is a madness and folly to say God takes no notice of, nor is angry at the sins of his people. It was a doctrine not known in [*these*] days, though I grant there is great difference between God's taking notice of, and being angry at his people when they sin, and others.

7. The angriest time that God has towards his people, he is careful of their good, and lets out a word of direction to them. He never gives up with them, but has a respect to their gain and advantage.

8. There is no taking away of sin, even to the justified, but by sacrifice. This way the Lord laid down to keep them in mind of a Mediator, and it were good we should not speak, nor think of pardon of sin, but in God's ordinary way.

9. Observe lastly on this second part of the chapter, that God will add threatenings to put his people to duty, and threatenings should have their own weight in stirring them up to duty.

10. Observe three things in their obedience, and Job's praying for them. (1) Their deniedness and humility, who after so long debate with Job, stoop to, and think no shame to go to Job, and bid him pray for them. When God calls us to seek help one of another in prayer, we should not disdain [it].

(2) This help that God prescribes is a main means to knit their affections together, to write and make them one, and it is for the rooting out of prejudices. And it is a good way, if God would put us to it, to heal the divisions, and remove the differences that are among us.[2]

---

2 Perhaps this is another reference to the Protester/Resolutioner controversy. See previous footnote, pp. 11-12.

(3) Job prays for them, and heartily, for God accepts him. It is an evidence of a humble frame when we can pray heartily for them who have wronged us.

11. On the last part [III:1], from the time when God turns Job's captivity, it is when he prayed for his friends, observe that people would sometimes come as good speed for themselves if they were busy in prayer for others, especially such as have wronged them, as if they were praying for themselves. This is not spoken as if people should not be busy for themselves, but to teach us not to be selfish. David gives himself to prayer for his enemies (Psa. 35:15), and his prayer returns to his own bosom. We exhort you more to this duty, to interpose between God and others more, and you shall come more speed for yourselves. God sanctify what has been said. *Amen.*

12. Look now on the event and <u>outgate</u> [*outcome; deliverance*] God gave Job, and see if it is not better than anything Job prescribed or expected. It is best to give God his will in our afflictions. The outgate he carves is often better than our own; yea, is it not better to Job now, than if he had not such an exercise? Which is a manifest proof of God's faithfulness, who makes all things turn to the best.

Finis.